THE BEAST WITHIN

THE BEAST WITHIN

"Living With OCD"

Angela Todd O'Neal

Copyright © 2005 by Angela Todd O'Neal.

Library of Congress Number: 2005900892
ISBN : Hardcover 1-4134-8488-3
Softcover 1-4134-8487-5

All rights reserved. No part of this book may be reproduced or transmitted in any form or by any means, electronic or mechanical, including photocopying, recording, or by any information storage and retrieval system, without permission in writing from the copyright owner.

This book was printed in the United States of America.

To order additional copies of this book, contact:
Xlibris Corporation
1-888-795-4274
www.Xlibris.com
Orders@Xlibris.com

CONTENTS

FLAVOR OF THE MONTH 11
IT'S NOT NORMAL TO BE ABNORMAL 16
KINDERCARE 22
SPONTANEOUS COMBUSTION 29
IT TAKES A VILLAGE TO RAISE A CHILD 33
IMAGINARY HATE MATE 43
"YEAH, AH 'SEEN IT" 47
ONE, TWO, THREE STRIKES 59
THROW IN A MONKEY WRENCH 66
OPEN CLASSROOMS, CLOSED MINDS 70
AN APPLE A DAY 84
YOU'RE A GENIUS 88
"ATTENTION—DON'T TAKE THE LITTLE BROWN PILLS!" 103
SEA SALT AND HOLY ROLLERS 114
LITTLE TRANSYLVANIA 125
PINK, GREEN, AND PAPAGALLO ALL OVER 131
WHEN I SAY 'JUMP,' YOU ASK 'HOW HIGH!' 149
IT'S MORE POPULAR TO BE A CHEERLEADER 152
I KNOW WHAT YOU DID THAT SUMMER 166
ON THE OUTSKIRTS OF SOCIETY 176
ISLAND OF THE MISFITS 200
BE CAREFUL WHAT YOU WISH FOR 232
FOUR-LEGGED FRIEND 241
WAKE UP AND SMELL THE COFFEE 244
A DOSE OF YOUR OWN MEDICINE 254
ANOTHER SUBURBAN FAMILY MORNING 269
BIG HAIR ROCKS ON 276
BLESS THE BEASTS 282
ALL IN A DAY'S WORK 288

COLLEGE CO-ED	306
THE BRIDGES OF ROBESON COUNTY	313
WORKAHOLICS ANONYMOUS	322
FAMILY TREE WITH MISSING BRANCHES	335
YOU REAP WHAT YOU SOW	342
QUESTIONS WITHOUT ANSWERS	360
EPILOGUE	375

In Loving Memory of Reverend "T" Dunstan

*(You will never know how much you meant to my family—
as well as to so many others.)*

*__Thank you for making a difference—
for choosing to "toss the starfish."__*

** Most names have been changed
with respect to individuals' rights to privacy*

FLAVOR OF THE MONTH

". . . . *And* he has ADHD."

She says this as though she is proud. The very blond woman who just wheeled her cart in front of me, like I am not even here. Maybe I'm not. Maybe no one can really see me. Maybe I am invisible. What if I don't exist? Believe me—it's not the first time I've wondered this.

I know I should say something enlightening, like '*Excuse me, but you just broke in line.*' And though I know this is what I *should* do, what is it that I *actually* do? I swallow it, of course, like always, concentrating on the contents of her basket instead. And apparently, she is some kind of health nut because her basket is filled with all kinds of trendy good-for-you stuff like soymilk, tofu, goat cheese and these expensive-looking organic vegetables. Not that I've ever bought any where I'd know what they actually cost, but just the packaging alone speaks volumes. Then, as if in complete contradiction, she has an assortment of colorful cartoonish packages labeled 'lunch-ums,' and also several six-packs of juice boxes, filling the other corner of her cart. Still talking to her friend, she begins to casually unload her purchases onto the conveyer belt, being careful not to snag her sculpted nails as she carries on her important conversation.

"And who do you have working with him right now?" Woman Number Two asks. Like she really cares. Who knows? Maybe she does.

"We just finished up a session with Triangle Psychology," Fake Blond Hair is chirping. "And he really seemed to get a lot out of that. You know, as far as redirecting his anger, and saying how he really feels. Because that's very important, you know."

"Yes," Number Two agrees wholeheartedly. "You have to *really* insist that they express themselves. Because it can be so harmful—keeping everything bottled up inside like that."

Fake Hair puts her hand on her hip then, adding, "Well, that's what I've been trying to express to Rick—"

But neither one of us will know now whatever it was that Rick didn't get, because a little boy—blond-headed, too, and probably around six or so—pushes past me in line, walloping Fake Hair on the backside with his fist. Oh well, at least he has a pretty ample target, I reason. I figure that this must be 'ADHD.'

Fake Hair smiles then, saying, "Now Dalton, what have we discussed about hitting? Do you remember?"

I want to roll my eyes. Of course he does.

The little boy shrugs, then deviously punches his mother in the butt again. Hard. She attempts to turn away from his assault, putting her hands down in front of her, kind of like shields, as she says, "Dalton, that's not how we show our 'friendly feelings,' is it?"

Now he is laughing, punching fist over fist. Lucky for her she's got that extra padding back there to absorb the blows. Otherwise, she'd be in pretty bad shape. She reaches for his hands instead then, saying excitedly, like she just thought of it or something, "Tell Miss Kimberly where you're going!"

Number Two sucks in her breath, asking, "Are you going somewhere, Dalton?" Like she can't believe it.

He quits punching long enough to nod. But then the miniature fist barrage continues, right where it left off.

"Where are you going?" Number Two asks, her eyes bulging with exaggerated suspense.

When he still doesn't answer, Fake Hair speaks up for him. "The *beach*! Can you tell Miss Kimberly you're going to the beach?"

He shakes his head, reaching in the rack beside him for a candy bar instead. "Get me this. I want *this*." And he holds up the king-sized chocolate bar for his mother to observe.

"But we've already bought you the lunch-ums, Sweetie—and the juice boxes, too. Isn't that what you said you wanted?" she asks.

"Yup." He nods, looking kind of guppie-ish. "But I want *this*, too."

"Do you have your allowance with you, Dalton?" she asks. "Remember that things cost money. You can't just take them. Do you remember what we call that? When people just take things?"

He starts making this buzzing sound then, flying the candy bar through the air like it's a plane or something. When it becomes obvious that he's not going to answer, she reminds him, herself, saying, "That's what we call '*stealing*.' When we take things that don't belong to us. And that's not good."

He continues to ignore her, now threatening to crash the 'plane' into the magazines that line the register.

"Dalton, Sweetie—why don't we *not* do that?" she suggests pleasantly, then asks again, "Where's your money? You need to count out the right amount if you're going to pay for it when we get to the register."

"I'm *not*," he informs her.

"No? You're not paying? Don't you have money today, Sweetie?"

"No." He tosses the candy bar into the cart. "But *you* do."

Again, she turns, shaking her head, as she laughs to Number Two, "Honestly, they know *exactly* what they want, don't they?" Still, she makes no attempt to remove the candy bar from her cart, no attempt at saying 'Not today.' In fact, she makes no attempt whatsoever to show Little Dalton the value of this experience, the value of actually carrying his *own* money with him. God, I feel sorry for his future girlfriend.

The checkout woman is waiting more or less impatiently for the line to move along before Fake Blond actually notices that she has created a hold-up.

"Here, Dalton. Help Mommy put the groceries up on the register so the girl can ring them up. Because we have to pay, you know."

Instead, he skips off towards the gum machines, totally ignoring this woman that is supposedly his mother. And if I were her? I wouldn't claim him, anyway.

She shakes her head in feigned exasperation, turning towards Number Two again. "He has absolutely *no* attention span. It's really becoming more and more of a challenge every day just to keep him on-task."

"Well," Number Two sighs. "You know what they say about gifted children."

Gifted, my ass! Because I can pretty much tell her what the problem is right now—right while we're all standing here. And she wouldn't even *need* to waste her money on a stupid psychologist. Somehow, though, I don't think she'd buy it.

Don't get me wrong. I'm not saying that children should be beaten into submission. Nothing like that. Because truly, I like kids. But when they are given to us, I believe it is with the expectation that we will make the effort to *raise* them, get our hands dirty with the actual exercise of 'parenting.' And yes, that means accepting responsibility in situations that might be a little uncomfortable. We, after all, are the adults. And if we want our kids to grow into responsible adults, too, then at some point, we have to take credit, or blame—whichever happens to be the case—for their actions. Which, in turn, brings me to the beef. ADHD. Okay, so maybe he really *does* have it. I'm no doctor, so who am I to judge? Maybe there's no such thing as over-diagnosing, anyway. After all, if anyone should know that these chemical imbalances really *do* exist, it would have to be me. Hands down. Still, if I ever *did* have kids of my own, I know I'd never seek something like this out. I'd never choose '*chemical imbalance*' as a label for my child. And certainly not just because it's the '*in*' thing to do right now, the 'flavor of the month,' so to speak. These people just don't know, simply have no clue what it's like to actually live in a chemically-imbalanced body. Because if they did, they'd understand that there's nothing rewarding about it at all, nothing to be proud of, nothing to boast about. It's just not something you'd ever want your kids to experience, no matter what—not if you really loved them.

It's the main reason I elected *not* to have kids. Sometimes I feel like I've missed out on something really important in life, though. Especially when I see all these young, suburban mothers, pushing their little mini-me's in politically correct strollers, or wheeling them through the grocery store in the built-in child seats. Still, regardless of how I feel, I know it's not worth bringing someone else into this world—not when he has the chance of inheriting—or I guess I should say of being cursed with—his mother's genes. Sure, it's a gamble—he might get his father's, after all. But for me, that's just too much of a risk—and one that I'm not willing to take.

As I begin to unload my groceries onto the conveyer belt, I glance up at the sliding 'exit' doors just in time to see ADHD running out ahead of Fake Blond. "Now Dalton—you need to *wait* for Mommy . . . ."

Personally, I think Dalton needs a good, old-fashioned spanking. It'd sure fix a lot more than labeling him '*chemically imbalanced*' ever could. Because there *are* no excuses, no convenient outlets. So deal with it, already—your child is not perfect, and neither is he supposed to be, so why should this even be an issue? And though I'm not a parent, my guess is that it never should.

IT'S NOT NORMAL TO BE ABNORMAL

My earliest memories go all the way back to the crib, believe it or not. Literally. I mean, back to the day when I decided it was time for me to get a 'big kid' bed, so I actually devised this plan to make my parents think the crib had suddenly become too small for me, that somehow I'd just happened to outgrow it while they weren't looking. This seemed like a pretty good idea to me, and to this day, I can still remember climbing up over the pink and blue spindles and lying on my back, scrunching way down on the mattress so that my feet hung out of the bars at the end. I also remember the way my parents looked down at me, there in the crib—smiling, no less— while I was trying so hard to be completely somber. But for whatever reason, it worked, and shortly thereafter, I had my first 'real' bed—

what my mother called a 'bonnet bed.' The bed, itself, was pretty plain, but on the wall above me, there hung a wonderful valance covered in flowered chintz, and across the wall behind it as well as flowing down the sides, fell these pink filmy dotted-swiss curtains. And my mother'd fixed the dresser to match as well, gathering a dotted-swiss skirt around the vanity and covering the little wrought-iron stool cushion in the same flowered material as the valance. I knew no one else with anything like it, and I thought it was a room made for a princess.

Sometimes at night, I would lie in bed, pretending that I *was* a real princess, and that my bed was my castle. I even imagined that it took wing and 'flew away' on certain nights, riding me all over town, past my friends' houses where I could look down and see them sleeping in their beds, too. This was before the debut of 'Bed Knobs and Broomsticks,' so I had no trouble giving myself credit for the idea behind the magical bed in that movie, too, even if nobody else knew it, but me.

These are the evenings that should have been filled with catching crickets in cotton nightgowns, with picking wild strawberries and bathing before vacation Bible school. All the things you'd do in a small town. And I'd be lying if I said that they weren't. Because I had a wonderful childhood in every sense of the concept—despite the other part of me—the other person who lived inside of me.

* * *

Okay, fast forward—all the way to 1993. I am a newly released college graduate. I've managed to land a good sales job, splurged on some really cool clothes, and as I drive down the highway in my new red convertible (top down, of course), I feel like I've finally made it in this world. Regardless of my differences, regardless of the difficulties it actually took to finally get here. And looking back, I have to admit, I feel like the little lizard in the Geico commercial. Because if anyone else could ever understand the significance of being totally different in such an unforgiving world, it would be him. The most important thing to remember through all of this, though, is to be good at what you do. In other words, *appear* normal. You never want to call attention to yourself by letting anyone see your differences—because they translate *not* into simple 'weaknesses,' but instead into complex incapacitating 'abnormalities.' Hence, you are now the *weirdo* that everyone avoids. Or sure, they smile at you, and they're nice enough, friendly and all—just as long as you keep your distance. Like they think it's contagious or something. Who says the concept of Leprosy's a thing of the past? Because when people discover that there's something different about you, something that they can neither understand nor explain, they officially hand over your cowbell and 'unclean' sign. I mean, I became aware of this very early in life—the fact that a behavioral revelation on my part has disastrous consequences. Because there's nothing worse than *not* being normal. Especially when you are in high school. College—now that's a different story. People thrive on their differences there, talk about them, display them. They become learning experiences for everyone around you. You are proud of your differences because they contribute in large part to who you are as an individual. And in college, that's important—being an individual. Being your own person.

And of the corporate world? I wish I could say the same. But when you reach that plateau, that ultimate point in your 'education,' this is where the cold, hard reality hits you, completely without warning. All of a sudden, it's no longer about you as an individual, but instead about your *position* as a team player. No one cares whether you can make the basket, just that you can toss the ball. And if you have anything they even *perceive* as a slight difference, no matter how subtle or insignificant it may be, they will never pick you to play on their team. And if you're somehow already a part of the team when they finally radar in to it? Forget it—you're ostracized. There *is* no second chance. And when the *other* teams out there get wind that the *first* team you played on didn't want you, you can forget that, too. Moving on, I mean. Getting a fresh, new start. It'll never happen. Because you've just committed corporate suicide. For lack of a better way to explain, all I can say is it's like being back in 7th grade P.E. all over again. When the jock-ass coach names the two most athletic kids in the class to be his team 'captains,' giving them total power to pick whomever they want for their respective sides. And you—*you* stand there, waiting like a complete dummy—because you have been blessed with the privilege of being the 98-pound-class-dork, whether you asked for it or not. And will you ever experience being first? Sure, when you stand in the middle of the dodge-ball circle in that same P.E. class, you will be the very *first* one all the jocks aim for, and they don't care how hard they hit you with the ball, either. Just so they get you 'out.' Think it's juvenile? Think again. Because the corporate world is under no obligation to play by anyone else's rules—only its own. And yes, they *can* make up the rules as they go. I let the cowbell rest.

If I'd had any choice about it, I'd have been born normal. Totally. But if I *had* to pick my own disability, if there was simply no way around it, I'd definitely take something physical over *this* any day—over this mental stress, this crippling fear that's spawned out of absolutely nothing. Fear that won't let me leave the house at times. Fear that makes me do repetitive, mundane things—like, for instance, turning a light switch on and off. Over and over again. Until the Fear inside is finally satisfied that I've done it enough times, that I've earned the right to sidestep any evil it has threatened me with—*this* time. And if it lets you off easy, like you only have to do it one or two times extra, you're damned lucky. But this unknown Fear drives a hard bargain—and you are more than likely going to be bullied into doing it an infinite number of times, usually consisting of groups of 2's or 4's—sometimes if it's really bad, groups of 8's or more. As for myself, it usually wants me to do things in pairs like this—in even numbers. Then everything balances out.

Now imagine you live with this torture day in and day out. Panic attacks followed by desperate repetitive motions, followed by more panic attacks that you'd hoped to ward off with the repetitive motions. Not exactly the panic attacks, themselves, since they're just the result of the unknown Fear, but instead to ward off whatever it is the Fear has threatened you *with*. For me, it was getting sick for the most part. And anytime I came down with an ailment, I'd always wonder what it was I'd done wrong, why the Fear had allowed this to happen. Oh, it threatens you with other things, too. Like telling you your house is going to burn down, your favorite pet is going to run away never to be seen again, or your parents are about to be killed. Anything. It's not choosy. Sometimes it even likes to be humorous and scare you into believing that your skirt is going to suddenly fall down, that you're going to trip over your own feet, blurt out something stupid, and that everyone will laugh at you. But overall, the thing it really focuses on—where it shows the most prevalence, is zeroing in on the one thing you are scared of the most, and that's how it gets control of you. Your private life becomes this series of rituals, apologies and hostile frustrations, while publicly, you are trying to appear cool, collected—and you are constantly thinking of excuses, of believable explanations that you'll give people when they accidentally 'catch' you in the act, and want to know exactly what the heck it is you're *doing* with the light switch. Or the cold water faucet, or the remote control. Whatever. It doesn't matter what the item is, or whether its even tangible or not. Because nothing that actually exists in your world (and even some things that *don't* exist) is immune to the ritualistic bargaining that the Fear tortures you with every single day of your life.

So far, I have been lucky. I have finally gotten through college—NC State University—even made honor roll several times. And I've actually managed to land a real job—a *professional* one where I have my own office space and personalized business cards. I have learned not to fight the Fear anymore, but rather, to work *with* it. This has created a flexibility, though a subtle one, to where I can actually function. Because as a child, I'd always believed I'd eventually outgrow it—this voice of Fear that constantly invaded my thoughts, controlled my actions. Strangely though, as I have grown, gotten older, it, too has grown, taking root and claiming a stronger life of its own to steadily take over my whole body in some remotely parasitic way—to the point where there is no room in there—in my own body—for *me* anymore.

Sometimes I am angry and I just want to know 'why,' especially when I remember the overwhelming dump truck load being dropped all over me as a very little child, the way I had to fight so hard every single day, just to keep from giving in and letting it suffocate me. It is so completely unfair. No child should ever be burdened with such an adult illness. I don't know how I ever managed to grow up. Because to this day, no matter what I've learned or how old I am, just out of the blue and completely without warning, it can still bring me down to my knees—just like it did when I was six.

KINDERCARE

In 1993, at age 27, I am still searching for answers. I am driving my red convertible towards a place I haven't been in a very long time. A place where my strongest memories of the Fear are spawned. The place where I can still vividly remember my first panic attack. I don't know exactly why I've decided to come back here, or what I'm hoping to find. But my hometown—Wendell—actually happens to be in my new sales territory, so to say I'd just be in the neighborhood wouldn't be completely inaccurate. 'Besides,' I rationalize. 'I'm not that scared little kid standing inside the fence anymore.'

Carver Kindergarten. Located just across the railroad tracks, kind of on the outskirts of town, it had been an exclusively Black school until the mid '60's. Until integration. The school, itself, was named for George Washington Carver, Jr., a renowned African-American scientist from the turn of the century whose work was mostly centered in Chemorgy, later known as Biochemical Engineering, which is a branch of science that deals with creating usable products from organic matter. Most people remember him best for his experimentation with peanuts, though.

I remember sitting at the breakfast table on my first day of school and asking my mother, "What do I call them?"

"What do you mean, 'what do you call them?'" she'd asked. "They're *people*, just like you and me. God doesn't differentiate among people."

She told me I should just ignore it when some of the others in town, especially the older ones, referred to them as 'colored'—or even worse.

I park my new convertible in the area where the buses used to stop. But it is just after midday now, so there's no reason to worry about blocking the driveway, at least for a while yet.

It is a nice fall afternoon—around 75ish and breezy. Random clouds dot the otherwise sunny sky as I follow the walkway towards the side door—the one that leads into the cafeteria—the same route I'd taken daily some twenty-two years ago. But I still maintain that I can handle it now. I'm all grown up, and have long ago put away the theory that monsters exist.

The first thing that strikes me is how little everything is; the low tables, the miniature chairs. As I make my way through the cafeteria, I can hear the steam washer hissing somewhere back in the kitchen. Voices of children float in from the surrounding hallways, the playground, though none of them are actually visible.

I push the doors open at the opposite end of the cafeteria and walk out towards the classrooms where the voices now become more pronounced. The second thing I notice is the forgotten smell. Kind of a mixture of Clorox and mildewed papyrus. It hits me hard, the smell. Funny how the things that you *don't* recall can actually be the sharpest thorns when your memory is unexpectedly pricked by them. These are the things that make you bleed.

She is here somewhere. I can feel her. I half expect to walk around a corner and suddenly see her standing there, waiting for me. She will immediately know who I am, what I'm there for. Because in her mind, I am the imaginary savior she has conjured up. She will want me to help her, and I wish so much that I could. But I am at a complete loss, and I have absolutely no idea what to say to her. Because the ability to actually touch her—to reach and grab her outstretched hands, to take her with me—is a complete impossibility. We exist on different planes. She will not understand this. It won't matter how hard I try to explain. It'll all be pointless. Because in the end, I, too—the shining savior she has created—will be yet just another grown-up to let her down.

I push the feeling away, trying to focus instead on the reason that I've come here, and I know I have to let go—to be strong—to leave her behind, no matter how hard it is. Still, it makes me feel like I did the morning they discovered my cat had cancer, and I had to leave him at the vet's to be put down. I knew he was old; I knew there was nothing I could do for him. Still, something screamed inside of me that day for actually *doing* it, for having the audacity to turn my back on him. For giving up so easily. Because how do you explain 'good-bye?' How do you find those last words?

I take a sharp left and walk towards the girl's bathroom. I am surprised to see that after all these years, the same motif still hangs on the wooden door, identifying which one it is; the faded silhouette of a girl's head cut from blue-flowered paper. I suddenly wonder who made it—who took the time to cut it out. Had it been a teacher? An aide? Or maybe a grade mother?

Inside the hushed bathroom, the only sound is the monotonous drip-dripping from one of the old, porcelain faucets. The smell is more prevalent in here, much more defined, adding a strong mixture of pine cleaner to the otherwise musty mix. I feel my stomach roll over as I turn to leave, but I catch myself right then. I will not go there.

Back out in the hallway, I retrace smaller footsteps towards the classrooms. First there is Mrs. Hedrick's room, on the right. I can still remember when we got our class assignments, how disappointed I'd felt when I hadn't been in Mrs. Hedrick's room. Instead, I'd gotten the new teacher. But my best friend, Christie, got Mrs. Hedrick, so that meant we weren't going to be together. I remember crying about that. I remember my mother telling me that I could still see Christie after school and on week-ends. She told me I'd make new friends in the other classroom. I told her I didn't want 'new' friends. But still, I promised her that I'd try.

Caddy-cornered and to the left is Mrs. Willard's room. I can see that the wooden door with its frosted glass pane is open, and I glance in timidly before entering. It is devoid of all children, but the back door leading out to the playground is propped open, and small voices float in with the breeze. Large, awkward drawings on Manila paper line the back wall, and they, too, lift and settle randomly with the gentle gusts of fall air.

"Hello."

I turn quickly at the sound of the voice to find an aide smiling up at me from a miniature table where she is grading papers. I don't recognize her.

"May I help you?"

It's amazing how such a simple question can, at the same time, actually be so loaded, so complicated. But I just return her smile. Better to keep things simple because how in the world do you explain twenty-two years of stuff you don't get, yourself?

"I was a student here," I tell her, then add quickly, "a long time ago."

I glance around again. "This was my classroom. I—I just wanted to come back and visit." I wonder why my voice sounds so thin.

"Oh, how nice!" she is saying.

"I don't remember everything being this small," I tell her, and she laughs.

"Well, it wasn't back then," she explains. Now it's my turn to smile.

"Who was your teacher?"

"Mrs. Willard," I say. "And Mrs. Holding was the aide."

"How about that?" she exclaims. "You know Mrs. Holding just retired this past year."

"No, I didn't know that," I tell her, genuinely surprised. But then I realize that what seems to be complete eons to me is actually, in reality, the normal span of a teacher's career. Or any career, for that matter. I've often wondered before why lives and events outside of your own don't seem so long and drawn-out, but when you try to think about your own past, it seems like it goes on forever. I finally came to the conclusion that this is because we have no concept of time at all before we are born, so to visualize our own lives *is* to visualize forever, in a sense. It's all we know.

The aide tells me to help myself, to have a look around, and I thank her. It doesn't occur to me at the time why I don't notice the things that I seem to remember most. Like whether the large, patchwork show-and-tell rug that used to fill the main right corner of the room is still there. The rug where we all had to pick a shape and sit Indian-style before we could start 'Magic Circle.' Or if the large, wooden sandbox still remained, standing on sturdy legs under one of the tall sections of windows lining the back wall; windows that were covered with varying lengths of dilapidated shades, brittle and yellowed with age. Or even the shelf beside the back door where Mrs. Willard kept a box of sewing pins; pins that she used to attach letters and correspondence to our dresses and shirts with as we lined up to leave in the afternoon—so we wouldn't lose them on the way home. The idea of using straight pins on kindergarteners today—for any purpose at all—seems completely absurd, maybe even a little humorous. But counteractively, I wonder what anyone would have said back then about the concept of e-mail, let alone computers? Strangely, as I am missing all these things, another forgotten memory rears itself out of the thorn bush. It's a song—one the teachers would always start, and we would join in as soon as we heard them. It was to get us to pick up our area before lunch, before going home. I hear the voices as clear as a bell; they're all around me in the empty room.

"Clean-up tiiime, get your things together! Clap your hands and let's get started!" How completely odd that I'd never even thought about that song until now, but yet, here were the words, coming back to me just as plain as day. Just like it was yesterday.

". . . . Get along, boys, it's clean-up tiiime! Get along, girls, it's clean-up tiiime!"

I leave the phantom voices behind, though they linger in the air, following me out into the hallway before finally fading away.

A little further down is the multi-purpose room. There are four large mats placed on the floor—one for each class—where we'd come to sit and watch a movie or have a guest librarian read a story to us. That was our mat, the one on the back left. Mrs. Hedrick's was the one in front of ours. Sometimes the teachers had to ask Mrs. Hedrick's class to lie down on their mat so that our class could see, too. Then there was the time when they hoarded us all down to the multi-purpose room in the morning, which was unusual since movies and story-reading always came in the afternoon, following nap time. It wasn't until we were loaded onto the yellow buses and driven to the elementary school several miles away that we were told where we were actually going; to a mass vaccination against a new strain of measles—Rubella, to be exact—conducted by the county health department. Then, at that point, there was nothing we could do but follow the teachers into the auditorium and all hold hands—whether to keep our line in-tact or to keep our knees from knocking, I can't actually recall—as we waited our turns for the nurses up front to give us each a shot. There were three of them, all dressed in white, complete with little semi-circle hats pinned to their respective beehives; one to actually do the injection, itself, and the other two for the sole purpose of keeping us immobile while Number One did her thing.

I have to laugh a little at the recollection. Because back then, they didn't play. If it was something that needed to get done, it got done. Period. Any questions? I didn't think so.

My eyes continue to trail further down the multi-purpose room, towards the back corner where, unbelievingly, the sterile little cot with starched sheets still sat. For some reason, I can't tear my eyes from it, and again, I unexpectedly feel my stomach tighten. I feel the conflict, the betrayal as I look around for the adult who had walked in here so confidently only minutes ago. Suddenly, I don't know who I am anymore, and my whole purpose for the visit is swept out from under me. Kind of like when you're standing at the edge of the ocean, and you can feel the sand rapidly breaking away under your feet while at the same time, the waves are pulling against you.

Carver School (later Carver Kindergarten)

Wendell Elementary

SPONTANEOUS COMBUSTION

Someone is calling me. I think I hear my name. Then the folded sheet placed over the back of my head for coolness is removed.

"Angie?" Though it is phrased like a question, it is actually more of statement.

I recognize the authoritative voice even before I see her. Mimi. I feel like I've been asleep, like I don't really know what's going on yet. She is standing over me in a khaki rain coat and clear plastic bonnet as the teachers try to explain what happened.

"Hyperventilated—passed out. Called both numbers, but couldn't get her mother on the phone."

For some reason, I am scared. Then it all comes crashing back, and I shiver because I feel so small. It's not the first time I've felt this Fear, but it's never gone this far before.

One of the kids in my class—Raymond—exploded. It was during nap time. But they just turned the lights back on and swept the remains up, then took him out of the room in a giant rolling trash can, like it was no big deal.

Realistically, he'd just become ill from hoovering too many cookies over lunch, and they'd simply whisked him away to the office to call his mother while the janitor cleaned up the mess. But at the time, I didn't know what was going on, and I truly believed that it was the cookies that had made him explode, and that we'd never see him again.

I can remember the panic setting in, how my fingertips felt so cold and my face so hot as I realized how easily people could just explode and disappear into nothingness. What if I was next? After all, I'd eaten a cookie at lunch, too. Feeling the panic gather in the pit of my stomach, I tried as hard as I could to tell Mrs. Holding that I was afraid the same thing was going to happen to me, that I'd eaten a snickerdoodle cookie, too. And I definitely didn't want to explode like Raymond, leaving my soul to float around Carver Kindergarten indefinitely. No, I wanted to become an angel when I died. The kind you see on Christmas cards that have glossy wings and haloes. And who're usually playing golden horns, sometimes harps. But if you exploded, I didn't know if you still could. Because then there wouldn't be anything left of you that they could turn into an angel. What if when you exploded, you became nothing? Nobody could see you, nobody could hear you. You'd just be floating around out there in this inky blackness forever, all by yourself.

The fear I felt at that moment I can never explain; the cold, desperate hopelessness of it. The aloneness. The complete wave of terror that was swallowing me up. I began to cry.

This was it—the exact moment when the fear became the Fear, rearing its ugly head in what would be only one of uncountable times from then on for the rest of my life.

"Are you sick, too? Like Raymond?" Mrs. Holding asks, leaning down. But I can't answer. All I can manage to say is, "Please don't let it happen to me!"

Mrs. Willard has already started herding our class down the hall towards the multipurpose room for afternoon movies when Mrs. Holding notices the true extent of my distress. I am shivering and crying as she leads me over to the large mat in the front of the room, telling me to lie on my back. Mrs. Willard, noticing that something is wrong, comes over quickly then.

"Please don't let it happen to me! *Please!*"

Mrs. Holding stretches my arms out on the mat while Mrs. Willard leans over me, telling me to relax and take deep breaths. But no matter how deep my breaths are, the Fear is catching up with me all the same, and the only thing I can do is breathe harder and harder—to keep on outrunning it. I can feel my hands going numb, hear ringing in my ears, and from somewhere far away, Mrs. Willard's voice telling me, "Just relax now."

The next thing I know, I am here on the cot, waking up as Mimi leans over me. I am feeling better now, but the raw hopelessness of the Fear still hovers just in the background, letting me know it is still there, that it will always be there.

We don't say much on the ride home, and Mimi drops me off in the driveway where Mama has just pulled in, recently returning from the grocery store. I run through the misting rain towards the kitchen door where Frieda steps up, wagging her tail, waiting for me to pat her. But I've got much more important issues now—like what I'm going to do with this unsolicited dump-load of Fear that's just been dropped all over me—and I sidestep her instead, leaving her behind to look in through the screen door I've just let slam in her face.

When I died, I planned to become an 'angel' and fly away.

'Main Street' in the small, close-knit community of Wendell.

IT TAKES A VILLAGE TO RAISE A CHILD

Anyone who's grown up in a small town knows the drill; that you don't screw up. You just don't go there. Because if you do, one thing you can count on is that your teacher will definitely call your mother who, in turn, will undoubtedly be waiting at the front door for you as soon as you get home from school. And after she finishes whipping you, she always says those infamous last six words, the ones you dread the most; '*Wait till your father gets home*!' Because in this day and age, there is no such thing as child abuse. And already tired from a long day at work, you can depend on his being much, much worse as he reminds you between licks, "*I-brought-you-into-this-world-and-I-can-take-you-right-back-out-of-it-too*!" Think your run-in with the Wall of Shame is over now? Don't forget about Sunday lunch, where your mother relays play-for-play exactly what it was you did to your stunned grandparents who declare in unison, "*Lordy* mercy! *Mm*-mm-*mm!*" and "Hush! You *know* she didn't!"

Whoever it was that said '*sticks and stones may break my bones, but words can never hurt me,*' obviously never had a run-in with my grandparents—or any other small town grandparents for that matter. Because I'd gladly take another whipping over *this* any day. *Now* think its over? Guess again. Because when you go to your *great*-grandmother's house for Sunday *supper* and *she* finds out what you did, there are no words to describe your shame. Because she doesn't even have to say anything. Motney just has this way of looking over her glasses at you, and whatever it was that you'd done instantly becomes a dead issue; it'll never happen again. Not in *your* lifetime. You *swear* it! Only don't let *her* hear anything about you—or anyone else for that matter—actually 'swearing.' Because if she does, that's when the obligatory Bible comes out, and the pages just know—they just automatically fall open—right to the dooming scripture she will undoubtedly read—and you will undoubtedly hear. No, you definitely don't want to screw up.

Once when she was keeping Kay and me, we were playing around when I called my sister an 'old fool.' Just as Kay was saying, "No *you're* the old fool," Motney appears in the doorway. All six feet of her. The Bible in her hand falls open to a passage from Proverbs and she gravely reads us a scripture—one that says '*Thou shalt not call thy brother a fool.*' While Kay is busy pointing out, "But Motney, we're not *brothers*, we're *sisters*," I am amused, wondering what she'd say if she knew what we *really* called each other—when we were actually mad; 'Dig-a-Dig,' 'Little Pig' or 'Big, Fat Pig' (depending on the severity of what you'd done), 'Habitrail'—which is Kay's personal favorite for me because it refers to my incessant touching of objects. Oh, and don't forget 'stupid' and 'dummy.'

"In God's eyes, we're *all* brothers," Motney tells her, then returns to the kitchen to stir her butter beans.

At first, we'd just thought Motney was telepathic, that maybe she had ESP or something. Now, though we've pretty much figured it out—come to the only explicable conclusion there is—that she, herself, *wrote* the Bible.

Realistically, Motney is an icon, in and of herself. In fact, if you looked up the word 'grand' in the dictionary, it'd be her picture you'd find there among the definitions. Her real name is Martha. But when my father was a little boy, he'd been unable to say 'Miss Martha,' and somehow turned 'Martha into 'Motney,' which she's been ever since. She's who our youngest sister, Martie, is named for. She is one of the founding corner stones of Wendell Christian Church, where every Sunday, without fail, she plays the organ, and each year, she donates large quantities of money to its cause. Motney's husband, Mallie, whom we never met because he'd died of cancer back when my father was still in high school, was just as much of an icon as she was. Serving as town mayor, he was also the president of the 'Bank of Wendell,' where it was a well-known fact what lenient terms he placed on his loans, especially in hard times. And though he is no longer with us in the physical sense, he is still among us; the family has seen to it that his love and generosity (not to mention his peculiaralities) did not go to the grave with him.

Remarrying was not an option for Motney. She probably never even thought of it. Instead, she traveled. All over the world. Even to countries whose names you were scared to speak, like Cuba and Russia. Kay and I had a wonderful collection of foreign dolls that we kept lined up on our dressers. They were the kind you didn't play with, though. They were the kind you just looked at. And when she wasn't traveling? You could always find Motney in the yard with her straw hat, planting flowers or pulling up weeds. She is the only person I know who can not only tell you what each flower is, but also exactly what each weed is. Sometimes when Mama goes to pick corn or snap beans, Motney goes with us. And while Kay and I sit waiting in the stifling Plymouth Fury, all four doors propped wide open as we try to come up with new and exciting ways to torture each other, Mama and Motney are busy filling up their bushel baskets with what will be our winter rations. Later, we will go sit on Motney's back yard swing and shuck the corn, then snap the beans. It'll be much cooler then, and as long as I don't have any run-ins with corn worms, I'll be fine. Kay likes the corn worms, likes to play with them because they're furry and cute. She *would*.

Motney has two children; Granddaddy and his older sister, Sue. Aunt Sue is the 'funnest' person I know. She rides a bicycle with a flowered basket strapped to the handle bars, and the time we asked her to go to the State Fair with us, she came skipping out Motney's backdoor, all smiles, with her bright sweater in tow. She's the one who taught me how to ride the Ferris wheel, how to look up at the sky so my stomach didn't feel like it was rolling up in my chest. Aunt Sue liked to take us to the swimming pool, too, where we'd stay for hours; she didn't believe in that *going-for-30-minutes* crap. No, if Aunt Sue took you to the pool, you could rest assured that the only thing to cut it short of an all-day event would be a thunderstorm. A *severe* one. She didn't just sit on the side of the pool, either. She actually got in and splashed around with the rest of us. And she didn't even care if anyone laughed at her rubber swimming cap. Later, when we'd finally get back to her house to clean up, Aunt Sue would see nothing wrong with running out on her back deck (*underdressed*) to hang her wet bathing suit over the railing. Sometimes she even waved to the next door neighbor, if he happened to be out, cutting his grass. When we acted surprised, Sue would just say, "This is the body God gave me, wrinkles, flab and everything. He made it, so why should I be ashamed of it?"

Most of the family didn't really study it too hard; they just laughed and said that Sue tended to be a touch like Mallie. I wasn't sure whether this was good or not, but I didn't care because either way, I planned to be just like Sue when I grew up.

On the opposite end of the Fujita scale is Granddaddy. I mean, if their lives could be outlined using coloring books as a simile, then Granddaddy's picture would be exactly the way you'd expect. The sky would be blue, the sun yellow, the grass green, and all the trousers and obligatory ties would match, embodying the same shade of subdued brown. Everything would be in its proper place, and there would be absolutely no stray marks outside of the lines. It'd be the kind of picture you'd tear out of the book and hang on the bulletin board for PTA Night. Sue, on the other hand, would not have been the least bit confined by lines at all. Instead, she'd have made her own picture—right over the one that was already there. And a blue sky? Why in the world would you want to do that? No, in contrast, Sue's picture would be the kind that all the teachers would refer to in a tongue-in-cheek sort of way as resembling 'modern art' (*bless her heart*).

Though Granddaddy didn't really posses any of the idiosyncrasies that Mallie had, he *did* follow in his father's footsteps in other ways. He, too, ran his own business, 'Todd Electric,' a successful appliance and T.V. store. And like his father, it was a known fact what lenient terms he placed on his financing as well. Up into the '90's, his business was one of the only ones around that still catered to customer service the way that his did. And like his father, too, Granddaddy served as town mayor until his arthritis became too much to bear. Then he served on the town council—all the way up until his death in 1994.

Granddaddy was a strong and intelligent man. He was a genius when it came to managing money and financial situations, and lucky for me, also when it came to algebra problems. I can still remember the endless nights I cried on the phone to him, reading out my algebra problems so he could write them down, figure them out on his own paper and then explain to me how they worked. Unlike my teachers, though, Granddaddy refused to use any of the short-cuts they taught us in school. Instead, he went through each and every grueling step. But by the time he'd finished, I could work the problem backwards and forwards, even with my eyes closed. Sometimes to this day, I still find myself thinking things through in much the same way that Granddaddy taught me how to do algebra, even though these things really have nothing to do with math at all.

Granddaddy had rheumatoid arthritis—the crippling kind. He'd gotten it in his early twenties following a car accident in which he'd injured his spleen. The arthritis had progressed severely—until he'd later had his spleen removed. But by that time, his hands were already bent into the shape of claws, his feet, almost club-like. Each year when he and Mimi traveled to the mountains for their annual vacation, he'd schedule an appointment with a man he knew there who would make special shoes for him. Looking back, I realize how utterly painful his condition must have been. But at the time, it didn't strike me as such. Though he limped, he never complained, and the shape of his hands and feet were simply distinguishing characteristics as far as I was concerned. They were just a part of what made him who he was—of what made him 'Granddaddy.'

And of Mimi? He'd done real well in finding her. She is a true southern belle, through and through. Originally from Georgia, she'd met him, of all places, in a dentist's office where she worked as a hygienist. A recent graduate of NC State University, he was putting his electrical engineering degree to use, working for Southern Bell Phone Company. At the time, he'd been transferred temporarily to Georgia, where he'd had the uncanny luck of developing a cavity. The rest is history.

Mimi, herself, is a very complex person embodied neatly in a petite frame. In her early twenties, she'd sung with a traveling band by night, then worked as a dental hygienist by day to make ends meet. Sometimes she plays the records for us that she made back in those days, and the low, sultry voice that emanates from the speakers, filling the room around us is beautiful, mysterious—holds a longing that is almost painful. We ask her why she traded all that in—why she gave all that up, just for a small-town church choir.

She doesn't hesitate.

"Because I loved your granddaddy."

Not just her voice is beautiful. Mimi, herself, is, too. She is always dressed to the nines, and anything she chooses to put on, she wears exceptionally well. She is the most beautiful woman in Wendell, hands down. Anyone here could tell you that. And though I intend to inherit Aunt Sue's free spirit, I also aspire to inherit Mimi's poise and grace. Especially since I already know I did not inherit her voice.

One Christmas, back when Granddaddy was serving as mayor, a newspaper article written on the family had referred to her as the First Lady of Wendell. At the time, it didn't make sense to me. Because I knew there were lots of women who'd been here much longer than she had. But after I asked, Mama explained to me what the term 'First Lady' actually meant, and then I finally understood its implications. Not only is she a beautiful person on the outside, but Mimi is also very well-respected, both personally and politically. And when she speaks, everyone listens. This, too, is something anyone here could tell you. Because if you live in Wendell, it's simply a given.

Overall, our extended family is a large and diverse group. Probably just like anyone else's. But then we have our peculiarities to deal with as well. Like, for instance, there's 'Aunt Gladys.' No one knows whose aunt she actually is or where she came from. But for the past hundred years, she has religiously shown up at every family function without fail. Usually dishless and empty-handed, she is instead armed with a broad range of opinions, useless information, and hoards of advice that no one really wants to hear. I try to console myself with the fact that probably every family has its own 'Aunt Gladys,' that there's no way it can just be us. But still, I've never quite been able to bring myself to ask any of my friends about this, though.

(Ooops!) Take two . . . .

(from left) Kay, Motney, Me
(back row) Daddy, Granddaddy, Aunt Sue, Mimi, Mama

'Motney' (a.k.a. the definition of 'Grand.')

*Wendell Christian Church
(of which Motney was one of the founding cornerstones)*

*Motney, Aunt Sue and Granddaddy
(as a young family in the 1920's)*

Mimi in her 'Singing Days'

IMAGINARY HATE MATE

Most kids have imaginary playmates. Like, for instance, my younger sister, Martie had three; Khaki, Grainger and Deevis. Khaki and Grainger were girls. Deevis, I believe, was androgynous. And often you could hear her in her room, jabbering away to these non-existent people who were always a handy outlet when she happened to get in trouble; she could always blame it on Khaki.

But Kay and I, we didn't have just a few imaginary playmates. Instead, we had the '*Wincarter Book*.' It was this whole imaginary *lifestyle*. In The Book, there were three of us, the third being a runaway whom we'd rescued and taken in to live with us as an equal sister. (Her character was based on an early movie we'd seen called 'Flight of the Doves,' in which two children were running away from home. The movie starred Jack Wild (on whom we both had a painfully unrequited crush and whom most people would remember best from his role as 'Jimmy' on H.R. Puffinstuff), and a young, new actress with blond curly hair, who played his sister. Her name was Helen Ray, and we thought she was absolutely perfect.)

The Wincarter Book, itself, consisted of nothing more than old half-used composition books, their ragged wires bent into submission, loose-leaf paper with varying degrees of lineage, and leftover drawing paper. But to us, it might as well've been etched in gold. Whereas someone else might think the scribbled drawings of stick figures and what appeared to be tornadoes and UFO's were simply the doodlings of a bored child, he, unfortunately, just wasn't getting the whole picture, no pun intended. Because for us, there was an hour-long story behind each and every drawing, which we could recite, word-for-word, any time we read The Book, an activity that took, on the whole, about a week to do. Sometimes we drew new pictures to add to The Book, other times, we just sat around Kay's room, 'reading' it.

Had it just been the story of three happy girls who lived in a place called Lucky Duck Land where nothing bad ever happened, it might seem more justifiable as a child's imaginary creation. But no, that wasn't good enough. We had to have a force of evil as well; someone who was not only mean, herself, but to whom we could be mean in return. The whole concept worried Mama, who, on more than one occasion, took The Wincarter Book away, due to its abusive content. We had originally based The Book on one of my sister's friends with whom she'd had a fight. But Mama refused to give it back until we took the little girl out, saying it was cruel and uncalled for. This is the point at which we were forced to look for surrogate enemies. And we finally found one; a guest star on the T.V. show, 'Family Affair,' who'd been really mean to Buffy and Jody, named none other than 'Win Carter.' Thus, was born 'The *Wincarter* Book.'

Like Aunt Gladys, no one really knew where Wincarter came from or to whom she was actually related. She was more of an entity than a being, and she embodied many different forms. Sometimes she was a stick figure like the rest of us. Other times, she appeared as an F-5 tornado, trying to destroy everything in her wake, which, of course, she couldn't do because we lived in Lucky Duck Land where nothing bad ever happened. Most often, though, she appeared as a large floating bubble complete with an ugly face, to which a string was attached, and one of the three of us always held in tow, like a giant helium balloon.

Wincarter, herself, had only one friend, Thingamajig, who was in her class at school and who lived just up the street. There were 101 Majigs in all, and the family lived in a three-bedroom house. Sometimes, if Wincarter was really good, which wasn't often, Mother would let her go spend the night at Thingamajig's house, where all the Majigs would be vying for a place to sleep as it was. And in the morning when she came home, what did she have for breakfast? Bread and water. But what if there weren't any end-pieces left over and what if it didn't happen to be raining? Then we hated it for her. Because at that point, she was just shit out of luck.

The absolute worst thing that could happen to you in those days was that you'd get 'changed bad,' where your character became Wincarter, and she became you. My sister had the sole power to do this since she kept The Book in her room, and if I made her mad enough in some way or another, she could always retaliate with those three dreaded words; *"You're changed bad!"*

Though I hate to admit it now, The Wincarter Book, in reality, was probably my earliest attempt at what would later become my so-called writing 'career.'

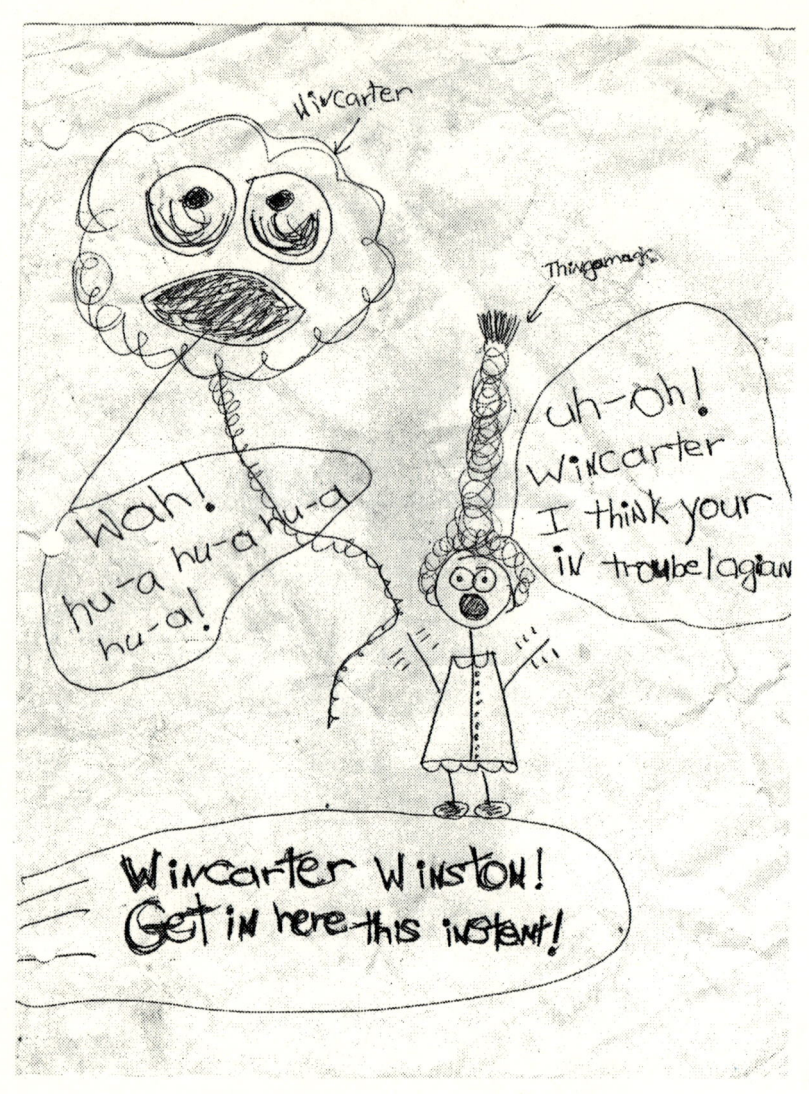

*Vintage picture from the 'Wincarter Book'
(starring 'Thingamajig' and 'Wincarter,' herself)*

"YEAH, AH 'SEEN IT"

"Once again, your action news reporter in the booth covering the disturbance at the basketball *playoffs*. Pardon *me*, sir—did you see what happened?"

"Yeah, ah 'seen it. Haff-time. Ah was up at the concession stand gettin' a *snow cone* when it happened . . . . all through the stands, across the basketball court. He wutten wearin' nuthin' but his *Ke-uds*. An' Ah hollered up at Ethel, Ah said, '*Don't look, Eth-el!*' But it was too late. She'd already got a *free* shot!"

We are laughing too hard to address Mama, who stands in the open doorway, looking like she can't decide whether to be shocked or pissed.

"*Whoa yes, they call 'em the streeek! Look-at-dat, look-at-dat!*"

Mama shakes her head, saying, "I can't believe your *daddy* brought you that record! I can't imagine *my* daddy ever even *thinking* about—I mean, my daddy would've *died* before he'd have *ever* brought something like that home to *his* daughter!"

We break down into peals of uncontrollable laughter, the image of Pop perusing the racks at Record Bar, let alone, even listening to Ray Stevens at all, way too much to grip. No, Pop's natural habitat was more likely in the A&P, his arms swinging like windmills on the junk food aisle. And he looked like the little cartoon man on the Hawaiian Punch commercial, too—the one who always got sucker-smacked right in the nose.

Overall, Pop is the sweetest little man in the world. He's always smiling and happy. We can never do anything wrong when he's around. And we find it hard to believe when Mama describes the whippings she claims that she and her three brothers used to get. Pop is a very busy person, too. He likes to always have something to do. Like Granddaddy, Pop had also graduated from NC State University. His degree was in engineering as well, but rather than 'electrical,' his was 'agricultural.' Pop had served his full thirty-five years working for the federal government in its agricultural department. But when he retired, he didn't just go home and rest like you were expected to. Instead, he got up every morning and wore his gold watch to a new job, one with a company called 'Crumpler Plastic Pipe,' and whenever he and 'Mom' (what we called my grandmother) came to visit, he would always bring a big pile of yellow notepads and orange pencils with the logo inscribed on them. They would also bring with them a huge assortment of shopping bags every time—from Belk's, Sears, K-Mart—wherever they happened to have shopped while they were in town, because Pop said there were no good places back home, in Lumberton. So they always saved their shopping sprees for when they came to visit us, or when they visited Mama's older brother who was a lawyer and lived in Atlanta. (Mama had two younger brothers as well; one who lived in Nashville and worked for a large, well-known beer distributing company, and an even younger one who was a hippy and who drove a convertible MG (a lot faster than he was supposed to, according to Mama). He was still in school at NC State, and had a pretty girlfriend who attended Peace College.

She'd made Kay and me these really cool Hollie Hobbie pillows for Christmas the year they came to visit.

Mom and Pop would always arrive on our doorstep as scheduled, Mom carrying one or two of the smaller bags, Pop, bringing up the rear with the brunt of them as well as Mom's four-pound pocketbook. (It was actually so heavy that Kay and I came up with the bright idea of sneaking it to the bathroom to weigh it one day, and that's what it actually registered—four whole pounds.) Because of this—the manner in which they arrived—Daddy referred to them in a tongue-in-cheek sort of way as 'the traveling gypsies.'

"That's not fair," Mama'd tell him. "I don't say anything like that about *your* mother!"

"Well, *my* mother doesn't land on the front porch with a whole posse of shopping bags, either," Daddy'd retort.

But that was probably the biggest difference in their upbringings. Daddy, who'd been an only child, had lived a quiet, private life in the same house throughout his entire childhood, whereas Mama and her three brothers had always shared a bathroom and had moved around a lot in order to accommodate Pop's job with the government. It was only after Jimmy, the baby, was in high school that they quit moving as much because Mom wanted Jimmy to be able to finish school with his friends. And it was during this time, when Jimmy was in high school, that Mom had her terrible wreck. It'd been raining, and she'd lost control of her car, running off into the ditch. She'd hit a dirt embankment, the impact throwing her into the back seat, where she'd landed on her neck. Jimmy's school bus had passed by the site, and he'd told the driver to stop, to let him off, because he'd thought that the car in the ditch looked an awful lot like his mother's. But the bus driver'd refused to put him out in the remote area, and with no other choice, he'd had to go on the rest of the way to school and then call his father from there.

Mom had ended up breaking her spine in the accident. The doctors were not hopeful that she would even make it through the night, what with the swelling in her neck. But she'd defied the odds, anyway, surprising everyone by pulling through. Though she had recovered, she'd been left with a paralyzed right arm. Still, she didn't let this slow her down much. And although she didn't drive anymore, she *did* sew and crochet since she still had the use of her fingers, and she'd taught herself to write all over again, using her left hand.

Sometimes Mom and Pop would wait to go shopping until after they'd get to our house, and we'd always beg to ride with them. The best time of all to tag along with Pop on one of his grocery outings was right after Halloween or Christmas, when all the candy was marked 50% off. Because you didn't even have to ask. He asked *you*, then dumped it in the cart, himself. "Hmmm—How about this? Marshmallows. You can get the king-size bag on sale for less than you can get the regular size. And look over here. If you buy one box of pop tarts, you get another one free." That was one of the neatest things about Mom and Pop visiting. They always had plenty of great food around. And you didn't have to wait until Saturday to eat sweet cereal, either. Not like here. Not like home, where we had to eat stupid Rice Krispies all week long (only two spoon-fuls of sugar allowed per bowl). No, we had to wait for Saturday to finally roll around before we could actually go into the kitchen and so much as touch the sweet cereal. Kay and I took turns picking out which kind we'd get—usually, for my week, it was Froot Loops. For her's it was Sugar Pops. But sometimes she'd just up and choose this weird stuff, for no apparent reason at all. Like she couldn't simply be normal. She had to go and pick out this totally weird cereal that no one'd ever heard of before. Like Ka-Boom, which had this funny-looking clown on the front of the box and tasted like a diluted cherry-and-grape version of Captain Crunch. Sometimes, though, she wouldn't go quite so far out into left-field, like when she picked Lucky Charms. For the most part, Lucky Charms cereal was good, at least until you ate up all the little moons and stars. Then you'd wind up with a whole bowl of this plain, left-over grainy cereal that wasn't any fun to eat. And in order to combat that, you had to keep adding more moons and stars from the box, until eventually, all you'd have left in the box, itself, was the grainy stuff that no one liked to eat. As far as I was concerned, it was a waste of good cereal—of what could have otherwise been a full box of some kind that was actually edible. The only reason Kay did this—pick out weird cereal—was to irritate me. I was sure of it. But still, anything's better than plain old Rice Krispies, and as long as we got up on our own Saturday morning and fixed it ourselves, we could eat all the sweet cereal we wanted—which usually involved the whole box—while we watched endless cartoons, like the 'Bugs Bunny Roadrunner Hour,' 'Sylvester and Tweetie,' 'Scooby Doo,' and 'Emergency + Four.'

Mama returns to my room, putting some folded shorts and tops in my bottom drawer—my summer drawer. She is still tight-lipped, shaking her head in disbelief.

"Ma-*ma*! It's *supposed* to be funny!" Kay tells her. She picks up the needle, starts the record over.

"Oh, it's *funny* alright. A *father* teaching his young *daughters* about streaking!"

But Daddy'd only pointed out, "It's not like they don't already know about it. Not when it's all over the news like it is right now."

"But you don't have to go spending *money* just to stick their noses in it!"

"I didn't spend any money," Daddy explains. "I got it at the station." He'd gotten the record—a demo—from the radio station where he worked at the time, and knowing how funny Kay and I found what Mama referred to as 'bathroom talk,' he figured we'd get a real kick out of it. And that summer—the summer of '73—was when, in addition to his radio-announcing gig, he'd started 'stringing' for the TV news stations as well, a position that would later become his full-time job. Mama, herself, had gone to work for the local newspaper that year, and with Daddy working two jobs now, they'd had to find something to do with me during the days, since school was out.

"Why can't I just stay here with Kay?" I'd whined.

"Because you'd kill each other," Mama tells me.

"But Mama—"

"No—no—*no*!"

It's over. Anything else I say is pointless. Because I know she means business when she slices her hands out to the sides like that, emphasizing every single 'no.'

So that summer, the summer after first grade, was the one I'd spend with the lady who lived all the way on the other side of town, and who, coincidentally, had a daughter about my age, named Stephanie. They'd thought it would be fun—getting to spend the summer with a new friend. But that, unfortunately, was the utopianistic version. The realistic version was that once together, we hated each other. Literally couldn't stand to breathe the same air. And we ended up spending more hours in 'time out' than I can even count, the little girl's exasperated mother continuously having to lecture us on the merits of getting along.

I hated going there, almost as much as I hated Stephanie, herself. I remember praying that I would stop having to go there. And I guess God finally felt sorry for me, too, because it wasn't a week later that Mimi paid us a visit one evening after supper, her plush car left idling in the driveway, a sign that 'this won't take very long.' Her alligator pumps click purposefully up the porch steps, and she raps lightly on the back door, just to let us know she's there, before letting herself in. She crosses her arms, looking pointedly at my parents.

"You *cannot* leave *that* child with *that* woman anymore!"

Both Mama and Daddy look dumbfounded, but Mimi goes on, completely unaffected.

"Do you know what they were doing this afternoon? Do you have any idea what *that* woman was letting them do? Those two little girls were out riding bicycles in a *thunderstorm!*"

Mama looks at me, surprised. "Is that true, Angie?"

I shrug. "I guess. But Stephanie's mother made us come in when it started raining."

"*That* woman *knows* better!" Mimi continues, incredulously. "*Everybody* knows that lightning always precedes the storm! And those two little girls out there, riding around on *metal* bicycles. Mm—mm—*mm!*"

Mama looks bewildered as she says, "Well, Judy, I don't know what we're going to do with her during the day, then."

Mimi flashes her look over in mine and Kay's direction. "Well if the two of *them* can't learn to behave like sisters are *supposed* to, then the child can just come stay with *me*!" There is a strongly implied '*I'll* set the two of them straight.'

Mama looks at Daddy. "I just don't know," she begins.

"There's nothing to know," Mimi informs her, matter-of-factly. "*That* woman cannot look after *that* child anymore! Uh-uh, uh-uh. No, siree! Abso-*lutely* not! I *won't* have it!"

And though Mimi doesn't slice her hands out to the side, we all know it's settled, anyway. Because when *she* means business, no one dares to argue with that. At least no one in their right mind.

I smile inwardly, realizing that I will never have to go to dumb old Stephanie's house ever again. I'll end up staying here with Kay, after all. They will talk seriously to us, threaten us, tell us we can do whatever we want, but there is no excuse—no reason at all—why we can't save the fighting till after they get home. Then we can kill each other if we want—they don't care. But during the day, while we're alone like that, they expect us to get along. They don't believe it's asking too much.

I look over at Kay, who smiles at me purposefully, silently implying, '*Hah! You just wait*!'

"Why can't I go stay with Mimi instead?" I whine.

Mama plants her hands on her hips. "Well, that's not very fair to Mimi, is it?" She indicates Daddy with her hand, saying, "Mimi's already *raised* her family. I'm not going to dare ask her to do it again!"

"But Mama—"

"Mimi has things that she has to do during the day, too. She has bridge club, and Thursday Morning club, and she has errands to run—a house to keep clean all by herself! No, you are *not* going over there every day and interrupting *her* life, just because you and *Kay* can't get along!"

I glance over at Kay. "But I don't want her *smiling* at me!"

"She's *not* going to smile at you."

"But Ma-*ma*! She's doing it right *now*!"

Daddy speaks for the first time. "This's going to have to change. Your mother and I shouldn't have to leave for work every morning, worrying about whether the two of you are going to kill each other or not!"

Then Mama starts in with the *I-don't-know-what's-wrong-with-the-two-of-you* speech. "When I was growing up, I'd have done anything to have a sister! You two just don't know how lucky you've got it!"

I roll my eyes. No, *she's* the one who just doesn't get it. Still, it's another victory for me because I know I will never have to go to Stephanie's again. Daddy will go pick up my bike and put it in the trunk of his car, bring it home, and that will be the end of it. Mimi *said* so.

Interestingly, years later, Stephanie will turn up in my eleventh-grade APP class at Sanderson High School. She is nice, quiet—really smart. And I can't believe I ever hated her. I guess that's just a part of Murphy's Law, though. Because probably if I'd never had to stay with her in the first place, we'd have wound up being best friends or something. Who knows?

'Mom' and 'Pop'

Daddy in 'broadcast mode' in the early '70's

Daddy's Family

Mama's Family

Mom's car after the accident that ended up leaving her partially paralyzed.

The best time to tag along grocery shopping with Pop was after Halloween or Christmas, when everything was marked half-price.

Kay's 'favorite' cereal
(The only reason she picked it out was to irritate me—I was sure of it.)

ONE, TWO, THREE STRIKES

There is something wrong with Mama. They aren't talking about it, though. At least not to us. It is making my stomach hurt something terrible. I can't help but remember the lady she worked with at the town newspaper—Ramona. Or maybe it was Geraldine. I can't remember exactly which one it was now, but the point is, it was one of them. Cancer. It had gotten to one of them, and I remember, too, Mama telling us about her cat. She had this special cat. And she'd requested that when she died, the cat immediately be put to sleep, too, and then buried with her. She maintained that the cat could never survive without her, that they were too close. But when the time came, the vet decided it was simply too cruel and unjust, and he'd elected on his own accord not to go through with it. Interestingly though, and to everyone's surprise, before they could even conduct her funeral, the cat, too, died of what was determined to be natural causes. So in the end, he did wind up being laid to rest with her.

Maybe Mama has cancer, too. Maybe that's what it is. It seems like everybody has cancer around here. Over in the corner, Mittens is haughtily grooming herself, completely removed from the rest of the family. But no matter how clean she is, I still can't see it. I just can't imagine Mama ever wanting Mittens in the casket with her. She doesn't even like Mittens on the couch. And the bed? Forget it. Still, what if she *did* want to take Mittens with her?

"Do you have cancer?" I suddenly blurt out.

I might as well've fired a shot gun. Because they all look at me then. Mama, Daddy, and my sister, Kay. Still, no one answers. But I don't care. I have to know.

"Well *do* you?" I demand. I'll never forgive her if she does.

Their shock turns into slight amusement, and they look at each other. Kay sits over to the side, trying to seem uninterested. But I know that she really is. Just as much as I am.

Mama leans her head over onto her hand, her amusement now turning into a smile. But it is Daddy who answers.

"No, Mama does *not* have cancer."

"Then what's wrong?" I refuse to give up. "Why does she always feel so bad?" I think I might start to cry then.

Again, they look at each other. And again, it is Daddy who finally answers.

"Mama's not sick. She's going to have a baby."

What? I think.

Instead, I say, "You mean a real *baby*?"

I look over at Kay, but her curiosity still isn't piqued.

"Well, we hope so," Daddy says.

I guess I must have given him a strange look then, because Mama speaks up, saying, "Now, John, don't tease her." Then turning to me, she says, "Yes, a *real* baby."

I look over at Kay who, strangely, still doesn't seem too excited at this point. But I don't care, and I start to whoop for joy, anyway. Because I know it will be a girl—it has to be—and the Wincarter book will finally come true! There will be three of us now, and Mama will name her 'Helen Ray.' But suddenly my own excitement dries up as quickly as it had flooded. A harsh thought strikes—right out of the blue—of broken crayons, headless dolls, red scribbles on petal-pink walls. And hands on hips, I plant myself defiantly, right in the middle of the floor.

"Well, it's not sleeping in *my* room!"

Kay looks at me. "Not mine, either . . . . And I'm *older.*"

"That's not fair!" I stomp my foot. "Mama, *tell* her—"

But Mama holds up her hand then, saying, "Just settle down a minute! It won't have to sleep in *anybody's* room. It's going to stay in mine and Daddy's room for now—until it's older. Until it can sleep by itself."

I look over at Kay, but she is back in Superior Land.

"Then what?" I ask Mama.

Again, she and Daddy look at each other, like they're trying to decide whether or not to tell us something.

"*Then* what?" I repeat.

"Well, we thought we might move to Raleigh. To a bigger house. With more bedrooms."

Strike two!

"It only makes sense," Mama continues. "Daddy's work is in Raleigh, and your school is, too. Just think—we won't have to carpool all these long distances anymore."

"*My* school's not in Raleigh!" I inform her. I'd gone to the Christian Academy this past year, a small, private school here in town with only one classroom for each grade. A huge improvement over Carver and then Wendell Elementary, where I'd suffered through first grade. And if she and Daddy don't quit looking at each other like that, I think I'm going to scream!

"Well, we thought you could go to Robinscrest next year, too. With Kay."

Steeer-IKE three!

From somewhere in her chair, Kay retrieves a huge bag of Doritos, which she begins crunching on as she informs them, "She won't be with me. Because I'll be in the *Middle* school next year." Crunch,

crunch. "And *she'll* still be in the *Lower* school!" She speaks slowly, being careful to point this out. But she might as well've just said it; '*With all the other babies!*' I stick my tongue out at her, then make a face I hope is horrible. She ignores me, wrapping herself up tighter in her favorite towel. Most kids have a favorite blanket. But not Kay. She is unique. She has a favorite towel. It's kind of plain—just beach-variety with the ocean on it—that and the silhouette of a couple of surfers. Around the edges, it has begun to fray with wear. But she still dons it royally. Like a queen who enshrouds herself in the finest ermingard.

The phone rings then, and Daddy goes into the kitchen to answer it.

"You know what I mean," Mama goes on. "Like last year—when you both went to Wendell Elementary. When Angie was in Mrs. Alexander's class and you were in Mrs. Kirby's. You were in different *rooms*, but still at the same *school.*"

She goes over to where Kay is sitting, leaning down to pick up some discarded socks.

"Well, this is different," Kay tells her pointedly, still crunching. "I'll be in a whole other *building*!"

Mama recoils then. "Please! Don't *breathe* on me after you eat those things!"

Kay holds the bag protectively against her. "Well, I *will* be. You said."

So did Kay already know about this? Before they'd even told me? She knows everything first! It's so unfair! I bet they've all been laughing behind my back, making bets on when they'd finally let me in on the juicy news. I glare at her.

From her superior perch, she eyes me, then lifts her chin and smiles. "*Hmph!*"

I hate it when she does that!

"Mama—she's *smiling* at me!"

"Girls, please don't start tonight," Mama says. "I don't feel good . . . . and I really can't handle it right now."

"But Mama—"

"Kay—*stop* smiling. And Angie—*stop* hollering. Otherwise, I'm going to put you *both* in your rooms!"

But then, as if on second thought, she turns, heading for her own bedroom instead.

In the silence that follows, we can hear Daddy still jabbering away on the kitchen phone, oblivious. We're not sure who he's talking to, but we gather it must be somebody pretty important because he is using his 'movie star voice.' The one he reserves only for announcing things on the radio or reporting a story on the evening news. I can feel Kay staring at me. She wants me to look at her. She's trying to get me to look over there just so she can smile at me again. But I refuse. I ignore her.

"*Hmph!*"

My patience is running thin, but I still hang on to my pride.

". . . . *dig-a-dig!*"

Neither one of us knows what a 'dig-a-dig' is, but regardless, we both know how much I hate it.

I glare at her.

She smiles, triumphant.

Probably the only thing in this world I hate worse than 'dig-a-dig' is its creator—my stupid, older sister, herself.

*Kay and me, sitting on the couch with Pop
(Kay is wrapped up in her infamous 'favorite towel.')*

On a trip to visit Mom and Pop while they lived in Edenton (We are 'swimming' at Cape Colony.)

Me, holding 'Mittens'

Kay and me posing beside the lamp post for an Easter picture (That would be 'Mittens' scratching and digging around my feet.)

The new 'bigger' house in Raleigh

THROW IN A MONKEY WRENCH

July, 1974. We have a new sister. Her name is not 'Helen Ray.' It's 'Martha Lambeth.' 'Martha,' after the Todd's side of the family, and 'Lambeth,' after my mother's side. We're supposed to call her 'Martie' for short, though. Martie with an 'ie.' Because it looks much more feminine than Marty with a 'y.' At first we were disappointed. Because who'd want to go through life with a name like 'Martha Lambeth,' especially when you could've had one like 'Helen Ray?' But this is Mama and Daddy's way of letting the family know they're finished. That this is it—this is all she wrote. The Final One has been Named.

She was born on the 5th, to be exact. Almost on the 4th, though. We were having a neighborhood block party, and it was right in the middle of the watermelon-seed—spitting contest, when Mama begin to 'feel like the baby was coming.' So we'd grabbed our pre-packed bags and headed over to Mimi's, only to have Daddy pick us up bright and early in the morning, giving us this stupid 'false alarm' explanation. The doctor'd said it would be at least two more weeks, that Mama should just go back home and rest quietly until then. But Mama'd only scoffed at that, fanning herself as she'd huffed, "I wonder how many babies *he's* had?"

We still haven't seen her yet—the new baby. Because this is the time when fathers are not allowed in the delivery room, when kids are never to darken the sterile hallways of hospitals. In fact, the closest we can actually get is to stand right here on the grassy hill outside of Rex Hospital, waving up towards her window. (That, by the way, would be the *old* Rex Hospital—the red brick one over on St. Mary's Street. Not the new and improved 'Rex Wellness Center' across town that now occupies three consecutive city blocks). I am holding my new transistor radio—the one Granddaddy'd brought me from his store, and there is a song playing that I really like. Something by *Seals and Croft*, according to the announcer. I like the images it paints in my mind; of curtains hanging in a window, the warm night air softly billowing through them; the scent of jasmine vines floating in along with the wind. It makes me think of days in the early spring, when Mama's daffodils are blooming, when she has our windows open to 'let in the fresh air.' She can't do this for many days, though. Because before long, it will be too hot, and in lieu of the tranquil, open windows, Daddy will clean out the filters of the two air-conditioning window units—the one in the den and the one back in their bedroom—and then he will turn them on for the summer. And it's very important that you remember to keep all the doors and windows closed when the air conditioning is running. Otherwise, you'll let all the cool air out.

From her top-floor window, Mama waves down to us, holding up the flowers we'd had delivered so that we could see them. At first I can't tell what it is she actually has, and I think the flowers might possibly be the baby.

"Is that it? Is that the baby?" I ask excitedly.

But Kay only looks at me then, rolling her eyes as she says, "*No*, Dumb-dumb! Those are the *flowers* we sent!" She follows with a short, nasty laugh. "You think she's gonna hold the *baby* up in the window like that? Just wait till we get home! You just wait till I tell everybody how stupid you are! How you're so stupid you can't even *see*!"

"I *can* see!"

"No you can't! And you're gonna have to get bifocals! Maybe even *tri*-focals!" Again, she laughs. "You'll look just like a bug! Just like a big, fat mosquito!" She makes these huge tunnel-things with her hands, holding them in front of her own eyes. "And Mama's gonna make you wear them to school, too!"

"No, she will *not*!"

"Yes, she *will*!"

"Will *not*!"

"Will *so*!"

"Will *not*!"

I look around at the grown-ups then—Mimi and granddaddy, Dick and Peggy Brantley, the Shores; Grace and Ernie. But they are too busy conversing with each other to hear anything that's gone on at about knee-level, and oblivious, Granddaddy takes my hand, saying, "Let's go eat. Go get some supper. How about Don Murray's? You like hush puppies don't you?" To which Mimi sternly replies as she herds us into the air-conditioned back seat of the car, "Now Curt—don't you go *starting* that! They are *not* going to sit there and fill up on hush puppies! Not before supper! I won't have it!"

She shuts the door firmly behind us. We are momentarily alone in the plush car. Kay looks at me, smiles. "Will *so*!"

Kay playing the 'Bean Bag Toss' game at the ill-fated 4th of July party

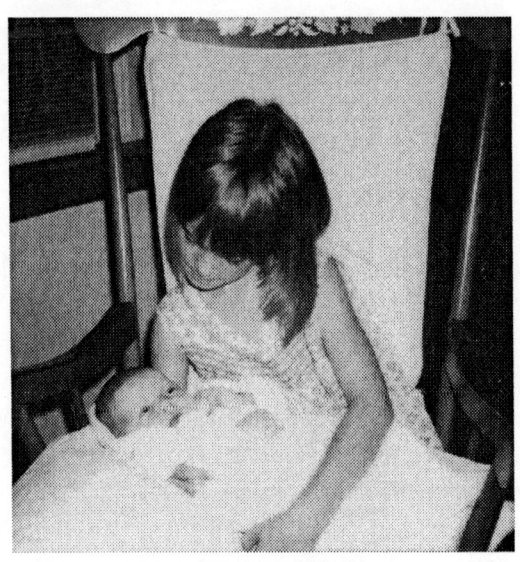

*Me holding the new baby
(In the far left corner above my head sits one of the two infamous
air conditioning window units that we proudly owned.)*

OPEN CLASSROOMS, CLOSED MINDS

The line of waiting cars seems to go on infinitely. It looks more like a fancy auto parade than what it actually is—just an early morning school drop-off. There are Mercedes Benz's with spoked wheels, shiny new Cadillac's, Lincoln Continentals with tinted windows, and in one case, even a Rolls Royce—complete with a white-gloved chauffer who runs dutifully around and opens the door for his small passenger when their turn comes.

And then there is Mama's bright green 1972 Buick Electra—the one that accommodates 8 comfortably in the back seat—idling along with the rest of them. Like it fits in.

We are in our usual traveling mode; Kay on one side, me on the other, with the baby in the middle, still gowned, but usually barefooted, and almost always diaperless. In fact, most mornings we are in such a rush that Mama ends up having to pull the baby right out of her high chair while we're on the way out the door. But she lets her carry the soggy zwieback toast along for the ride because it keeps her from crying. Somehow though, the toast always manages to wind up all over the back seat in the form of mushy crumbs, which is grosser than gross.

I figure this is Mama's wonderful idea to keep us from fighting—putting the baby between us like that. Because she figures we won't wallop the baby trying to get to each other, that it'll make us stop and think first. Oh, but she has no clue. I cut my eyes over at Kay, thinking about the brick wall it would actually take—

Mama is cheerfully oblivious, and she hums along with the radio which is set, like always, on WYYD. A stupid muzak station. The one the baby has to listen to. The one that has to be turned up to astronomical levels every single night in order for her to fall asleep. And if *she* has to listen to it, then, of course, that means *we* do, too. It's all about the baby. Everything's about the baby these days.

"Angie, have you got your stuff together?" Mama asks pleasantly from the front seat. "Because it's almost our turn—and you can't just sit here, piddling—not when there're all these other people waiting in line behind us."

I roll my eyes.

"Have you got your shoes tied?" she drones on.

I look down at the tangled laces. "Yes," I lie. Because it's much easier to lie than it is to have to perform all the rituals—let alone, to even *think* about all the rituals—it would actually take to get my shoes tied.

The right one's first—always the right one. And it has to be tied an even number of times. When I finally finish, the ends of my laces have to be completely even with each other, and the loops in the bow the exact same size, too. If they aren't, then I have to unlace my shoes, all the way down this time, and start over from the very beginning, making sure the laces match as they pass through each hole. Then I start on the left shoe. It always has to have the exact same pattern and number of things done to it as the right shoe, and in the end, it has to totally match the right shoe, with the laces both lining up and turning out the same length as those on the right shoe. I want to scream.

And getting out of the car? Forget it! That's a ritual in and of itself. First, I have to step out on my right foot. But I can't step on a crack in the sidewalk while I'm doing this. Otherwise, I have to sit back down in the car, making sure both feet are placed securely on the rubber floor mat, and then when it is determined that they finally are, I have to start all over again. Next, I have to pick up my books with my right hand first, then shift them over to my left arm so that I can pick up my lunch with my right hand, too. Now I *really* want to scream, but I just don't have the strength for it—not anymore.

Mama thinks I'm doing all this just to waste time, just to bug her or something. Usually, she is pretty patient, but sometimes she gets irritated and tries to rush me, which only makes the rituals come even faster and harder. The truth is, I have to do what the voice inside my head tells me; that is if I don't want anything bad to happen to *her*. I could never tell her this, though. That I'm doing all this to protect *her*. Or that other times I have to do it to keep the house from burning down, or to keep the whole family from getting sick. Maybe even sometimes to keep the cat from getting run over. One thing I know for sure is that she'd never understand it, so I just go on like that, just keep pretending that I'm only being a hateful brat. It's so much easier. Because whether they're right or wrong, at least a hateful brat has a say in the things she does, has control over herself. I, on the other hand, do not.

Robinscrest is truly a magnificent modernization of the educational concept. It is everything you'd expect, and then some. Age groups are paired up, such as first and second grade, then third and fourth grade. Each group has its own 'learning center' around which are arranged open classrooms; one grade occupying the left-side, the other, the right-side. Though kindergarten and fifth grade are in separate sections of the lower school, themselves, they, too, are open within their age groups. The theory behind the concept is that children learn much better in an open, unrestricted area where they are among peers and more or less free to express themselves.

And at lunchtime, we are not herded down to a large, clangey cafeteria where we are stopped to be threatened and shushed every few steps of the way. Instead, we remain right at our desks to wait for the large stainless steel catering vats to be rolled into the learning center. We are served in modernized Styrofoam boxes, that after finishing with, are tossed into a temporary trashcan that is quickly whisked away. In fact, five minutes after the lunch period has ended, no one would ever guess that food had been in the area at all.

And Robinscrest has other amenities that no public school, let alone, any other private school in the area can claim. The one I like best is the Olympic-sized, indoor swimming pool. Part of our regular PE class is swimming several times a year, usually for a week at a time. There are only two things I don't like about swimming. The first is the ugly, black one-piece bathing suits that we are issued from the laundry each day before class. Not just for their unattractiveness, but also because having always been on the puny side, there is never a bathing suit small enough to fit me, and the bottom usually ends up sagging, which is so totally *not* cool.

The second thing I don't like about swimming is when, after class, we have to stand in line and get alcohol squirted in both of our ears before entering the locker room. The idea is to prevent infection, something they call 'swimmer's ear,' but sometimes I wonder if the cure is actually worse than the cause.

Another amenity Robinscrest boasts is all kinds of music lessons. Kay and I are enrolled in piano class, which is conducted in its own room. There are several rows of electric pianos with the teacher's in front, facing ours. We practice under headphones, where the teacher can plug into our unit anytime she wants, whether to conduct regular instruction, or just to listen in quietly, making sure we are practicing what we are supposed to, and not goofing off. There are microphones attached to the headphones, and that is the way the teacher communicates with us. Likewise, if we have questions or need help, we can buzz into her piano as well, and she will eventually get to us. There is a large overhead projector up front where she places transparencies of the exercises we are supposed to work on or songs we are supposed to practice. We can also work out of our issued books. These are really cool, and when you carry them to school, everyone knows you are in the piano class. They are compact notebooks, kind of a sea-green, with flaps that fold over and attach with Velcro. Again, the whole concept is kind of new-age.

Sometimes it takes Mrs. Leech or Mrs. Newman—whoever happens to be teaching that day—a long time to get to each one of us, and the activities lit on the overhead become boring. Kay and I, having always played by ear, have trouble learning how to read the notes, anyway. Mama, who'd played the piano while growing up, would often sit down at our own at home, performing concert pieces from those days. And after two or three hearings, Kay and I could sit down behind her and pick the piece out, playing it completely by sound. The downside to this? You relied on your memory to play, not on the actual notes in front of you. And after playing the ridiculous scale exercises, or *'Mary Had a Little Lamb' in 'C' Major* over and over again, Kay and I, out of sheer boredom, would resort instead to playing Bach, Beethoven or Chopin. Sometimes pieces taken from Mozart. One further thing I'd found to amuse myself is playing these beautiful pieces off-key. There's absolutely nothing funnier than to hear the perfect beginning of 'Moonlight Sonata' or 'Fur Elise,' then when the melody kicks in (the part you play with your right hand), you hit a flat—a totally sour key—and you play the entire song that way—on the wrong keys—while your left hand, on the correct keys, plays perfectly the unmatched accompaniment. It's like wearing purple and orange together, or stripes with plaid. And besides piano class, where's the ultimate place to do this? Family reunions, of course. Like when you sneak off to Motney's sacred music room, the grand piano always so elegantly poised, opened largely at one end, the other decorated with freshly-cut flowers. When you sit down and play off-key like that, though, you have to be dead serious about it. You can't crack a smile at all. Because when everyone starts feeling compelled to find their way back to the music room, just to see where the awful noise is coming from, you've got to be sitting there, completely poker-faced. That way, they'll wind up coming to the conclusion that there is actually something wrong with *them* instead. And it's totally fun to watch as they stand there and squirm, trying to make heads or tails out of exactly what it is you're doing. But leave it to Aunt Gladys, though—leave it to *her* to break this hard-earned *emperor's-new-clothes* silence.

"You know what I think, Miss Martha?" she drones loudly. "I think you really need to get that piano tuned. It's not good to let one go like that, just sitting around, going to the bad, you know. You *ought* to call that man that Myrtle's sister-in-law uses. He doesn't come cheap though. No sir, you've got to be prepared to pay—to really get out your pocketbook, and *then* some. But he's worth it— worth every penny of what he charges. Because you always get what you pay for, you know."

Motney comes into the music room, drying her hands on her apron.

"Well, now, Gladys—I didn't know *you* had a piano."

"Well, I don't," she says. "You know me—I can't even carry a tune in a bucket with a *handle* on it."

I suddenly wonder, if she realizes this—why it is that she still sings in church.

"I'm just going by what Myrtle's sister-in-law told *her*," Aunt Gladys continues. "You know Myrtle—the one who lives in the house up there on the corner—the one with the nice yard. You know, I might be wrong, but I believe she's had 'Yard of the Month' five or six times— at least that many. You know, that isn't right, though. Her getting it that many times. Because I know for a fact that Mary Earlene works just as hard in *her* yard. I've seen her, myself, you know. Seen her out there in her dungarees just a-mowing and a-weeding, like it's all she's got in the world to do. And do you think anybody ever takes notice of *her* yard? That'll be the day! Probably when Myrtle's in a *rest* home! But I'll bet your last dollar I know what it is, though— Myrtle's gone and got in good with the Jaycees . . . . both them *and* the Garden Club. I'll bet you anything that's what she's done. Probably bakes *cookies* for all their meetings. That's what it is, you know. That's what she's done. I'll be darned if I wouldn't put money on it. Now that I think about it, I remember hearing something else, too— that her father's cousin's *aunt* is on the board. And if you have any relatives on the committee at all, then you're *supposed* to be ineligible. But not Myrtle! No sir! Not *her!* She's played her cards just right—because she's in good with the Jaycees now, you know. And then they feel like they *have* to give it to her. See, *that's* how it happens."

I want to roll my eyes. Instead, I hit a sour chord. Loud.

"But really, Miss Martha—you ought to get that piano tuned while it's still worth something," Aunt Gladys continues, as if she hasn't just been off in Loony Land. "And according to Myrtle's sister-in-law, Mavis, he's the best there is. She won't even call anybody else when her piano goes to the bad like that. No, sir! She absolutely *swears* by him."

Behind Motney's magnified, coke-bottle glasses, I can actually see her eyes flash. Too bad Aunt Gladys can't.

And Mimi? She is beside herself with the atrociousness of it all. As we sit at the dinner table, she inconspicuously squeezes my wrist in subtle reprimand, saying, "You have such a wonderful gift. A God-given talent for music. Why in the world you would want to honor Him in that way with His gift—making fun of it—is beyond me. Especially when all He's ever done is to love you."

I stifle a laugh, faking a cough instead. I don't dare look over at Kay who is kicking me under the table. Because then I know for sure I'll lose it, which would really not be the ideal thing to do right now. Especially since Mimi fails to see the humor in it.

I ask Mimi if that's the case about God, then why does he let the voices keep bothering me? Keep telling me all these things I've got to do?

"You don't hear voices," she tells me, matter-of-factly. "You just *think* you do."

"But Mimi—"

"It's all your imagination."

"I know, but—"

She looks around the table where everyone else is engaged in conversation—everyone, that is, except for Aunt Gladys who for once is quiet, as she pushes a full-sized biscuit into her mouth, poking at it with her index finger. Okay . . . . *gross*. I turn back to the lesser of the two evils.

"Just stop thinking about it, and they'll go away," Mimi hisses in an under-voice.

Yeah. *Right*.

And back at school, in piano class, you had to be careful about playing pieces that weren't assigned to you as well, especially playing them off-key. Because if Mrs. Leech happened to quietly plug into your piano and hear you off-task? Then you could pretty much figure you were screwed. And if Mrs. Newman caught you? She was even worse. You never wanted to go there. So, according to them, what is the problem with playing Chopin when you are supposed to be playing 'Mary Had a Little Lamb?' 'You are not ready for those pieces. They are too advanced. Not only have you not mastered reading basic music, itself, but you are using the wrong fingers on the keys as well, and this is completely unacceptable. To put it mildly, you are attempting to build a house without first securing a foundation.' Needless to say, Kay and I never advance very far in piano lessons.

One other perk offered to the students of Robinscrest is French lessons, which, at this time, is unheard of in elementary school. The theory here is that linguistically, children pick up new languages much better and much faster than adults do, so it is never too early to start. Unlike piano, though, in French, we learn through repetitive sound. We don't read or write. All we do is practice conversation with our teacher, Mrs. Simmons, who sits in the circle with us, holding up colorful pictures that illustrate situations as they are introduced. (And I guess the theory behind the early French lessons actually pays off. Because Kay will later go on to graduate from college, Cum Laude, with a major in French.)

So how had we come to learn about this wonderful new school? Mimi and Granddaddy, of course. They always knew where to find things of this nature, were very keen about where the hippest things were going on. Realistically, they had singing practice at the A. L. Fogley Center which is a large, activity-centered building, located on the campus of the upper school complex. Very modern, it has long, narrow windows that reach all the way down to the floor, which, in turn, is covered with orange shag carpet. The A. L. Fogley Center is also where the pool is located, and the highschool gym as well, which is painted in bright green and gold, honoring the school's colors. (Actually, there is a gym here for each complex; lower, middle and upper, though at the time, this doesn't seem too excessive. We just figure every school has three gyms at its disposal.) True to Mimi and Granddaddy's ravings, the school, itself, *is* wonderful, in every sense of the word. It is only when we are faced with the other students, when we try to mix with them, that we learn just *how* different the differences between us actually are. Most are the children of prestigious doctors and lawyers, some even the kids of politicians or presidents of very large and well-known corporations. They all live in huge, extravagant houses, sometimes in North Raleigh, though the majority reside inside the beltline, around the St. Mary's street area. Most have summer homes in exotic places like Jamaica or Bermuda. And if they don't have a second home, then they at least have a thirty-foot vacation yacht. These kids posses every single color of alligator shirt that exists, along with infinite pairs of Levis corduroys to match. They don't have Saturday chores. Instead, they have maids, housekeepers or nannies. This is ultimately where I learn first-hand that being different is, in reality, equal to being a weirdo. Because it's bad enough to not live in the right neighborhood, or to not wear the right clothes. But then when you go tossing all these obsessive compulsions into the mix, you are jumping straight out the frying pan, directly into the fire.

    At school, I am completely absorbed in my own world, doing things like counting steps to the gym (which, by the way, have to come up to an even number. Otherwise, I have to find some excuse to go back to the room—like I forgot something—and start all over again). And then there's arranging my desk so that none of the four feet are sitting on a crease in the carpet, so that the chair is exactly parallel with the desk. Sometimes, if I don't open a book right, I have to close it and re-open it over and over again until the powerful urge goes away. The other kids are looking at me, poking each other, snickering. "Look, Angela's *retarded*," they say, then laughingly add, "Yeah, that's why her *bathing suit* looks so stupid!" And the more they tease, the more I want so terribly to be normal. But when I really concentrate, try to make a conscious effort to appear normal, the rituals only come harder and faster, like they do when Mama's frustrated with me.

At lunchtime, I usually bring my own in a brown paper bag now. I've had to retire my 'Bobby Sherman' lunchbox—the one where he's wearing this really cool studded choker, and his picture is surrounded by pink hearts. Because to carry a lunch box to school now would absolutely be third-grade suicide. You just don't go there. Still, Mama's aware of the tough times we're both having, trying to fit it here, and she always tries to make life easier. One thing she does is to include these hidden notes somewhere in our lunch bags. We call them 'little man notes' because each one has a bald-headed clown in a dunce cap doing funny things. Like if it's Friday, he might be waving a banner that says 'Friday' on it. Or if it's near Halloween, he might be carving a pumpkin; likewise, if its Christmas, he'll be hanging ornaments on a tree. And he always says happy things like 'have a nice day.' The little man notes are a bright spot in my otherwise black-and-white days. Because Robinscrest is very different from the small-town community of Wendell, where everyone and their brother's cousin knows my family. Though it seems like the rituals have always been there, for some reason, they did not consume such a large part of my life back then. Not like now. Not like after we moved to Raleigh. Now, not only are the ones that I already have intensified, but new ones are routinely introducing themselves, only to add to my already overloaded ritual regimen.

For some reason, my clothes suddenly bother me. They itch and rub the wrong way, and I can't stand the way they feel against my skin. Trying to dress in the mornings has become absolute hell. I soon discover, though, that the task can be achieved much easier if I do it in the bathroom, using water from the sink to 'lubricate' my dried-out joints; inside my elbows, under my arms, behind my knees. And always my feet. This is the year that I will be allowed to enjoy the benefits of soggy feet—as well as severely chapped skin. And does the suffering get any better after this ritual has invaded? No. Of course not. Instead, it escalates until there are only one or two things that I can actually stand to put on my body. Unfortunately, neither one of them possesses an alligator or a Levis tag. And in a school like Robinscrest where it matters what you wear, what your parents' occupations are, and most importantly where you live, this, too, becomes elementary suicide.

Often in the mornings, when I arrive with water stains on my clothes due to the drawn-out rituals, the kids all laugh and point at me, saying, "Look at Angela! She *peed* on herself!"

"It's just water," I angrily point out, then try to explain further by adding, "I leaned up against the cabinet this morning, and it was wet." But this only makes them laugh harder, saying, "Yeah, *sure* you did!"

Soon following are the '*I Hate Angela'* games. I remember the ringleader to be this fat kid, named Chris, and he'd say things while the class was walking in line, like, "If you step on a crack, then you have to kiss *Angela*." Sometimes, if I was lucky enough to get in front of Chris when we were walking in line, he liked to see how hard he could knee me in the butt before he got a reaction. And though sometimes it hurt so bad it literally took my breath, I refused to give him the satisfaction and tried to keep on walking as normally as before.

This was just the beginning of the bullying. Soon, I couldn't even go to the bathroom without girls crashing the stall with me, scratching my face with their fingernails, or having one hold my arms behind my back while the other punched me in the stomach. Though I never really told Mama about it, she noticed the cuts and bruises, and finally put two and two together.

It is at this point that Mama swoops in unannounced, invading the school with an other-than-friendly visit. She proudly parks her bright green Buick across three discreet spaces just outside the lower school office. No one says anything to her about it; they seem to sense that it would not be wise. But the very next day, I am beckoned by the guidance counselor, Mrs. Collier, who leads me out of the third-fourth grade center, through the library, then into the adjoining first-second grade center. Her intention is to leave me there for an hour or so while she discusses the bullying problem with all the other third and fourth graders. Once there though, I look around and notice that there is no laughing fat kid hovering over me. In fact, I am surrounded only by other pint-sized people. One holds out a crayon, asking, "Wanna color?"

When Mrs. Collier returns to get me, I break the news to her. "I'm not going back."

"But that's your class," she tries to explain.

"I don't care," I tell her.

"But you've already learned all the things that the second graders are learning," she rationalizes. "You wouldn't have anything to do."

Still, I don't budge. I cross my arms, looking at her. I hope she has a crow bar, because that's what it's going to take to get me out of here.

"Oh, dear," Mrs. Collier says, though it is more to herself than to anyone else. "We can't just put you back a whole grade. I don't think the state would allow—"

"My mother told me this was a *private* school," I inform her. "And that's why she put me here. So that the public schools couldn't tell us what we have to do all the time."

At first she seems taken aback, kind of a cross between disbelief that I'd made such a crass comment, and further disbelief that I'd even know such things to begin with. Still, I don't care. They can think I'm retarded all they want, but one thing's for sure; I'm not stupid.

"Oh, *dear*," She repeats.

I glare.

"It's just not that easy—" she begins.

"Call my mother," I interrupt. "I want you to call my mother. Because *she'd* say it was okay."

That settles it. I stay in the second grade class for the rest of the day. Because I don't think anyone wants to experience my mother again. At least not any time soon. And true to what I'd claimed, after later discussing it with her, the school decides, on the whole, that I'd be better off in the second grade center, where the kids are more my size and there is no history of bullying. And of this decision, I have only one thing to say. *Yesss*!

*The only known photo to exist of **'The Buick.'***

A typical 'Sunday Lunch' at Motney's

Kay, 'the Baby' and me, enjoying some 'recreational' time together

*On a trip to Yaupon Beach, where the entire family
(all four-and-a-half of us), stayed in one single motel room together—
for three whole incredible nights*

AN APPLE A DAY

    I am standing in the bathtub, trying to get the water just right. The hot has to be turned on first, and the water has to come out of the faucet in a certain way or else I have to turn it off and start all over again. And if I have to start over, then it has to happen an even number of times. When this requirement is finally met, I can then start on the cold water. And like the shoes, the hot and cold faucets have to completely match, follow the exact same pattern. The bathroom door suddenly swings open, and there is Mama, looking all wild-eyed and clinched.
    "If you squeak that spicket one more time—*I swear*—they're going to have to come put me in *O'Berry*!"
    O'Berry? I panic. Why *O'Berry*? That's so far away! Why not Dorothea Dix? Then at least we could visit. I voice my fears.

"O'Berry? I don't want you to go all the way to O'Berry! Why can't they just put you in Dix Hill instead?" Because even if she goes bananas, I still want her around.

"Well, they're going to have to put me *somewhere!*" she concludes, exasperated, the door shutting hard behind her.

I look after her guiltily for a moment. I suddenly wonder why it is that all mental hospitals are built on a hill—*O'Berry* Hill, *Dix* Hill, *Holly* Hill—I mean, what's up with that? Maybe they think it's a deterrent or something. Kind of like Rapunzel—like maybe it'll make the crazy people think they can't escape. Who knows? All I know is that it's not cool to be crazy—for any reason. And if Mama goes to Dix Hill, what'll I tell the other kids at school, in the neighborhood? I fear I already know their response, though. "Well, what'd you expect? I mean, we already know *Angela's* retarded!" The cold, hard reality sinks in at this point, and I know I have got to do something. Because it can't happen. There's just absolutely no way I can go there. I weigh my options, then reluctantly decide that overall it'd probably be so much easier if I just told her, if I just came clean about the voices. I cannot imagine what life would be like without the voices constantly governing my every move. But one thing I *do* know is that if there is a way to make them disappear, Mama and Daddy will find it. I know they will. I'll have to be very careful about how I explain it, though. Because this is different than being crazy, and the absolute last thing I want them to do is to think that. What if they decided to put *me* in Dix Hill?

They'd already sent me to this doctor—one they called a *psychiatrist*—back in the second grade. He was supposed to figure out why I was having all these 'anxiety attacks,' then offer my parents magical ways to help me 'get hold of myself.' So every Tuesday afternoon, we drove to Raleigh where I'd meet with this man in Glenwood Village, the same medical complex where my pediatrician was. Only this doctor didn't wear a white coat, and there were no nurses around, either. Plus, he never wanted to look down my throat or in my ears. Instead, he wore turtleneck sweaters and sat behind his desk, chain-smoking as he asked, "What do *you* think about that?"

I found these visits to be confusing; I didn't know what he wanted me to say. And when I'd ask him about it, he'd just repeat his same, dumb question, like a stuck record—just like the stupid Partridge Family album we had at home that got hung in the same spot every time we listened to it; "What do *you* think you should say?"

The only thing I *did* know was that in an hour, we'd finally be finished, and Mama'd be back in the waiting room to get me. And once downstairs, she'd let me go in the vending area and get a snack for the ride home. That was always the highlight of the trip; getting a Sprite and a bag of Lance Gold-N-Cheese crackers, better known to me as 'stop sign crackers,' out of the vending machine.

I remember begging my parents to let me quit going there. I totally hated having to sit around and talk to a grown-up that I didn't even know, let alone, one I didn't particularly like. Finally, they caved, and I wanted to whoop for joy with my new-found freedom. Because this was a victory that meant no more confining weekly trips to Raleigh, no more endless cigarette smoke curling up my nose, burning my eyes. And best of all, no more feeling like a science experiment—like a bug under a microscope. But still, after all the time I'd spent with him in these things my parents called 'sessions,' he was never able to offer them any magical solutions. I knew they were disappointed, but hell, I could've told them that. Right from the start. He didn't have any special powers, so what'd they expected? He was just as clueless about me as I was. It was such a waste, all that time—the case of a blind kid leading an even blinder adult.

So if I tell them about the voices, will they make me go back to him again? Will I have to sit through these boring 'session-things' like before and talk about stupid stuff that has absolutely nothing to do with anything? Because if that's what they think, then they're dead wrong. There's no way I'll do it. Never again. All I want is a way out, an escape from the voices. Not to wind up getting confined even worse. And, trust me, if I knew what it was I '*thought about that,*' then I'd fix it, myself. I wouldn't spend time wasting *his* time, let alone, my own. The larger problem is that there are no answers. Sometimes things just happen because they do, and there is simply no explaining them away. And if you sit down and try to do that—make excuses, I mean—then you only end up making things worse on yourself.

YOU'RE A GENIUS

It's a school day, and I am doing what I like best—sitting on my bed at home, still wearing my pajamas. For everyone else, it's an ordinary day. Daddy's gone to work at the TV station, Kay's at school, and the baby's in her room, playing with her imaginary friends. Mama has given me her jewelry box to look through, something I've always enjoyed doing, ever since I was a very little kid.

Last night I did it—I told her about the voices. About how they make me do all these weird things, how they threaten me with bad things if I don't comply. I could tell she was scared, and that made me feel better. Not because she was scared, but because I knew that she believed me. And once that confession was finally over with, I felt more tired than I could ever remember feeling—at least in a very long time. After tucking me into bed and assuring me that everything would be alright, I could hear Mama go back down to the den and start talking quietly with Daddy. I knew it had to be important at this point—because that's the only time they got all quiet and serious like that—when something was important. And this morning, I woke up by myself, not in the usual way with Mama, telling me it's time to get ready for school. It was past school time, anyway, so curiously, I'd gone downstairs to find her. She'd been busy putting dishes away in the kitchen.

"I didn't think you needed to go to school today," she told me. "Daddy and I talked last night, and I'm going to make some phone calls today—so we can get to the bottom of this. See if we can figure out what's going on."

When I only continued to stand there, she'd suggested, "Why don't you go get my jewelry box down? I'll make some cinnamon toast and bring it up to you."

I'd already been heading for the stairs. "And can I have Coke instead of orange juice?"

She'd paused, but then consented, saying, "Well, I guess. Just this time, though."

Now, after filling up on cinnamon toast and sugared water, I am sitting in my bed, surrounded by familiar stuffed animals as I pilfer through her jewelry box. I know all the pieces by heart—where each came from, the story behind every one. The little net purse made out of thin, tightly-woven wire was my grandmother's. At one time, Mama told me it'd had pretty flowers painted on it. But somehow over the years, the colors had faded, and now it appeared only a dull silverish. Still, it's an interesting piece—like nothing I've ever seen before, and it makes me think of old-fashioned things.

There is a hollow silver bracelet that I love. Daddy bought it for Mama on their trip to Denmark when I was just a baby. They'd left Kay and me with Mimi and Granddaddy for the trip. Mama said they'd had a really good time, that they'd actually met Sonny and Cher, who were also traveling to Denmark on vacation. And afterwards, when we'd watch 'The Sonny and Cher Show' on Saturday night, we'd ask Mama and Daddy endless questions about them over and over again. We thought it was really cool that our parents had actually met and talked with real movie stars. But Mama only maintained her original position, saying that they were normal, nice down-to-earth people, just like everyone else. Mama'd also told me that while they were on that trip, she'd missed Kay and me something terrible. It was the first time since we'd been born that they'd actually been away without us like that. She said when they finally got home, she couldn't wait to see us. But by the time their plane had landed at Raleigh-Durham and they'd driven back into town, Mimi had already fed us, bathed us, and put us to bed for the night, and she didn't think it was such a good idea to disturb us then. Still, Mama insisted on at least looking in the crib before she and Daddy went home, and just as she was leaning over me, I woke up, apparently saw her standing there, and proceeded to scream—for the rest of the night, according to Mimi. To this day, Mimi insists that she should have never allowed Mama go into the room with me. And contrary, to this day, Mama swears that she should've just swept right in and taken us home, anyway—where we belonged. I laugh every time I hear that story, but still feel bad for being so mean—for keeping Mimi and Granddaddy awake like that. But both she and Mama disagree, telling me instead, "You weren't mean. You were just a baby." Still, I wonder if that incident foreshadowed what was to come. "You were always a 'spirited' baby," Mimi would tell me. "You never wanted to be held or rocked. You were always too busy for that."

Downstairs, I can hear Mama on the phone. I can't tell what she's saying, but I know it has something to do with me. I know because of the way her voice sounds; all serious and formal. It makes me feel important—knowing that she's using those voices to make phone calls about me. Still, I'd like to be important for other reasons, though. Not for being crazy. I pinch myself then, a harsh reminder that I am *not* crazy. This is something totally different. This is something I can't help. Everyone else seems to think I can, though—that it's just a matter of 'getting hold of myself.' And nobody can do it for me; I have to do it completely on my own. I have to want it bad enough to stand up and take control. And how are you supposed to do that? It's simple. You have to be strong. You can't give in to the urges, the Fear. You have to say 'no.' Still, when I weigh the options, I'm not so sure of anything anymore. I find that actually, I never was. It just makes the concept of my brain more tolerable to think that what's going on inside my head is *not* the same kind of thing that goes on in those of crazy people. Still, when I try to explain that I don't *want* the urges there, that I want nothing more than to make them go away, the most common response is, "Well, you must not want it bad enough." Because I have to consider the fact that all people have urges and fears. The difference is that they don't let these things consume their whole lives, the way I do. And I try. Really, I do. But it seems like the harder I try, the harder the Fear pushes back, and I honestly wonder how the rest of the world does it. I am completely in awe of the 99.9 percent of the population who live normally day-to-day because they don't give in to the Fear. I wonder what it is that makes me so inadequate when everyone else so obviously has such a strong handle on things.

* * *

I don't go to school the next day, either. Instead, Mama tells me to put my clothes on, that we're going to Wake Memorial Hospital to have some tests done. (That, by the way, would be the old, state-owned Wake Memorial Hospital—not the new larger-than-life *Wake Medical Center* with such advanced technology that trauma patients are literally flown in from all over, a fully-staffed gurney waiting on the helicopter pad to whisk them away immediately upon their arrival.) But when my eyes nearly pop out with fear at the suggestion, she assures me that there are no needles involved at all. Only looking at pictures and answering questions. I figure I can probably handle that, so without further adieu, I go into the bathroom to start the all-consuming ritual of getting dressed.

* * *

The nurse who leads me down the sterile hallway has long, dark hair pulled back in a ponytail. I'm not scared at all now because Mama has assured me again that there are absolutely no shots involved, only answering some simple questions about the voices. "Kind of like the questions the doctor over in Glenwood Village asked you." But already, I trust this person much more than I ever did *Mister-what-do-you-think-about-that*. Because at least she is wearing a white coat, and that, alone, automatically makes things official. It ought to be a rule; that all doctors have to wear white coats. Then you'd be able to tell right off which ones were legit. The same rule ought to apply to policemen as well. Because if they don't have on an official uniform, how do you know the good guys from the bad ones? Like the time Mama and I had been making our weekly trip to Raleigh and we'd wound up getting a flat tire about midway up Highway 64. We'd stopped on the side of the road, and with nothing else to do, she'd taken my hand, and we'd started hoofing it towards the nearest filling station where she could use the payphone to call Daddy. He'd come help us because men did things like that; knew how to change tires and all.

Though I realize that a flat tire isn't supposed to be a good thing, I am still happy because of the unexpected luck it has brought me. Without the car, we are stranded, and that, of course, means no session with turtle-neck-wearing-chain-smoking-Mister-what-do-you-think. I wonder when we finally make it to the filling station if Mama will let me get some stop sign crackers and a Sprite there since we obviously aren't going to make it to the vending machines today.

While I am contemplating my good fortune, a gold car swoops in, crackling to a stop in the gravel beside us. There is a dark-haired man behind the wheel, and he shows Mama a picture of some sort—kind of like a driver's license. I guess he figures she needs to be reassured that it's okay for him to be driving a car or something. But this is the sort of thing that Mama has warned Kay and me about over and over again. *Repeatedly.* And *now*—now that it's finally happening for *real*, it's pretty doggoned exciting, though in a scary sort of way. I am thoroughly surprised when Mama opens the passenger door of the waiting car, motioning for me to get in first. I look at her, signaling '*Are you crazy?*' But she catches my drift, saying, "It's okay. He works for the state." I wonder what that's supposed to mean as I slide into the center seat, right next to him. Mama shuts the door, and we pull off onto the road again.

In the car, there are lots of funny-looking radios and things. Kind of like the equipment Daddy has in his car for the T.V. station. I glance over at the man, himself, then, noticing that he seems friendly enough. So is that what he does, too? Does he work for some sort of a state T.V. station or something? I wonder what the difference is between a state T.V. station and Channel 5, where Daddy works. Curious, I glance in his windshield, but there is no coffee-stained '*press pass'* lying there.

While I'm thinking these things, the man slows to turn around through a break in the road, and before I know it, we are headed back in the other direction. The *wrong* direction.

"Hey!" I pipe up. "This isn't the way to the filling station!"

"Honey, he's taking us back to the car. He's going to help us with the tire," Mama explains.

Yeah, *right*! After all that warning, all those talks. And now here she is, falling for it, herself. Didn't she know better? Oh, I'm sure how it must've looked to *him*, alright. How we seemed to be such good and helpless targets to this evil predator—a young, petite mother on the side of the highway, holding the hand of a little kid so scrawny it looked like she'd snap a leg off if she so much as stepped in an ant hill. What was Mama thinking? And it is at that moment, groping for desperate ways for us to escape, that I finally notice it—the gun tucked against his side. I grab onto Mama's arm, whispering fiercely, "He's got a *gun!*" But apparently, I don't whisper it quietly enough because he looks over at us, kind of amused, and I know we're busted. I give him the meanest *'keep your distance'* glare I can manage, but Mama is only saying, "It's okay. He's *supposed* to have a gun. He's a policeman. A *state* policeman."

I maintain my glare. "Then why doesn't he have a uniform on?"

"Because state policemen don't wear uniforms. They wear suits."

He pulls in behind our disabled car then, asking Mama for her trunk keys. I squeeze her hand, silently warning, '*Don't do it!*' Didn't she have any clue? Didn't she know how long it'd be before they actually found our frozen bodies, stuffed in the trunk of her abandoned car on this remote stretch of Highway 64? Hopelessly, I guess she doesn't—because she readily hands over the keys. And now there is nothing else to do but just sit and wait in the warm car, watching warily through the windshield as he rolls up his sleeves, opens the trunk, wrestles with the full-size spare, then begins the dirty task of changing the tire, himself.

Before I know it, we are back in our own car, on our way again, and as he shuts the door behind Mama, telling her to drive safely, I give him one last scalding look—just in case.

Up the road, Mama pulls into the filling station anyway. She leaves the car idling, telling me to wait right there while she goes to the payphone to call the Turtleneck.

"What for?" I ask.

"To let him know we're running a little late, that's all . . . ."

Great.

* * *

"I dunno . . . . maybe two penguins . . . . holding hands or something?" What the hell was it supposed to look like?

"*Goo*-ood!" she croons. "Now . . . . what about *this* one?" She holds up the next card.

I cross my legs, try not to think about the bathroom just down the hall.

"Um—a house? With a flower growing out of the roof?" I pause, consider it from a new angle. "Or maybe it's a face. An upside down face."

"*Very* good!"

I stare at her. Is *she* stupid, or am I? I mean, here she is, showing me these cards with ridiculous, unidentifiable blobs slapped on them in psychedelic paint, and she acts like I've uncovered some deep, dark mystery every time I simply say what it looks like. Maybe I should've told her the truth about the penguins—what *they* really looked like. How initially, they'd really appeared to be a couple of naked old ladies, fighting over a banana. Somehow, though, I didn't figure this was the kind of thing she wanted to hear, even if it *was* the truth. I mean, what if she'd actually painted those pictures, herself? Then, if I said something like that, it might hurt her feelings. So I'd thought quickly, coming up with the penguin-theory instead.

Earlier, she'd shown me a whole bunch of real pictures—photographs—of different people with various expressions on their faces.

"What about *this* man? Is he happy or sad?" she'd ask.

"Um . . . . sad."

"Why do you think so?"

"Because he's frowning."

"Happy people don't frown sometimes, then?"

"Sometimes, maybe—but only when they're *not* happy."

"So it's possible for happy people to be *not*-happy people sometimes?"

I shrug. "Maybe." I suddenly wonder what's for lunch—where Mama will take me when we finally break for the morning. I hope it's McDonald's. And that I can get large french fries this time—the kind that come in the tall red container, not the kind in the little white pouch. Because when you get the pouch, you don't get nearly as many.

And now, sitting here, back in the same chair again, I wish I hadn't drunk so much Coke over lunch. I squirm, uncross my legs.

"Do you need to take a break?" the nurse asks me.

"No," I tell her. "But I *do* have to go to the bathroom, though."

"Of course," she is saying. "That's what I meant by taking a break."

But I thought she'd been asking if I'd wanted something else to eat—if I was ready for an afternoon snack, maybe. I couldn't imagine eating anything else right now, though. Not when I'm still overstuffed from lunch with catsup-drowned french fries. And as she is leading me down the hall to the bathroom, I figure something must *really* be wrong with me. Because Mama hadn't even questioned it when I'd asked for the over-sized order of fries along with a cheese burger *and* a big Coke, as well. Normally, she would've told me that I'd never eat that much, that I'd only end up wasting food. And today, when I'd done just that, throwing away over half the hamburger, she hadn't said a word.

Maybe I'm dying. Maybe that's it. Maybe I have some remote kind of disease for which there is, unfortunately, no treatment, and maybe everybody knows it, but me. At least if I died normally, though I could still become an angel and fly away. Then I could always come back and scare the crap out of Kay. Yeah, I like that. Because she wouldn't have any clue how all the stuff in her room was flying around in the air, completely by itself. And I could hide her favorite towel, too—put it somewhere she wouldn't dream of looking. And best of all, she'd never even see me. Because when I became an angel, I could be invisible anytime I wanted. Yeah, that sounds like fun. Not at all like if I had exploded. Like if I had been left to float indefinitely out in the middle of nowhere. That's the kind of invisible that wouldn't be fun—the kind where you couldn't help being invisible, and you just had to stay that way, no matter what. And if you exploded, then you wouldn't have other angels around to play with, either. You'd just be out there, all by yourself. Alone.

I can feel the Fear start to crawl up my spine again. It is not a good feeling, and it completely overshadows any of the fun things I'd contemplated on doing to Kay. Even though I knew how crazy it sounded, how it didn't make any sense—people just didn't up and explode like that. After all, Raymond had come back to school the very next day, still in one piece, smiling and as good as ever. So it's not like I actually believed he'd exploded at that point. But by then, the Fear had already been spawned, had already taken root, so reality and logic didn't matter anymore. Because once you've felt the Fear, there's absolutely no turning back. None, whatsoever. It has you in its grip for eternity.

I quickly leave the bathroom, trying to shut the Fear in behind me. And as I follow the dark-haired nurse back down the hall to the small examination room, my whole attitude has changed. All I want is for this appointment to finally be over with, to just go home and sit in my own room, where everything is familiar. Because whenever I'm away from home, I'm always tricked into believing that home's the only place where I'm safe, the only place that the Fear cannot get me. Still, regardless, it creeps up on me at home just the same as it does anywhere else. So I really can't figure out why it is I've convinced myself that every time the Fear rears its ugly head, I absolutely have to go running home. But that's the thing about the Fear and the voices. They constantly promise relief that they never intend to deliver. It's like bargaining with the enemy—the one without a conscience. Or kind of like one of those rippling mirages you always see in hot summer streets. You think there is water pooled in these low spots, and when you ride over it, its coolness will splash up onto the car and reduce the stuffiness. And you anticipate as you ride towards it. But right when you get there, just in the nick of time, the sparkling water-image dries up—evaporates right there into nothingness before your very eyes. And you'd think that after you saw enough mirages, witnessed this strange phenomena enough times, you'd finally learn. You'd finally figure it out. But still, if you're not paying attention, it'll get you every time.

  For a while, I thought that maybe—just *maybe*—this was the ultimate answer in learning to controlling the Fear, the voices; always being alert, paying close attention, therefore, never giving them the opportunity to sneak up on me again like they'd always done so relentlessly in the past. But at this, my futile attempt to take control of the much larger force that ruled me, I find that I am a failure as well. Because have you ever thought about what it'd be like if you had to constantly remind your own body to do its regular, mundane functions? Like blinking your eyes, for instance, or breathing. Suppose you had to actually *tell* your body to take a breath every single time it needed air? *Every single friggin' time.* It'd absolutely take over your entire conscious existence, forget about your *un*-conscious existence. Because you'd never be able to sleep again for fear of suffocation. Ultimately, this mundane task would end up swallowing your whole life. And you'd have to let it, too—that is, if you wanted to survive. And this is exactly the way it is when you to try to control the Fear. It, too, is automatic, unconscious—operates on complete autopilot—so to try to stop it is virtually impossible. It's just not going to happen, no matter how hard you try, no matter how bad you want it to.

* * *

The authorities at Wake Memorial give me a clean bill of health. They deem that I am highly intelligent, healthy and overall, normal. About the voices, all they can do is scratch their heads, and when they can offer nothing further, they refer me to the 'experts' in Chapel Hill.

I end up going through the same battery of tests there that I had at Wake Memorial, only this time, they give me little academic tests, too. Like I have a picture of three jugs in front of me, and I have to put a big 'X' over the one that is about a third full. They give me some simple fractions, too, which is lucky for me since I suck so royally at math. And there are these passages I have to read within a given amount of time as well, then answer questions without looking back at the text. But since I love to read, this is not a problem at all, though.

The interviewers are young—at least younger than any of the doctors I've seen up to this point—and kind of hippyish, too. They are not exactly doctors, according to Mama. Not in the sense I know, anyway. They are instead expert *psychologists* who work under the tutelage of Chapel Hill Memorial, a hospital located right on the campus of UNC. Interestingly though, these psychologists don't work out of the hospital, itself, but instead, out of an off-campus complex, which is near the mall. And it is here that Mama and I go for lunch, eating hamburgers and french fries from Scotty's, then walking around for the remainder of the hour, looking at all the stylish displays of upcoming fall fashions. The mannequins in the store windows look so cool and elegant, and I wish I could wear the kinds of clothes that they are so easily sporting; plaid, knee-length kilts paired with bright cowl neck sweaters and sturdy-looking penny loafers. My eyes trail further down the line of poised mannequins to notice that almost all of them wear a tiny Kuala bear clipped to their collars. Or if not a Kuala bear, then these long hatpin-looking things—Mama calls them 'stick pins'—that are each decorated differently on top; some with butterflies, others with scrolly initials, even some with miniature frogs and ladybugs. I can't seem to decide, though—if I could actually get one—which pin I'd want to have. But overall, it'd be a toss-up. Probably between the little frog down there on the very end, and the ladybug, right here on the second one over.

I am in complete awe of anyone who can actually wear such wonderful clothes without them feeling all itchy and scratchy. And I suddenly want more than anything to be able to look normal—to look stylish like that. To look *trendy*. Like the girls on TV. Like the ones modeling in the Sears catalog. Like these mannequins. They all seemed to have 'it.' I, on the other hand, do not, and this only makes me want it more. But there're so many factors to consider here, like first of all, actually being able to put stylish things on and not feel physically uncomfortable. Then there is the way clothes look on you, how they fit, the aura you present when you walk into a room; because there is a definite difference between simply putting on an outfit and actually *wearing* that outfit. And me in a kilt? It's not a pretty thought; we're talking two toothpicks sticking out of a cauliflower here.

I am actually starting to believe that I will never grow up. Because at nearly ten years old, I only weigh a mere 45 pounds, and I still wear a child's size 6X—the same size I've worn since the age of five. I am constantly trying to put on weight so I can grow up and be strong. My biggest dream is to ride Daddy's horse, Cappy, in the Wendell Lions Club Horse Show. But Daddy says it's a rule; that I have to weigh at least 50 pounds before I can do that. And I try. Honestly, I do. I mean, I can literally have a night of complete feasting—everything I can get my hands on—double crust pizza, caramel popcorn, ice cream (I have to have a little of all three kinds when I eat it), and an entire box of chocolate cookies, usually chased with a huge glass of Coke. And the next morning, hardly able to contain my excitement when I readily jump on the scales in Mama's bathroom, I quickly turn instead into a popped balloon—completely deflated. 44 pounds. I step off the scales, then step back on, much harder this time. The needle comes to rest again. *44 friggin' pounds.* Would someone please explain this injustice to me? How it's possible for a person to eat all night like that, and then actually end up *losing* a pound in the morning? It just doesn't make sense at all. Mimi insists that I need to go to the doctor and get checked for a tapeworm. Mama, on the other hand, always tells me to quit worrying, that being small is a good thing. She is constantly reminding me that 'the best things always come in small packages.' Plus, she also points out the fact that as long as my feet reach the floor, I really have nothing to worry about, anyway.

Back in the expert psychologists' office, I continue my 'testing.' One thing I like about these psychologists is that they seem to be pretty hip. They leave the radio on quietly while I work, and we listen to the hit parade, not some stupid muzak station. It is only after I hear Gwen McCray's *'Rocking Chair'* playing for the third time, and then *'More, More, More'* by the Andrea True Connection for the second, that I realize just how long I've actually been here. Still, I'm definitely not complaining, though. Because this is a huge improvement over most doctors' offices where more than likely, you'll be introduced to the elevator-revised version of '*I Left My Heart in San Francisco.*'

Overall, the testing goes about the same as it did in Raleigh. The psychologists finish tallying up my scores, then call Mama into the room with us. They tell us that everything appears perfectly normal. And like the 'specialists' at Wake Memorial, the 'experts' at Chapel Hill, too, are stumped. Especially since the scores I'd earned while testing with them placed me way up the academic food chain. According to them, my scores were so high up there, they almost placed me at genius-level.

"Maybe that's why she thinks she hears voices," the female psychologist suggests to Mama—like I'm not even in the room anymore. "She's *so* intelligent, in fact, that she's actually tapping into parts of her brain that other people aren't capable of using."

I want to laugh, but decide on the whole that it's probably better not to. If only I could invite her into my brain for a day. Then she'd see how far off-base she really was.

I cock my head over to the side, studying her for a moment longer, just before we stand up to leave. Because none of this makes any sense at all. And *how* many years was it that she'd gone to 'expert' school in order to actually learn the valuable skill of coming up with great theories like this one?

I can only hope that somewhere downstairs there's a vending machine. Otherwise, it's all been in vain.

'The Baby,' playing with her imaginary friends
(One of her favorite activities was cooking for them on her miniature
'Suzy Homemaker' stove.)

A scrawny me, with my cousin, Andy
(My biggest dream at that time was to actually get up to a full 50 pounds—
soaking wet or not.)

"ATTENTION— DON'T TAKE THE LITTLE BROWN PILLS!"

"How does that make you feel?"

I spin around in the modern pleather chair so that I'm facing the other wall. "I dunno," I say to the paneling.

"Angry?" she suggests.

"I guess," I tell her, turning back around. "Wouldn't it make you?"

True to Mama and Daddy's word, they did not make me go back to the Turtleneck. Instead, I am now attending sessions with a new doctor—a *lady* one this time. Because Mama thought it'd probably be a whole lot easier for me to relate to a woman, instead of some strange man. She is supposed to be an 'expert child psychiatrist.'

And unlike the Turtleneck, she believes in treating *two* ways—through combined counseling *and* medication. Mama and Daddy decide this is a pretty good idea. "There're lots of new medications out there that can help now," Mama explains to me. "I've been reading about them." So now I come to see her every Wednesday afternoon, where she asks me a bunch of dumb questions, then slaps a new prescription down on the desk for me to take to Mama.

Like the Turtleneck, she has earned a name all of her own, as well. In accordance with the endless supply of polyester suits she possesses, I have dubbed her likewise—*Polly-Esther*. I mean, every week—she has a different one for every single *week*. Sometimes it's a jacket, complete with matching elastic-waisted, seamed pants. Other times it's this horrid little top-thing; short, puffed sleeves, high waist, and a sash—a friggin' polyester *sash*—that ties behind the back. And with those tops, too, she has a wide variety of pants to match. Then there are the endless textured patterns to deal with. Just like somebody's old living room drapes or something. It's absolutely enough to make your eyes cross. But regardless of the patterns, colors or textures, one thing you can count on for sure is that it'll always be polyester. *Definitely* polyester. And like the Turtleneck, she, too, smokes, though at least not when I'm in the room with her. Still, I'd really hate to be around when she strikes a match. Because given her fashion sense and style, the results could be devastating.

There are vending machines downstairs here as well. They even have this one machine that fixes the drink for you. When you put your money in and push the button, a cup drops down and fills with ice, then the drink pours in after it. When it stops, you can open the plastic door and take the cup out. It's pretty neat.

Taking this endless supply of medications is not so neat, though. I mean, one week the knit-woman'll give me one thing, and the next week, another. Mama takes the prescriptions up to the drug store to get them filled each time. And I always know if they're supposed to have some kind of weird side effect because she'll try to ask me about it, but in this roundabout way, so I won't figure out what she's doing. But I bust her every time because she uses these words that she normally wouldn't. Like she'll ask me, "Are you feeling a little drowsy yet?" I mean, what is *that*? Does she think I'm dumb? Because normally she'd just say, "If you're so *sleepy*, why don't you go take a nap?" Or "If you're so *tired*, then maybe we ought to change your bed time back earlier." But '*drowsy*?' That's a pill-taking word in and of itself. Seriously—you can find that right on the side of the Dramamine box; '*May cause drowsiness*.' Once when I'd started taking this new medicine that Polly-Esther'd prescribed, Mama actually asked me, "Do your gums feel a little dry?" Okay—so what the hell kind of question is that? I mean, it's just not the kind of thing you go and pull right out of thin air. It reminded me of this skit they did on Saturday Night Live one time where the husband says, "*You know, Dear, I haven't been feeling too well lately.*" And the wife instantly replies, "*You know, Dear, maybe it's your pancreas.*" I mean, talk about elephant footprints in the Jello!

Actually, I am surprised that Mama is even going along with this little medicine scheme, anyway. Especially since she is so anti-drug. I mean, she doesn't even like to give us aspirin. She's always worried that we'll get 'hooked on drugs' or something, like so many of the other kids she's read about and seen on TV. She doesn't have to worry, though. Because who'd want to go around drowsy all the time, and with their gums feeling dry, too?

I remember one day when she fixed lunch for us—me a deviled egg sandwich, and Kay, a hard-boiled egg, itself. After we'd sat down at the table, for some reason or another, Kay decides she isn't hungry anymore. Instead, she picks up the hard-boiled egg, looks at it with interest, then without warning, suddenly squashes it in her hands. At first, I am stunned, but when she picks up the trashed remains, squashing it even flatter, I can't control the silly laughter any longer. Mama comes to the door to see what's so funny, and she gets this horrified look on her face. "Kay! What is the *matter* with you?" But suddenly, her expression shifts, gets almost paranoid, and she asks accusingly, "Are *you* on *drugs*?"

"*Yesss!*" Kay tells her, picking up what still remained of the egg, then going for the squash again. "*Psychedelic* ones!"

"*Where* in the world would you even *get* drugs?" Mama demands, pulling her out of the chair and escorting her to the bathroom where she deftly turns on the tub faucet. "*Certainly* not from that million-dollar school that *Mimi* sends you to!"

Kay laughs. "Out of the medicine cabinet! Where d'you think?"

"What medicine cabinet?" Mama asks her.

"*That* one!" She points to the closet in the bathroom, still laughing.

"What in the world did you take out of there?"

"Daddy's Co-pyornil!"

"You took Daddy's *Co-pyornil*?" Mama asks incredulously.

She is still laughing as Mama pulls the soiled dress over her head. "*Yesss*! But not the little *brown* ones. Only the little *red* ones!"

"That's not even the color that Co-pyornil—" Mama begins. But then she gets this enlightened look on her face again, asking, "Daddy let you watch that thing they did on *Woodstock* the other night, didn't he?" She thinks back for a moment. "The night I went to bridge club!"

But Kay is laughing too hard to even answer.

"Damnit! I *told* him not to let you watch that!"

She helps Kay into the bathtub, then turns around, seeing me still laughing in the doorway.

"Okay, that's it! *No* more TV after nine o'clock!" She pulls a fresh towel out of the linen closet. "You should be in bed by that time, anyway!"

But again, she has nothing to worry about. Because we've seen how Daddy is when he has Hay Fever, when he has to take his Co-pyornil. He has to lie on his bed with a sun lamp aimed at his face and a towel over his eyes until the pressure goes away. There's no way I ever want to have Hay Fever, let alone, anything that's associated with it. That's why this whole drug-thing with the knit-woman is so strange. Because it just doesn't seem like something that Mama and Daddy'd agree to do. Especially when some of the medicine she gives me does such weird things. Like working the opposite way than it is supposed to. Like the little white pills that appeared too small to do anything at all. But when Mama gave me one, I began to feel pissed off. And the longer I sat there, the more pissed off I got.

"Are you feeling a little light-headed?" Mama asks.

"No!" I holler. "So just leave me alone!"

"Well what's the matter then? Why are you acting like this?"

"I *said* just leave me alone!"

She calls Polly-Esther then, telling her how I'm behaving.

"Another one?" Mama says into the phone. She listens for a moment, then says, "Well, okay."

She opens the bottle, places another of the small pills near the back of my throat so that I can swallow it easier. But it isn't long before I'm sitting on the kitchen floor, crying uncontrollably. I don't know why I'm crying, only that I can't stop, and that I'm terribly, terribly angry. I feel like I'm going to absolutely bust. I don't know how to make the anger go away, how to get rid of it, and burning up inside, I hear myself start to growl. Mama watches me, looking more and more worried. She picks up the phone, calls Polly-Esther back.

"I just don't know what to do," she says. Again, she pauses, then says, "How many? I don't know. Hold on—let me look."

She opens the bottle, looks inside, then says into the phone, "There're three left."

A brief silence follows before she comes back with, "*All* of them? Are you *sure*?" Then, "Well, okay . . . . I'll try that."

Before I know it, she is handing me the rest of the pills along with a glass of water. I don't want to take them. I'm way too pissed off. But she insists, so I let her put the pills on my tongue, one at a time, and I dutifully swallow, though I want to scream instead, to tear something up. I gnash my teeth. Scream. Beat my head on the floor. There is spit running out of my mouth. I am really scared because I've never been this mad before.

Moments later, Mama is back on the phone. "I don't know what to do! She's completely out of control! Do what? The hospital? How? She's acting just like a wild animal! I can't put her in the car like this! And assuming I could even get her to the car, there's no way I can *drive* her like this! She'll end up causing me to have a wreck and kill us both!"

She looks haggard as she listens. "But she wasn't acting like this until I gave her the medicine."

She puts her hand to her face in exasperation. "Put her *where*?" In a *closet*? Why? Why do you think she's going to *hurt* herself?" Mama tries to sit down on the floor beside me, but the phone cord won't reach. She puts her hand on my back instead. But that only pisses me off worse, and I shove her away.

"A *reverse* reaction?" she is saying harriedly into the phone. "Then why did you tell me to give her the rest of the bottle? Well *that's* certainly a fine way to experiment!"

The next thing I know, she is leading me to the den closet, where there are coats and things and it is relatively soft. She puts me in, shuts the door. I scream, bang from the inside. I'm not scared at all. I'm too angry to be scared. I just want to tear something up, and she is keeping me from doing that.

I'll bet I'm not in the closet thirty seconds when she quickly swings the door back open again. She is crying as she wrestles this Tasmanian monster that I've become into the little half-bath. She kicks the furry toilet seat down, pulling me onto her lap. She wraps her arms around me, holding me still, and she rocks back and forth. She is crying as she says, "I don't know what the answer is. Honest to God, I don't. But I know it isn't *this*!"

* * *

Polly-Esther is not impressed by my emotional display. She seems to think that *I've* caused the medicine to create this kind of reaction. Because she assures Mama that it's really a fine medication, highly tested, and used liberally by all of her colleagues. Still, Mama refuses to ever give it to me again.

"There's one more we can try," Polly-Esther says removing her large owl glasses. "It's relatively new. It's actually for kids who are hyperactive, but I don't think it would hurt to try it at this point."

Mama looks skeptical. "What kind of side effects does it have?"

Polly-Esther replaces her glasses, beginning to scribble out a new prescription as she says, "Well, the most common one is weight gain."

What had she said? Had I actually heard her right?

"Well, I don't know," Mama is saying while at the same time I am exclaiming, "I'll *take* it!"

But Mama holds up a hand then, saying, "I don't know. I'll have to talk to Daddy about it. Then we'll see."

But I couldn't ever imagine her keeping this wonderful new drug from me, especially when it could make me gain weight. Then I'd finally look normal. People would finally like me. The concept's almost too much to grasp.

Polly-Esther finishes writing out the prescription, handing it over the desk to Mama.

"It's called Ritalin," she says. "And if you decide you want to try it, just go ahead and fill this." As she indicates the prescription, I can see that her hands are fidgeting, that she really wants a cigarette, that she can't wait for us to leave. She stands up, moving towards the door. "Just let me know what you decide first," she tells Mama, holding it open for us.

But as far as I'm concerned, there is no decision. I will have that medicine, come hell or high water. Because nothing's keeping me from becoming normal—nothing at all.

* * *

There are only two things I can put on my body now. Not because of their comfort level or lack thereof, but because they're the only ones I can actually squeeze into anymore. Because in two month's time, I have gone from 45 pounds to a whopping 75 pounds. I am not simply 'healthy' or even 'pleasingly plump." I am downright fat, and there's no getting around that. Mama doesn't call if 'fat,' though. Instead, she calls it 'bloated' from the medicine. "Nobody gains that much weight in such a short time," she tells me. "Especially not someone with a metabolism like yours."

Sure, I'd hated being scrawny. But this was much worse. Because Mama's right. I don't simply look like a chubby kid, but instead, like a beached whale—bloated, like she says, and kind of sallowed-out. Not that I've ever been a pretty child to begin with. But at least when I was skinny, I was cute. And besides, my face, having gotten fat, too, only better frames my severe malocclusion problem. Whereas before I may have looked like a sunny little woodchuck, I now more or less resemble an overgrown sow—one who could actually eat corn through a chain-link fence.

And on top of that, the knit-woman decided that what Mama and I really needed was time away from each other. And at a full eleven years old, she suggested that Mama and Daddy put me in after-school daycare. Yeah, right. That'll be a good sight. Needless to say, I am not happy at all when Mama and Daddy agree to give this a try.

They end up sending me to this place called 'Creative Days,' a center pretty far away, kind of across town. After school, there is a van that comes directly to Robinscrest and picks me up—along with two other first-graders—and drives us there. The lady who drives the van is named Becky. She is skinny, blond. She doesn't wear any make-up and seems more androgynous than female. She takes corners too fast, and she likes to sing along with the radio while she drives, too.

"*Keep on a—rockin' me, ba-beee—keep on a-rockin' me, ba-beee!*"

She opens the van door to let us off at the center. "*I been to Phoenix, Arizona, all the way to Tacoma, Philadelphia, Atlanta, LA—*"

As we disembark, she shuts the door behind us, then pulls into the adjoining lot where she backs the van into a parking space. Embarrassed as always, I follow the two first-graders around the building to the classroom where we are supposed to enter, 'A-Room,' slouching way down so that no one'll really notice how much older the 'fat kid' is than the rest of them. It's like prison, leaving one school and then going directly to another. I wonder what I should've done differently, what I could've maybe done to avoid this punishment. Mama and Daddy say it's not punishment, that it's just a way for Mama and me to get some time away from each other. But they just don't know. They have no clue what it's like to be around a bunch of babies all afternoon, let alone, to be *treated* like one as well.

The only other kid here who is my age is this tall, gangly guy who is mentally retarded. And sometimes when he has tantrums, the teachers at Creative Days do the same thing to him that Polly-Esther'd tried to get Mama to do to me; they shut him in a closet and hold the door. The sounds that come out of the closet are scary, sometimes unbelievable; yelling, angry name-calling, the door being kicked so hard the wall literally shakes. They have us all sitting Indian-style on the rug in 'B-Room' one day when he goes crazy like this. Ed and Becky force him into the closet up front where Ed holds the door hard against the angry yanking and pulling. The wall shakes again. Becky turns off the lights, a sign that we need to get quiet. My stomach is knotting up, listening to the desperation of the muffled sounds. Some kids are laughing, though. Like this is actually amusing or something.

From the front of the room, Becky crosses her arms, looking hard at all of us perched there on the rug.

"For those of you who think it's funny, you can laugh your *pretty little heads* off somewhere in a corner!"

The laughter quickly dries up, turns into muted snickers instead.

I look at the clock, see that it's only 4:15. Mama won't be here to get me until at least 5:00. I raise my hand, and when I am finally acknowledged, I ask for permission to go to the bathroom. Closing the door behind me, I immediately begin trying to hear music. It's something I've learned to do—hear music like that. Because I've discovered that if you shut everything else out and concentrate really hard on a song that you know, eventually you'll actually hear it for real—outside your own head. I like doing this best with 'Nadia's Theme' because it's such a beautiful song. Plus, it's easier to 'hear' than most other songs. I don't know why, but for some reason, it just is, and the faster I can hear music, the sooner I don't have to listen to what's going on out in the other room.

I am angry, mostly at the knit-woman, but also at Mama and Daddy. Because how can they do this? I am part of the family, too—just like Kay and the baby—and I should be there, with them, not stuffed away here, in this babysitting hellhole, like I don't even exist. At home, I beg Mama and Daddy to let me quit going there. I promise to come home from school and go straight to my room every single day where I'll play quietly until supper time. But again, Mama and

Daddy tell me it's not about that at all. It's just to give the two of us some much-needed time apart. When I am insistent, they finally agree to talk with the knit-woman about it, see what her opinion is.

This is all her fault! I hate that stupid woman! Because Mama and Daddy would've never come up with something this heinous on their own. Not without *her* input. And while I'm tucked conveniently away in this prison-like environment every single afternoon, Polly-Esther, herself, is probably at home, eating all the cookies she wants—not being limited to a Dixie cup of Kool-Aid and only three cookies from the plastic serving dish.

I go into Mama and Daddy's bedroom, pick up the phone book. After I find it, I dial Polly-Esther's home number, listening as it rings once, then twice.

"Hello—"

"AAAWWWooOOOCK!" I screech into the receiver, hoping I sound just like a big, fat pterodactyl. One that'll fly over and crap on her car. I slam the phone down. There. I feel much better now.

Me, reading to 'the Baby'
(at a whopping 75 Ritalin-induced pounds)

Kay, 'the Baby' and me on Easter Sunday
(in the front yard, before church)

SEA SALT AND HOLY ROLLERS

Mama is taking on new interests. Daddy doesn't want her to work now, like she did when we lived in Wendell. Instead, he wants her to stay home so she can be with the baby, so she can pick the two of us up from school in the afternoons. He doesn't want us to become 'latchkey kids.' So like most of the other mothers in the neighborhood, this is what she does.

They don't make me go to Creative Days anymore. Not since Polly-Esther insisted that after school was out, I needed to attend summer camp as well—a decision that had ultimately earned her another phone call from me. Because when Mama learned how unhappy I'd been for that whole week, how the other kids had teased me and called me 'fat,' she'd said, "That's it! This is *my* child, and

I'm raising her the way *I* want to!" And as if to cooberate that, to finalize her decision, she flushes the remainder of the Ritalin down the toilet. And within weeks of this twisted Boston Tea Party she has regally hosted, something interesting starts to happen; I begin to be not so fat anymore.

The house begins to fill up with plants—lots of them. Some sit on stands in decorative pots, others are clustered together on the floor in front of a large, sunny window. Some hang from macramé ropes. But regardless of their manner of display, they are everywhere. Mama says plants are good for you, that they provide oxygen, help you breathe better. I can't help but wonder how it was we ever breathed at all when we lived in Wendell, when the house was sealed up like an Egyptian tomb with respect to the two air-conditioning units.

In this house, we have a different kind of air-conditioning. It blows through vents hidden in the shag carpet, and it cuts on and off all by itself. All you have to do is set the thermostat in the hall, and it does everything for you. The rooms all feel the same, too. Not freezing in one and hot in another. Daddy calls it 'central air,' and he says it's much more economical to use than window units. (Actually, I've been introduced to central air before, only I didn't know it. Daddy claims that Mimi's always had central air in her house—ever since it was first available. But I'd never really thought to question why her house was always so nice and cool. I'd just assumed that being hers, it wouldn't dare to do otherwise.) But for whatever reasons, Mama says this change has been good for Daddy, too, because he hardly ever gets Hay Fever anymore.

Mama has begun to join clubs with the other neighborhood mothers as well; the garden club on Tuesdays, a morning Bible study on Thursdays—and she is even taking guitar lessons from one of the mothers who lives just behind us. They all get together after supper on Wednesday nights and sit in a circle over at her house, learning how to create new chords. Sometimes she practices at home, and I just can't get used to it—seeing her that way on the floor and all. I mean, she'd been totally against the idea of Woodstock, saying that it was nothing but a huge gathering of hippies with nothing better to do than take drugs and stand around, dancing foolishly. She didn't think there was any purpose to it at all. And when Kay and I had asked Mama and Daddy if they'd actually wanted to go to Woodstock, too, they'd share the same word in unison; "*No!*"

In the mornings after her clubs and meetings, Mama has started watching this new hour-long TV program. It is religious, though in a modern sort of way, and they'd had this guest on recently who'd talked about preservatives and toxins, how these maim the body, keep it so unpurified. He claimed that people don't need all that sugar and all those preservatives, how a movement back to the basics is not only of the utmost importance, but also definitely necessary. He has written a book on this pressing issue, and Mama goes out to buy it.

Whenever she is not watching the show, which now occupies *two* full hours of morning network time, she is reading the book, checking the labels on the food in our cabinets.

"Polysorbate, soy lecithin, xanthan gum—*aluminum sulfate*?" She shakes her head at Daddy. "And we wonder why she's hyperactive." She throws the box of fake Twinkies into the trash compactor, deftly turning it on. She taps the book, saying, "It tells you right here—in the first two chapters—that if an ingredient is one you've never heard of before, or if it has a weird and unnatural spelling, then you can pretty much count on the ingredient, itself being unnatural—a *toxin*."

Needless to say, sweet cereal days have come to a screeching halt, and I wonder, too, if this means the end of the delectable sugar cookies Mama has always baked for special occasions.

Ultimately, it does. Because this is the year that we will become 'enlightened,' in more than one way. It is 1976, and Mama has thrown out all of our food. Every bit of it. You couldn't find a preservative in our house now if your life depended on it. Instead, our cabinets are filled with ingredients like sea salt and honey, wheat germ and yeast. And our refrigerator is even scarier. Because other than some rubber cheese and this welfare peanut butter, it is completely bare, too—devoid of all the normal and regulated items that you would expect to find there for routine human consumption.

"It is *not* welfare peanut butter!" Mama tells us. "It's very expensive—all natural. It came from the health food store."

But somehow, I just can't understand how they can charge *more* for a jar of peanut butter that requires so much work, just to make it fit to eat. To start with, the peanut butter and oil come separated in these gross, obvious layers, and when you open the jar for the first time, you have to stir it all together. But the peanut butter, itself is so hard, you end up having to get a bowl out instead, dumping everything together for some serious rounds of chopping just to break up the clumps. Then, to keep it from tasting like cardboard, Mama adds a touch of her sea salt to the mixture. And poor Daddy—since there's no more sugar in the house, he has to drink his coffee with a teaspoon of honey instead.

Actually, the rubber cheese turns out to be pretty good. It comes in a sealed wax container so it's always fresh when you cut it open. You can slice off a few slabs and put it on the whole-grain crackers that Mama bought, or you can put it in the oven and melt it over some wheat bread. And either way, it's surprisingly pretty good. She always gets two different kinds of cheese; Edam for us which is mild, and Gouda for Daddy because it's sharper-tasting. But you always have to be careful to keep the wax container *with* the cheese when you open it, not just stick the plain slab back in a baggy by itself. Because other than the color of the wax, the cheese looks exactly alike, and you may end up cutting the spicy Gouda for your crackers instead of the mild Edam.

This healthy snack has replaced Daddy's afternoon beers as well. Now when he comes home from work, instead of popping an aluminum can top, Mama fixes him a little plate with cheese and crackers, then pours a glass of wine which she takes out to his model train workshop behind the garage. This is Daddy's quiet time—when he goes out to the train room after work—and Mama says we aren't supposed to bother him when he's 'winding down.' Still, we've discovered that if you sneak out there when Mama's not looking and knock on the door, he'll let you in, anyway.

Interestingly, the health food diet ends up greatly improving over time. As Mama gets more into it, she learns how to make some really good things. Like the wonderful snacks she always has freshly baked and waiting for us when get home from school. She has gone through her cookbooks and modified all the recipes so that they are healthy, substituting honey for sugar, real butter for margarine, sea salt for regular salt. We have cinnamon buns complete with raisins and glaze, homemade potato chips, apple turnovers, cheese straws, and even homemade bread. We have to be careful to walk very lightly when she's making bread, though. If we come thundering through the kitchen when it's sitting under a warm towel trying to rise, then we could cause it to cave in. And we definitely don't want to do anything to ruin the bread. Because in all my life, I have never smelled anything better than fresh, warm bread baking.

Mama's show, called 'The PTL Club,' now comes on several times a day. Along with the health food diet, she and Daddy have made one other huge change; they have become 'Born Again' Christians. Now on Sundays, they visit around, looking for a new church—one that'll meet their new needs—instead of attending the conservative Presbyterian church where we'd gone since moving to Raleigh. It is the new trend, this 'Born Again' Christian thing—and all of the mothers in the neighborhood are going this route, the fathers dutifully following. It is an advanced form of Christianity where modern ballads are sung instead of hymns, where attending alternative churches requires only that you be there, not that you be dressed to the nines. "It's not about trying to impress anyone," Mama tells us. "It's about getting together to honor the Holy Spirit—to praise God." Most of these new-age churches that we attend are not big, brick buildings with steeples in well-established parts of town. Instead, they are in small, temporary buildings with corrugated siding, or remote trailers out in the woods of North Raleigh. Anything that you would normally equate with a traditional church setting has now become null and void. Because those traditional churches do not teach what is important. They focus on the Old Testament rather than the New. They are too strict and narrow-minded. In fact, they don't elaborate at all on the fact that Jesus is coming back to rescue every single one of us—anytime now—and we need to be ready for that, for 'The

Rapture,' when it happens. Because none of us wants to be left behind. And those of us who have actually taken this huge step towards salvation—become 'Born Again' Christians—can readily expect to have a hard time fighting the devil off. Because he will do anything in his power to win us over, to make us stumble along the path to salvation. But we have to be aware of this, to constantly fight him, to 'bind' the devil from doing these things.

Mama and Daddy have become convinced that the voices and the Fear are actually demons that have entered my body. And from one of the churches they've attended, they invite the minister to our house to pray over me, to bind the devil, to call the demons out for good. His name is Reverend Coster and he is red-faced, fat. He wears a suit and tie, carries a handkerchief in his sweaty palm, which he uses to mop his forehead periodically.

We sit in the living room with the doors pulled shut; Mama and Daddy standing beside Reverend Coster who sits in the leather chair. I am kneeling on the floor in front of him. From his coat pocket, he retrieves a small bottle of olive oil, which he uses to anoint my head before he lays his hands on me in prayer.

He is stoic, methodic—and somewhere during the exorcism, I cough—something that I do pretty often due to the dry air in the house. But afterwards, Reverend Coster tells Mama and Daddy that the cough was actually the demons leaving my body, that I would be healed now.

Strangely, when I am released from the living room, I am disappointed to find that I am still counting steps, that I still feel compelled to touch the light switch over and over again. Though I don't know what it actually feels like to be 'healed,' I have all ideas it's not like this. I should feel free, weightless, completely unburdened. Not the same as I did before. Maybe I did something wrong. Maybe there was something I was supposed to do while he was praying over me, and I didn't do it. But if that were the case, wouldn't he have told me beforehand what it was I needed to contribute? Now what I feel is confused, tired. And all I want to do is return to my comfort zone, where I know what to expect and how to feel. So what if the voices are still there? At least it's what I'm used to.

One other way we have become 'enlightened' this year is when Mama and Daddy visit our school on a mandatory parent night. The whole meeting turns out to be the school telling the parents how they are not contributing enough money to school funds, and that this is going to have to change. The school will now go out and evaluate each family's potential, and then it will decide, itself, the individual amounts of the newly-imposed 'gratuity' that each family will owe.

"And don't think you can just write down any amount," the chairman tells the parents matter-of-factly. "Because we will ride out to everyone's house and look to *see* what size boat you have parked in the driveway. There's no way around this, folks. I'm sorry, but it has to be done. Since no one's bothered to contribute even a *portion* of their fair share, we have, unfortunately, had to resort to these measures. And knowing how well-off you all are, anyway, this should not be a problem for a single one of you."

I can honestly say that if you'd managed to snag the Roadrunner's Acme slingshot itself, you couldn't have gotten us out of that school faster than Mama did.

"That's ridiculous!" she fumes "I don't care if I have a million dollars, nobody's going to tell me what I have to give! Already, it costs us more to send *each* of you to Robinscrest for *one* year than it did for Pop to send me to Meredith College for the entire time I was there!"

Mimi offers to pay the 'gift,' but Mama waves it away, saying, "It's not about the money, Judy! I am *not* going to be threatened—and—and *manipulated* into meeting the demands of a school that's so snobby it'll completely drown if it simply tries to lift its head in a *rainshower!*"

I have the feeling I am not supposed to be listening to this, but still, it's good shit, so I maintain my position just outside the doorway.

"They can go to *public* school, with all the other kids in the neighborhood! And no one'll have to pay a *penny!*"

What had she said? You mean public school is *free*? This was certainly news to me!

"Why can't you just send them to the little Christian school?" Mimi asks. "The one where Angie went."

'*Yes!*' I think, triumphantly. '*Then we can move back home!*'

"Do you know what they tried to make us do?" Mama is saying to Mimi. "Do you have any idea? Because that's why *Angie* didn't go there anymore! That's why we decided to put her in Robinscrest with Kay, in the first place!"

"No, I don't think I'm aware—" Mimi breaks off.

"They told John and me that we'd have to sign this petition—if we planned to put Angie there the next year, we had to sign this *petition*—saying that we'd do everything—absolutely *everything* in our power—to keep Blacks out of the school! Now, you tell me— how Christian is *that*?"

I am shocked. I never knew, never understood exactly why they'd pulled me out of the little school I'd actually liked. But now it all makes sense. Because after moving to Raleigh, those issues—the racial ones—that we'd been constantly faced with living in a small town didn't hold nearly as much 'value' here. For lack of a better term, they became more or less 'dead issues' when you were in a much larger community.

"I will *not* have my children raised in an environment where they are taught the virtues of *superiority!*" Mama continues. "And that is *precisely* what Robinscrest is attempting to do! Maybe it's not racial, maybe it wears a different disguise, but the concept's still the same, and I won't have my children on *either* end of the stick! They will never live to make *others* feel bad, and neither will they live to let others make *them* feel bad! No, they are going to *public* school, with all of their friends! And they can ride the bus—throw spitballs—just like everyone else!"

I want to peep around the corner so badly—just to see if Mama's actually slicing her hands at Mimi. But I don't dare because I can't risk having them see me there, eavesdropping. Anyway, who was it that said 'eavesdroppers seldom learn anything beneficial?' Because I would have to challenge that since obviously, they've never lived in my house before.

* * *

It is the Tuesday after Labor Day—1977—and it is also the night before my first day of normal school, in a regular public setting, at least since the first grade. I am very excited, especially about getting to ride the bus in the morning. I will be entering the 5th grade at Northridge Elementary, where all of the other neighborhood kids go. While trying to pick out something to wear tomorrow for my big debut, there is a huge sonic boom outside. All of a sudden, everything goes completely black. I am too excited to be scared, though, and as I feel my way to the staircase, the baby begins to cry. Mama meets me half-way up with a flashlight in her hand.

"It's alright," she tells me. "A transformer blew, that's all. Probably just a circuit overload or something."

At the landing, I meet Daddy who is opening the front door, walking onto the porch. I take advantage of the situation, follow him out. And it is like we just stepped off a space ship or something, right out into new and unfounded territory. The other neighborhood families, too, are spilling out of their front doors in curiosity, and all of us kids run together, converge, excited with this new and unexpected adventure. It's very dark, though not as pitch-black as it is inside the house. The air is still, hushed—devoid of the continuous hum from all the central air conditioning units. And there is no monotonous buzzing coming from the now darkened streetlights.

Over in the driveway, Mama is standing beside Daddy now. She is holding the bewildered baby who is irritatedly rubbing her eyes. A little further up, Kay stands with some of the other kids because like them, she thinks she is too old to play flashlight tag. She is going to junior high now, and that has changed everything. (She'd actually gotten to leave Robinscrest after Christmas last year and start at the local junior high school, West Millbrook, in January. I, on the other hand, had to finish out the year at Robinscrest.) And since she's been going there—to public junior high school—she's a whole different person. Now she gets up in the mornings and curls her hair, puts on eyeshadow. And in the afternoons, she talks on the phone for hours—until Mama makes her hang up and do her homework.

From the darkened street, I motion for her to come over and join us because we are getting ready to play hide-and-seek now, but she still hangs back with the others, listening to her transistor radio instead. And the song that is playing adds a mysterious air to the already bewitching night. *"Mirrors on the ceiling, pink champagne on ice—and she said, 'We are all just prisoners here, of our own device.' And in the master's chambers we gather for the feast. They stab it with their steely knives, but they just can't kill the beast . . . ."*

CP&L doesn't get the lights back on until 11:00, and no one is forced to go in, to rush into bed, until normalcy is finally restored. And now, finally lying here in my own bed, the hall light brightly soothing, I know I will never be able to fall asleep. Not in a million years.

The house begins to fill up with plants . . . .

. . . . they are everywhere

In the driveway, posing beside Daddy's 'work car' ('The Baby' is giving the infamous 'Fonz' AAAAAAY thumb.)

LITTLE TRANSYLVANIA

The baby is standing at the front door, the new little dog—a 'Benji' look-alike—standing right beside her, wagging his tail excitedly. (Actually, the dumb dog has no clue why he's happy. He just figures that since everyone else is, he is supposed to be, too.) They are waiting for Pop to come down. He has gone back upstairs to retrieve his hat from my room where he and Mom have spent the night. (I, unfortunately, after having drawn the losing straw, landed the wonderful luck of sleeping in Kay's room, where she shuts the door up tight, insisting that everything be pitch-black.) Pop is riding along with Mama to take the baby to pre-school, and this is something the baby, herself finds totally irresistible.

She is wearing her favorite dress, a Ronald McDonald number, complete with red and white stripes and these orange, puffy sleeves. It even has the stupid McDonald's logo sewed on the pocket. To top it all off, she has on tights to match with black patent leather shoes. And her hair, so long she can sit on it, is pulled up high in these stupid matching pigtails, each one tied with a red ribbon. I'd sure hate to be the one to break the news to her, to tell her the truth—that in reality, she looks a heck of a lot more like the little 'Hamburgler' than she ever will the tall, red-headed clown.

"Oh, how *nice*!" I say sarcastically. "The baby's getting ready for *school*!"

She scowls at me.

I smile.

"You don't have to teach her to hate school," Mama tells me, coming into the entry way. "Just because you don't like it doesn't mean she doesn't have to."

"Well, if that baby's got any sense—" I began.

"And *stop* calling her 'the baby'!" Mama insists. "She is *not* a baby! She's almost four years old!"

I cut my eyes over at her then—at *not-the-baby*—who has taken on the same confronting stance as Mama; arms crossed, looking at me pointedly.

"Well, as far as I'm concerned," I say, "she will *always* be 'the baby'!"

"If that's the case," Mama rationalizes, "then so are you. And so is Kay." She indicates Pop who is coming down the stairs. "And me, too, for that matter."

"No, this is different," I tell her. "Because the baby will *always* be 'the baby'!"

"Well, her name is *Martie*, and you *need* to start calling her that," Mama tells me as the three of them walk out the front door on the way to their little happy-go-lucky journey—which, in reality, consists of only about a half-block up the street. I snort. Because now I will be forced to create new and exciting names with which to address the baby. And frankly, I can think of nothing else that fits.

Mom comes out of my bedroom then. As she is going in the bathroom to get dressed, she calls down to me, "Pop and I brought you some souvenirs—some little trinkets and things—from our trip. They're in one of those shopping bags down there if you want to look for them."

She shuts the bathroom door, turns on the water.

Suddenly, the clouds of confusion open up and a beaming ray of sunlight enlightens me, brightens my entire day.

Trinket!

Because Mama will think the baby's new name means something cute and special—like a small reminder you'd purchase at a neat place you visited. But only the baby and I will know the truth, what a trinket *really* is; a piece of impulse-junk you'd pick up on a spur-of-the-moment tourist-trap stop—like at *South of the Border*, for instance—when in reality, you're final destination is someplace much, much better, like *Myrtle Beach*. I smile. It's just too perfect! And I relish in my good fortune as I head for the small half-bath to start the ritual of getting dressed for school, too.

* * *

One other form of 'enlightenment' comes to Mama and Daddy that year; they finally notice the glaring fact that I have teeth growing out of places where teeth should never be. Whether they notice this on their own, or whether it's a result of Kay's new name for me— 'Count *Drrra*-cu-la,' which now takes full precedence over '*Habitrail*'— I'm not sure. But either way, I'm not one to argue the point. At least they're willing to do something about it. Because not everyone can be born with perfect teeth, like Kay. They take me to the dentist; he sends me to the orthodontist. It turns out braces are very expensive, but the orthodontist tells Mama and Daddy not to worry, that he will work out a payment plan with them. It is not often that he gets a mouth as 'challenging' as mine, and he really wants to work with me, regardless. Translation? *'Come on, Folks! You can't be serious! You just can't let your kid grow up, looking like that! It's inhumane. The only thing she'll be prepared for in life is accepting sympathy donations in a tin cup, or if she gets real lucky, maybe a part in Ringling*

Brother's side show!' But whatever it is that he *really* says to them finally hits home because it is at this point that I start the grueling 10-step program for '*Orthodontics Anonymous.*' And it is truly amazing, all the things I have to go through first, just in preparation for the actual braces, themselves. To begin with, I have to have several teeth pulled because my mouth is simply too crowded to even hope for any kind of corrective movement, lateral or otherwise. I then have to undergo oral surgery to remove impacted teeth that will later come through, wrecking all the progress the orthodontist has actually managed to make. Finally, after all that has taken place, I will have to wear this thing he calls a 'palatal spreading appliance' for at least six months, maybe longer. Translation here? '*Ancient Chinese Torture, reincarnated.*' What this device actually does is unbelievable, and at first, Mama won't agree to it. It is this metal bar that goes over the roof of my mouth, attached on each corner by a band to the respective tooth. The bar, itself, is divided in half, and it is held together by a long screw with a series of holes in it. Twice a day, Daddy has to take a small key and put it in the next hole, cranking the bars another notch apart and stretching my mouth a little further out each time. The idea is to gradually separate the bone in the roof of my mouth, causing new bone to grow in and fill up the hole, thus making my mouth wider.

"By the time we get her palatal bone separated far enough," the orthodontist explains, "she should be able to get a half-deck of cards in the space between her two front teeth."

Lovely!

"But as the new bone grows in, her teeth will close back up, right along with it."

He'd better hope so!

"Oh, and one other thing," he tells us, just before we leave. "If she starts seeing double, call me right away. Because that will mean we've stretched the mouth too far too quickly, and we'll have to go in and let some of the tension off the jaws." He smiles as he holds the conference room door open. "You all have a nice day, now."

Is he kidding?

But he misinterprets my look, saying, "Don't worry, Angie. When this is all over with, it'll literally rearrange everything, give you a whole new face. You'll see."

Gee! *Thanks*! But still, it's a comforting thought, since regardless, I realize I need all the help I can get. Because if Kay calls me '*Dracula*' one more time, there's no question about it at all—I *will* be out for blood—*hers*.

'The Baby,' all decked out in her favorite Ronald McDonald dress (Pop is riding along with her on the one-block trip to pre-school.)

'Count Drrracula' teeth

The new little dog—a 'Benji' look-alike

PINK, GREEN, AND PAPAGALLO ALL OVER

Daddy has been offered a good job; one as the manager of a new TV station scheduled to go on the air in less than six months. The catch?

"It's in Winston-Salem," they tell us.

I let the math book fall from my hands. "Isn't that where all those witches are supposed to be?"

Kay rolls her eyes. "*No*, dumb-butt! That's Salem, *Massachusetts!*"

"Well—what's the difference?" I ask defiantly.

"Lots, *stupid*! *Winston*-Salem is where *Old* Salem is. You know, where you always go on field trips. Where you get Moravian cookies and visit all those old shops and things."

"*I've* never been there," I say. "So how would *I* know?" I stick my tongue out at her.

"Oh, that's *right*," she replies, sarcastically. "I *forgot* how you won't ride a *bus* for any length of time—you know, for any long distance—when you can't just stop and *pee* any time you want."

"That's not fair!" I tell her. "I can't help it if I have to use the bathroom a lot!"

"Oh, *yes*, you can," Kay smiles.

"Mama—make her stop!"

"Alright—*both* of you!" she warns. "Cut it out! *Now!*"

Daddy leans back in his chair, casually lighting his pipe as if there's been no interruption at all. "Your mother and I will be going up there several times in the next month or so to look for a new house."

"So it's all settled?" I demand. "Just like that?"

Mama nods. "We think so."

"But I don't *want* to move again!" I wail, at the same time Kay is asking, "Will we get to go up there, too? *With* you?"

Mama shakes her head, telling Kay, "No, we've arranged for Mom and Pop to come stay with you while we're looking. That way you won't have to miss any school."

I cut my eyes over at Kay, crossing my arms over my chest. "Well, they're not sleeping in *my* room this time!"

Mama holds a hand up, saying, "They can sleep in mine and Daddy's room. We won't even be here."

I feel like the bottom has absolutely fallen out from under me. I cannot believe what I'm actually hearing. We are moving, and pretty far away from here, at that. The only consolation I have in all this sudden turmoil is that at least with Mom and Pop here, there'll be some good food in the house for a change. Even if it *is* temporary. 'Besides,' I think, trying to cheer myself up. 'Maybe they won't even find a house at all. And if that happens, we'll wind up staying right here.'

But no such luck. It isn't long before they return home from one of their outings, all happy and smiling, because they've finally found 'the one'—a Williamsburg-style house, around fifty years old or so. "A real fixer-upper!" they tell us, excitedly.

Unfortunately, we can never be prepared enough for the actual truth that simple statement holds.

* * *

It is late January, 1979, all the necessary arrangements have been made, and we are finally heading for Winston-Salem. Everything that we can't fit into the Buick gets loaded into a rented moving van instead.

They are calling for snow in the immediate forecast. Lots of it. It is late in the afternoon when we finally leave the house in Raleigh for the very last time, but Daddy still thinks we can beat the storm. He says we'll stop in Greensboro for supper, then go the rest of the way from there.

The animals have been drugged into submission; the dog, Sam, sleeps on the front seat of the truck, between Daddy and me. The two cats, Robert and Willard, completely oblivious to this sudden upheaval of their immediate environment, are passed out, sleeping comfortably in the trunk of the Buick. Daddy and I are following behind in one of Granddaddy's 'Todd Electric' trucks because they'd decided we could fit a whole lot more into one of his trucks than we could in Daddy's car. At some point in time, we will have to return the service truck, and I plan to ride along for the trip, just so I can see 'home' one last time.

"You act like we're moving to Siberia," Mama tells me. "We haven't even gone out-of-state. We're not going to be but two hours away."

Still, when you've basically lived in the same area for all of your life, two hours' difference might as well be Siberia. Especially when Mama's told us that we can't just run to the phone anytime we want and call our friends anymore. "It'll be long distance," she'd explained. "And you have to pay for that—for every minute you talk." We must've looked unhappy then because Mama adds, "Besides, you're going to make new friends in Winston-Salem, and you'll want to talk to them on the phone, too. So it's not like you won't be talking to *anybody*."

Maybe we won't make new friends. Maybe we'll hate everybody there, and everybody there will hate us, too. Like Robinscrest. But Mama says that's silly, and she refuses to even entertain that notion. "Why wouldn't you make friends?" she'd asked. "Especially when you're both such likeable people."

I can't help but wonder what it is exactly that a mother sees in her offspring which, for some unknown reason, happens to elude everyone else?

* * *

It seems like we have been riding forever before we finally turn into a tree-lined drive that winds its way uphill and through a dark, wooded yard. Mama and Daddy pull the car and truck up side by side, and as we push open the doors, disoriented and tired, Mama says, "Everybody grab something to take in, and we'll be that much further ahead unpacking."

We follow them up some brick steps, onto a brief walkway, then into a glass-enclosed sun porch. It is unfathomably cold, and the frigid air cuts right through me, straight to my bones, just like I'm not wearing any skin at all. Daddy unlocks the side door and we walk in warily behind him. The first thing that hits me is the smell; like mildew—*old* mildew. He flips on a light switch, illuminating a small den-like room with a fireplace. Trinket yawns, looking around before finally asking, "Where's my bed?"

"Brrr!" Kay shivers. "Why is it so cold in here?" She wraps up tighter in her puffy jacket.

"Daddy's got to go down to the basement and turn on the furnace," Mama tells us. "He's got to light the pilot before the heat will come on."

Basement? *Furnace*? She has got to be kidding! Because in this—the latter part of the 20th century—the only other person I even know of who still has a furnace, let alone a basement to keep it in, is Motney. And even she doesn't use it anymore, hasn't since electrical heat was first introduced, then later when forced-air heat became available residentially, she'd switched over to that, too, making the idea of a furnace even more obsolete.

"Why don't you girls go look around while Daddy and I get the house warmed up?" Mama suggests.

That seems easy enough, and we head off, trailed by the group of hung-over animals who make an effort to follow. But we haven't even gotten past the living room when one of the cats gives up, dropping down right where he is, opting to lick himself instead.

The living room is dark and has no overhead light. There are brass-plated switches on the wall, but Mama says we have to plug in lamps to get those to work. There is another fireplace in here as well, but a freezing draft wafts from it, so we quickly turn instead, retracing our steps back towards the kitchen where Kay flips on the light. And though there is an overhead fixture in here, we suddenly wish otherwise when we see what it so brightly displays; a life-size Suzy Homemaker all-in-one kitchen set—just like Trinket's playhouse one, come to life—so large that it actually takes up almost a whole wall, and it even covers over half the window behind it as well. It looks like some kind of consolation prize straight off the Newly Wed Game—a 50's-style retro brown contraption, baring commercial emblems of about equal age. And all we can do is stand there and look, totally speechless.

"That thing's going," Mama says, breaking the silence as she comes up behind us. "As soon as the moving van gets here in the morning, Daddy's going to put in the stove that Granddaddy sent. And the refrigerator, too."

Kay flips off the light, leaving the showcase prize in immediate darkness. We can only hope.

Upstairs, we find three bedrooms. The largest stretches from the front of the house all the way to the back, and it has multiple closets as well as wooden drawers and cabinets built right into the walls. The second bedroom is normal-sized, and the last is small, one whole wall slanted to accommodate its unusual placement. Against its odd-sized wall there are built-in shelves and a little desk that runs the length of the room. Probably only a single bed will fit in here, so it will definitely be Trinket's. I look over at Kay then. But what about the two of us? What can this mean? That we're actually going to have to *share* a room?

"Ma-*MA*!"

* * *

"Now just hold on a minute! *Nobody's* going to have to sleep with *anybody*! Daddy and I are going to sleep in the little den downstairs," she explains. "That will be our bedroom. And eventually, we're going to enclose the sun porch—to make it part of the room, as well."

I have only one question. "Then where are we going to watch TV?"

"In the living room," Mama tells me.

"But there're no lights!"

"Yes, there are. You just have to use lamps because the plugs are connected to the light switch."

"So I don't have to sleep in a room with *her*?" I indicate Kay with an elbow.

"No. Daddy and I figured that since she's the oldest, she can have the biggest room. You can have the one right across the hall, and Martie's will be next to yours."

She says this matter-of-factly, and no one argues. Probably because we're all way too tired to even think of going there.

The house still feels like a Dixie Deep-Freeze when we get back downstairs, and Daddy is kneeling on the hearth in the den, lighting a fire. He turns to find us all standing there, watching him.

"There's a little problem with the furnace," he explains. "Nothing serious. I'll have to work on it tomorrow—when I have my tools here."

"So we have no heat?" Kay suggests, irritatedly.

"Of course we have heat," Daddy contradicts her. "It just isn't working tonight, that's all."

She crosses her arms. "So what are we going to do then?"

Daddy adds some newspaper to the growing fire. "Well, I thought we could get the blankets out. You know, all sleep in here tonight."

"You mean *together*?" Kay asks. "*All* of us?"

"Sure—something wrong with that?" Daddy returns, his voice irritatingly pleasant.

"Oh, come on!" Mama says. "It'll be fun. Just like a big slumber party!"

She drops an arm over each of our shoulders.

Kay scowls. "Well, if that *dog* so much as puts his greasy snout anywhere near *my* side of the blanket, he's dead!"

"Sam always sleeps with *me*," I tell her. "You know that."

"Well, I just don't want that hairy mutt getting any ideas, that's all."

I hug the dog, burying my face in his sandy-colored fur, saying, "Don't worry. He doesn't even *like* you!"

Kay looks around disgustedly at the rest of us. "You guys can have your little slumber party down here if you want, but I'm going upstairs—to sleep in *my* room!"

She grabs her down jacket and a blanket.

"Kay!" Mama exclaims. "You'll freeze up there by yourself!"

She looks back at the four of us, then at the smiling dog. "Well, I can *definitely* think of worse tortures."

Mama shakes her head, then turns to start spreading the blankets out on the floor, right over the mildewed carpet.

"Speaking of animals," she begins. "Did you fix a litter box for your cats yet?"

I wonder why it always is they suddenly become *my* cats whenever they need to be fed or have their litter changed.

I hold my hands out exasperatedly, saying, "I don't even know where the litter *is*!"

"It's in the kitchen. Right beside the back door," Mama informs me. "And you'd better go ahead and take care of that right now, too. Because I'm not having those cats mess up *this* house!"

I roll my eyes, wondering what more they could possibly do to it.

I'm serious," Mama continues. "As soon as they get their wits back, they're going outside. Do you hear me?"

I go into the kitchen to retrieve their box and the bag of litter. I don't turn on the light this time because I'm afraid the Suzy Homemaker monstrosity will give me nightmares if I have to look at it again.

There is a small bathroom in the hallway just outside the den, and right across from the squat door that leads down to the basement. I go there with bright ideas of putting the litter box in the shower. That way, it's not so hard to clean up afterwards. But when I open the cracked glass door, the first thing that hits me instead is a large piece of plaster as it hurdles to the rusty floor. And standing here, blanketed in humiliation with white powdery residue, I have a serious revelation; one that tells me, '*This is it—we've finally done it—we have finally managed to hit rock bottom.*' Because there's no way—not in a million years—no *way* it can ever get any worse than this. But unfortunately, this revelation comes a little too early—*before* I discover the mushrooms. The ones growing right out of the floor in the upstairs bathroom, like they think they belong there. The scary thing is, they probably do.

* * *

True to their word, the house is really coming along. Mama and Daddy have gone in, ripped everything out, painted, re-floored and changed the out-dated appliances, even polished all the brass doorknobs and light switches. And Mama's added her special decorating touch to each of the rooms, too, making them appear magazine-picture ready. They've used colors like deep gold, trimmed in eggshell, slate blue accented with winter white, and a touch of rust to match the bricks they've added to the wall in the kitchen. They've ripped up all the old, gray carpet, polished the hardwood floors underneath into a warm shine, and then scattered Oriental rugs all over instead. And when the old carpet finally goes out the door, so does the mildew smell. The house, situated on over an acre of land, has truly become a show place.

The first couple of months we'd been here, it had snowed relentlessly, causing school to be turned out over and over again. That first semester had been hard, making new friends and all, because every time we'd just about get situated, it'd snow again, and we'd be out for another week or so.

Neither of us has ever seen so much snow before in our lives, and we stand at the back window in Kay's room, looking out over the winter wonderland. Off in the distance, kind of beyond the trees, there are these two purplish lumps. They are weird-shaped and have what appear to be snowdrifts dotting them at random intervals.

"What are *those*?" I ask, pointing, as Mama enters the room, a stack of clean, folded clothes in her arms. She comes to stand beside me, following my gaze.

"Those are mountains," she tells me.

Mountains? "Are we really that close to the *mountains*?" I ask, incredulously.

"Well, yes *and* no," she explains. "The real mountains—the Blue Ridge Mountains—are about an hour further west. But those are actually two mountains that are left over from an old range that used to be there, many years ago. They're all that's left of it now."

"So they're not the real mountains?" I ask, trying to clarify.

"Oh, yes—they're definitely real mountains. Just not part of the actual Blue Ridge." She points them out then, telling me, "The long one that's kind of slanted over there is called 'Hanging Rock Mountain.' And that other one, over to the right—the one with the knob-like thing on top—is called 'Pilot Mountain.'"

"Well, if they're not part of the real mountains, then what are they doing there?"

"They're just all that's left of the old range," she tells me.

"I didn't know mountains were supposed to look like that."

Mama looks at me, kind of surprised. "You've never seen mountains before?" she asks.

"No, When would I have seen mountains?"

"Well, I guess I just assumed—" she begins, then breaks off, saying instead, "Well, we'll have to go riding one Sunday, go up to the Blue Ridge Parkway. Let you and Kay see what a real mountain range looks like." She begins putting the clothes away, adding, "Whenever this snow finally melts enough, we'll take a day trip up there, spend the afternoon looking out over the scenic points along the parkway."

This sounds like fun, and I realize that with the move up here, Mama and Daddy have begun to be more outgoing, more interested in doing things as a family, which is pretty exciting to me.

One other wonderful thing we've discovered in Winston-Salem is Dewey's Bakery. Located in Thru-Way Shopping Center, an outdated 50's style strip mall, it is kind of set back from the sidewalk, illuminated inside only by a dim row of soda fountain lights that hang over the serving counter. Most people, if they didn't know it was there, would probably walk right past the dark, cave-like store. But for the 'regulars,' and the ones of us who have discovered its existence, this is not an option. Because inside is the most wonderful Moravian Sugar Cake you have ever tasted in your life. There is absolutely nothing that compares to it—not by a long shot. And sometimes you'll just be sitting there, doing absolutely nothing, when, out of the blue, you find yourself craving it for no apparent reason at all, and there is nothing else to do, but pile in the Buick and take a road trip across town for the sole purpose of satisfying a sugar cake fix. Though Mama insists that he's teasing about this, Daddy swears up and down that the little old ladies who work in the back probably slip cocaine in the dough when they're mixing it up.

Winston-Salem, a quaint tourist town with plenty of historic places to visit, is fun to explore. Sometimes we ride over to Old Salem. You always know when you arrive because there is this huge teapot at the entrance, surrounded by carefully groomed bushes. For some reason, it fascinates me. We drive down tree-lined streets towards the 'Welcome Center,' where we park in the 'visitor' spaces. Once inside the gate, we walk around the old, cobblestone streets, taking in the ancient wood and stone buildings, and we honestly find it hard to believe that people actually lived like this at one time.

But Old Salem, in reality, more or less reflects the entire existence of its host town. Whereas Raleigh is pretty much commercially and professionally oriented, Winston-Salem, in contrast, is more of an industrial town, its largest employer, a tobacco factory, called R.J. Reynolds. And lots of things in Winston-Salem embody the 'Reynolds' name as well; there is the senior high school, named R.J. Reynolds, itself. Then there is 'Reynolda Road,' 'Reynolda Village,' Reynolda Manor,' and even a 'Reynolda Shopping Center' where we go to the Thrifty-Mart each week to buy groceries. There are no 'Big Stars' around or 'A&P's, for that matter. In fact, other than a lone 'Piggly Wiggly,' everything's pretty much a Thrifty-Mart here. Inside, though, the actual store, itself is arranged about the same way as any other grocery store is.

Whereas in Raleigh, tall, glass office buildings with modular designs are springing up all over, here in Winston-Salem, the old brick warehouses have probably never seen renovations, and their smoke stacks add a constant haze over the surrounding sky. The only modern thing this town can claim at all is the 27-story Wachovia building, where Daddy's TV station occupies the entire top floor. And anywhere you go in town, you can see it, sticking out like a sore thumb, high above everything else. I always feel comforted by that, though. Especially when we first moved here, and I was trying to adjust to a new and unfamiliar school. It made me feel like it didn't matter if the other kids picked on me or made fun of my strange compulsions, because in a sense, Daddy was always right there, looking down on me.

If it's not old-fashioned here, then it's completely backwards; like the brown police cars and the yellow fire trucks, the local restaurants that boast the best 'stew beef' in town. Even the 'exit' ramps off the boulevard seem to go in the opposite direction than the ones back home had, and for this reason, Kay and I have elected to appropriately re-name the town 'Salem-Winston.'

One area where the town is definitely not backwards or even slow, for that matter, is where fashion is concerned. Because everyone here—even the ones in my new junior high school (which is actually another old warehouse-type building, complete with high ceilings, huge stone columns and old-fashioned metal fire escapes)—is very stylishly dressed. Everything is 'preppy,' and if you have money, then those things come from the LL Bean catalog. Still, this isn't Robinscrest, so as long as it simply looks like the original, it'll do just fine. I trade my two favorite outfits in for khaki pants, Calvin Klein skirts, oxford shirts with button-down collars, pink and green patchwork sweaters. I even start to 'accessorize,' wearing these interchangeable belts with twin ladybug buckles, ladybug earrings to match, and a gold add-a-bead necklace. All my socks have to be Argyle, and my shoes, the coveted 'bean style,' complete with the rugged, outdoorsy-style laces. And for PE, it's all about white leather Nikes, with the swoosh shape punched out in small, matching circles to decorate the sides.

For some reason, it has suddenly become painfully important to me to be 'normal.' I want to look like everyone else, dress like everyone else, and most importantly, act like everyone else. Miraculously, my teeth have made drastic changes and no longer poke out of strange and unnatural places. Instead, they are now more or less in a straight line, and my full set of braces has actually become rather stylish. I get up early, wash my hair and feather it back with the curling iron, then put on lip-gloss before trekking out to the bus stop every morning. And the thing I want most in the world? A Papagallo pocketbook—a small one with matching wooden handles that has a variety of button-on covers, one to go with each outfit. Mama says that maybe I'll get one for Christmas. I figure if Kay gets one, too, we'll have a double selection of matching covers, and then we can share them, which will be pretty neat.

The hardest thing for me in this huge self-transition is to try to *act* normal. Because whereas I might be able to subdue the obvious outward compulsions to a degree, they instead manifest themselves in the form of mental challenges, such as reading the same passage over and over again, repeating words and phrases in my head until I think I might scream from the frustration. But screaming is definitely not a 'normal' thing to do, so I choose to refrain from this instead. And the more compulsions I subdue, the harder and faster the anxiety attacks hit, and on many days, shaking with uncontrollable fear, I find myself calling Mama to come pick me up from school, to take me home, where it's safe. Where I can finally let the compulsions have free-run and be released from this torture. I can only hope that when I have one of these days—panic-filled and desperate to go home—that it's not raining. Because if it is, that ultimately means our phone will not be working, nor will any of our neighbors'. Though we don't understand why this happens and Daddy has called the phone company on more than one occasion regarding this issue, no one seems to be able to pinpoint why it's actually happening. It simply becomes something we have to live with here in Winston-Salem.

On the days that I *do* have to call her though, Mama is pretty understanding about all of this. She knows I have anxiety attacks—something Daddy has always had as well—and though she doesn't understand them, she makes an effort to try. She still thinks I should get a hold of myself when this happens, but she understands that sometimes, I just can't. The downside to this it that none of my teachers understands my consistent absences, and assume incorrectly, that I'm just lazy. I wish I could make them see that nothing could be further from the truth, how motivated I truly am to do well and to be liked. But unfortunately, this is a perception that will follow me throughout my entire school-career.

Though I try with everything I've got to control the overwhelming Fear, it is no more possible for me to do this than it is for a diabetic to mentally control his blood sugar. Or for my grandmother, Mom, for example, to simply think about it and just because she wants to, all of a sudden, raise her paralyzed arm. Though I don't understand what causes this Fear in me, I do know one thing for certain—there is nothing I can do about it. And as the teachers get more and more frustrated with me due to my sporadic attendance, I begin to feel worse and worse about myself. I realize that I am a failure—a total failure at everything I attempt. Because you would have to be when you cannot even do the normal, mundane things that everyone else takes for granted. The few times that I have tried to explain this to one teacher or another—how I have these anxiety attacks, how I can't help it—they pretty much just looked at me and rolled their eyes. Because by the time I finally got up the nerve to say something to any of them, it was too late. They'd already formed their perceptions of me, and there was no changing that. Besides, according to them, this was something I could reason with, something I could fix.

One teacher, in particular, tells me, "It's not like you have to deal with being in a wheelchair or something. If I were you, I think I'd just concentrate on counting my blessings instead." I try to explain to this teacher that sometimes the Fear really is so bad, that I actually *can't* walk. And though I simply want her to understand how very real the Fear is, how it controls so much of my life, she just doesn't get it. And worse-case-scenario, she actually turns on me then, angrily telling me in a voice loud enough for all the other students to hear, "Don't you *ever* say something that heartless again! If *you* don't want to come to school, that's completely fine. That's *your* business! But don't ever—*ever* again—compare yourself with someone who really *does* have to physically struggle just to get here! That's about the *sorriest* thing I have ever heard in my life! Does your *mother* know you say things like that?" She shakes her head at me in disgusted disbelief. "I'll bet she'd absolutely *die* if she did! The teacher looks at me then, as if viewing things from a new angle. "Unless, of course, *she's* sorry, too."

I cannot look up as I make my way back to my desk. I try not to catch the eyes of other students or notice their expressions, some of whom are even snickering. Because her words have just humiliated me beyond explanation, not to mention really hurt me, cutting clean down to the bone where the pain is very real. I know I am going to cry. And there's nothing I can do about it. It's the kind of crying where you sob so hard you choke yourself. I turn back around, trying to reach her desk before the first sob actually breaks. I am only halfway down the isle when I know I'm going to lose it, and I ask from there if I can go to the bathroom.

"No you can-*not*!" She shakes her head defiantly. "We are reading *literature* right now, and you need to go back to your desk and do that."

"But—" It's too late. I'm already crying. "But I'm *sick*!" I tell her, desperately contemplating any escape route I can think of.

"Well, I'm *sorry* if you're *sick*," she returns calmly. "But you need to think about those things before you go making such cruel, thoughtless *comments* like the one you just made to me. If *I* said something like that, it would probably make *me* sick, too."

She picks her book back up, telling me, "No, you need to go back to your seat and read, like everyone else is doing."

Now sobbing uncontrollably, I am terrorized—everyone is staring at me, a few still snickering, though most are now looking on with genuine sympathy. And seeing their faces, I know it will be impossible to stay in this room. As I bolt out the heavy door, the teacher follows after me, calling, "I *said* no! You *cannot* go to the bathroom! You *need* to come back here right *now!*"

I ignore her and continue running for the stairwell. I know I am going to be in so much trouble, and I feel absolutely terrible for causing it. Finally downstairs, I go into the office, breathlessly asking the secretary if I can see Mrs. Hayes, my guidance counselor. (Mrs. Hayes had once confessed to me that she, too, had anxiety attacks, and if I ever needed help, I could always come to her.) The secretary looks up, starting to ask the routine question; whether or not I have a note from my teacher. But when she notices the completely distressed state I am in, she simply escorts me back to the guidance office.

Mrs. Hayes, thinking I am having an anxiety attack, calls my mother. I try to calm down enough to tell her what happened—what the teacher had said to me, everything she'd done. Mrs. Hayes listens in silence, jotting a note down now and then.

"And now I'm going to be in *so* much trouble!" I finish, the tears gearing up all over again.

"No, you are *not* going to be in trouble," she tells me. She pulls the door to, leaving me sitting there in her office with a box of Kleenex as she walks up to the classroom to retrieve my books and purse from the desk where I'd left them. I don't know what she ends up saying to the teacher, but not only does the teacher refrain from ever making crass statements like that to me ever again, she also hands me the pass anytime I need to go to the bathroom, asking no questions at all. Still, regardless, I will always remember what she said to me, how she made me feel so humiliated in front of all my classmates. And just when I was starting to appear normal, too.

Now they will all know the truth. I am afraid my existence as a normal kid is completely over—gone before I even have a chance to see what it feels like to be on the other side. And though mercifully, no one ever says anything about the incident again, I can never forgive her for what she has done. Ever. Because now, she, too, has joined ranks with Polly-Esther and the Turtleneck. She has officially earned a spot on my 'List.'

The Winston-Salem kitchen as we found it on move-in night (featuring the life-size 'Suzy Homemaker Monstrosity')

. . . . and the very next day, while a record-breaking snowstorm rages around us . . . .

(left) The 'new' bathroom—obviously at some point in time, blue paint had been on serious sale (And yes, that is plaster falling from the ceiling above the shower.) (right) One of the 'record-breaking' snow storms as photographed from our front door

Finally! The 'renovated' house

WHEN I SAY 'JUMP,' YOU ASK 'HOW HIGH!'

It's a Monday night, and I am setting my alarm clock for 1:00 AM. Normally, I wouldn't be getting up until around 5:00 or so, but this morning is different. This morning it's important that I wake up right on time—right when Daddy gets home. Because I haven't seen him in forever—something like two weeks straight. As the manager of this new TV station, he literally works around the clock. In the mornings when I get up for school, he is either still asleep, or sometimes he's already left for work, himself. And at night, he works until after we're all in bed, and though I've tried to stay awake just long enough to see him, I am never able to hold my eyes open that long. Earlier, I'd told Mama what I was doing so she wouldn't hear my alarm clock go off in the middle of the night and totally freak out.

Things have become so different. It's like we're completely on our own now, the four of us. Mama's taken on the role as 'decision maker,' and she has the final say in everything now. There's no more claiming "Daddy said it's alright with *him* if it's alright with *you*." Or, "Daddy said to come ask *you* first." No, now everything's completely up to her. And sometimes her decisions suck. Out loud.

"Daddy's not going to be home for supper again?" I ask.

Mama sets the plates on the table. "You know he's working."

"Why does he have to work so much?"

"Because he's the boss, and he has to be there incase anything goes wrong."

"But what sorts of things go wrong all the time like that?"

"Well, they don't always go wrong. But he has to be there incase they do."

"Couldn't they just call him? I mean, I don't understand why they just can't call him if they need him—you know, here, at home. Then, if something happened, he could drive over there. Why can't they do that?"

"Eat your supper."

The truth of the matter is, Daddy's never been one of those absentee, workaholic fathers. He's always been there for us, no matter what. And we simply don't know how to deal with this. Daddy, himself, is not very happy about the situation he's in. Just through eavesdropping on phone calls between him and Mama, I have learned a lot about this. Though Daddy's the boss, he still has to deal with the brothers who actually own the TV station, and while they have plenty of money and strong business sense, they are not as knowledgeable about the actual running of a TV station, itself. Daddy, who's been in radio and broadcast television all his life, tries to explain to them why some of their ideas won't work. He knows this because he's already been there, done that—many times before. Still, the brothers insist that he follow their orders, and then when the exact thing happens that Daddy told them would happen, they blame it all on him. They also force him to fire people who don't need firing; people with whom he's worked closely ever since day one. He tells Mama that the money's pretty good, though. That he thinks he should try and stick it out. And true, Kay and I have had more new clothes this year than we've ever had before. They've raised our allowance every week, and come to think of it, anything we've asked for since we've been here, we've gotten. They've even traded the Buick for a less conspicuous, up-to-date Chevrolet Impala. But still, weighing the options, there aren't enough modern cars or pink and green clothes in the world to take Daddy's place, and I'd much rather have him around than all these extra things.

My alarm clock doesn't go off. Instead, I am awakened by Daddy, himself, when he sits down on the edge of my bed. He is still wearing his suit, and he looks tired.

"Mama said you wanted to see me," he says.

I reach up, hug him. It is the best feeling I've had in a long time. The only way I know to describe it is to say it's kind of like if somebody had died or something, and now I am actually getting an unheard of second chance; to say all the things I never said, to tell him how I really feel, let him know how much I truly appreciate him. How much we all need him here. And I don't want to ever let go because there's no guarantee when the next time will be that I can see him again.

He sits with me for a while like that, on the edge of the bed. But after he's gone, I feel cold, alone. I go into Trinket's room, haul her out of her own bed, then carry her back to mine. She doesn't really even wake up as I put her on the other side, pulling the covers up over her. But regardless, I feel better now because her warmth is reassuring, and I am no longer alone.

IT'S MORE POPULAR TO BE A CHEERLEADER

It is the Spring of a new decade—1980—and we have just moved back to Raleigh. Mama and Daddy decided together that the TV station in Winston-Salem was simply too demanding, that we'd all be much better off with Daddy around more often—and *he'd* be better off, too, when he was no longer being pushed to do things that he knew weren't right. And to say the least, we are very excited about the prospect of moving back home.

Our new house is in an older, established neighborhood which is right across the street from North Hills Mall. I figure that's pretty cool because then we can ride bikes up there anytime we want and look at preppy clothes. Actually, Kay won't have to ride her bike because she has her driver's license now.

Sometimes, they'll let Kay and me go places together in the family car, but Trinket can't ride along with us when we're both in the car like that, though. They say we'll get to fighting and have a wreck or something, and it'd be bad enough if they have to lose *two* us that way, but at least they can spare *Martie's* innocent little life. Okay—and so this means what? That they *want* the two of us to ride in the car together? Maybe they simply figure a little Russian Roulette wouldn't be so bad. Anyway, I figure that all the years of constant fighting've finally taken their toll, and so Mama and Daddy can't really be blamed for any psychotic ideas that they happen to come up with at this point.

When they'd broken the news to us—that Daddy had a new job with a TV station in the Raleigh area, and that we'd be moving back there—we'd whooped for joy. And though they'd tried to find a house in the same school districts we'd been in before, they'd been unable to find one in both, and had ultimately decided on a house in the Sanderson High district. They explained that Kay would be a senior next year, and that they thought this was the fairest thing to do. Because she wouldn't have as much time to make new friends as I would, it would be best to put her back in the same school as before with all her friends.

"So where do I have to go?" I ask. "Hopefully, not Carroll!" Because Kay had told me that this was the last place I wanted to go since they'd had some kind of nasty fungus growing all down in the water fountain pipes that had made everybody sick.

"Well, it *is* in the Carroll district," Mama tells me. "So close you can walk, too. You won't even have to ride the bus to get there. Wouldn't that be nice?"

Walk? What if it was raining? Didn't she know what humidity did to my hair?

"I'm sure if it's raining Daddy or I one can drive you to school. Now stop worrying."

"How can I stop worrying?" I demand. "Especially when I know they have this nasty water fountain fungus that makes everybody sick when they're simply dying of thirst and have no choice but to drink from it?"

"*Water* fountain fungus? Where in the world did you hear that?"

I put my hands on my hips. "Kay told me that her friend Carol told her about a girl she knew named Kim who went there, and she almost died from it."

Mama shakes her head. "Well, even if there ever *was* such a thing, the school would never be allowed to operate like that. The county health board would shut it down first."

"But Mama—"

"Just finish this year. That's all I ask. It' already March, so it's not like you'll have to be there very long or anything. Then, if you still feel the same way in June, we'll talk about transferring you to another school."

I hate it when she does that; creatively solve a situation in a manner that I don't like, but doing it in a way that leaves me no grounds to argue with her.

So okay—I'll *go* to Carroll—I'll humor her. *This* time. But I vow— on my very *life*—to *never* put my mouth anywhere *near* the water fountains there, no matter what. I'll die of dehydration first. Then they'll be sorry they ever made me go to that stupid school in the first place.

* * *

The first thing that strikes me about Carroll Junior High is its zoo-like atmosphere. It scares the absolute crap out of me. Because just a few weeks ago, at my school in Winston-Salem, when the bells rang, you lined up at the door, then left as a group for your next class. And you had a certain side of the hall to walk on, too, depending on whether you were coming or going. And at lunch time, you went down to the cafeteria in a single-file line with your Language Arts block, and then you sat at your class's assigned table for a period of twenty minutes—after which you stood up and followed your teacher back to class in the same type of quiet, uniform line. Here at Carroll, when the bells rang, everyone just jumped up at once—whether the teacher was finished or not—and completely flooded the hallways. The boys jumped up, hung from doorjambs, made these ape-like noises. And the girls, just as bad, hollered loudly to each other from one end of the crowded hallway all the way down to the other—right over the extreme racket of locker doors being seriously abused. And at lunch, we had a whole hour; a whole *period* to spend, just like it was a class, itself. And when the lunch bell rang, everyone swarmed the cafeteria at once—in the same manner in which they exited class—and your choice was simple; either follow or be trampled.

Inside the cafeteria, everyone sits exactly where they want, including in some instances, right on the tables, themselves—sometimes even perched on the flimsy backs of chairs. Native drumbeats break out randomly, pounded rhythmically on the surrounding Formica table tops. Each one becomes a little louder, a little more obnoxious than the last, as they all try to out-do each other. From the other tables, there is a liberal accompanying air show of left-over food. And when everyone finishes trashing the cafeteria? They morph outside, spend the rest of the hour walking the track or hanging out on the benches. The kids who wear the Izod shirts play football with an unfortunate book someone left behind. The ones who wear the lumberjack shirts, unbuttoned so that their thermals underneath show, slink off into the woods behind the football field instead. Everyone refers to these kids as the 'freaks,' though in a strange sort of manner, they are popular in ways that other kids aren't.

One of my first friends here is Haley, who also happens to live just down the street from us. Her father has recently died of a massive heart attack, and now Haley and her two older brothers live there together with their mother. I can't imagine how awful that would feel—losing your father like that. But I know it's something I never want to find out. Haley's oldest brother is college-age and not home very much. The next oldest, Drake, is Kay's age, and he is very protective of his younger sister, as well as all of her friends. He is loads of fun and drives us anywhere we want to go. He teaches us the proper way to blow on grass blades so they squeak really loud, as well as the best way to hurl toilet paper rolls into neighboring trees so that you get the most foliage out of each toss. He always says it's best to wedge rocks into the cardboard cylinder in the middle. That way, you're assured that gravity'll return the unused portion, therefore, eliminating excess waste of the toilet paper. And Drake can draw, too—I mean, like nobody else's business. I wish so much that I could draw like that, but I can't even manage to connect the dots in one of those coloring book pictures; not without it ending up looking like some kind of deranged road map instead.

The very next year—8th grade—Haley and I wind up with the worst possible English teacher in the worst possible class; first period. This is the woman that all the rising freshmen warn you about; the one who keeps her gray hair slicked back severely in a bun, who wears these old-fashioned gingham dresses, and who always has a sweater fastened around her neck with this ancient brooch—even when it's 85 degrees outside. Though no one knows for sure, it is believed that she is close to a hundred years old, and everyone knows that she's senile and that she should've retired a very long time ago. But because she's been a teacher for so many decades—maybe even eons—she has earned this thing called 'tenure,' so there's nothing the school board can do about it.

Her name is Mrs. Waddelson and she has these huge, magnifying glasses, worse than Motney's ever thought about being, and she does not look over her glasses at you when you do something wrong. Instead, she looks right through them, and her eyes turn into these huge, black pits from which there is no escape. And once she's zeroed in on you, got you in her crosshairs, that's it. You're screwed.

What's even weirder about Mrs. Waddelson is that she doesn't drive, like all the other teachers do—not to mention, for that matter, most other normal adults. Instead, her husband brings her to school every morning and drops her off. And one afternoon, just as Haley and I were leaving school, we saw her getting into the same car—into the *back* seat, though. Okay—so what is *that*? Haley suggests that maybe her husband is simply a frustrated taxi driver. But I disagree. Because it's just like Mrs. Waddelson to do something all Pilgrimish like that—all prim and prudish, like nobody knows any better. Still, the alternative is a screamingly scary thought, so I decide that on the whole, the Puritan-thing is a much better bargain.

And in class, it didn't take much for Mrs. Waddelson to go off on you, either. I mean, if she simply didn't like the expression on your face, she'd call you out for it in front of the whole room, try her best to embarrass you. Like the time she yelled at me—right in the middle of a grammar lesson in which she was preaching about the eighth deadly sin—the use of dangling modifiers.

"*Miss* Todd! Don't sit there all poised and pretty, like you think you're getting ready to have your picture made. I won't have it! This is *English* class, not the *Barbizon School of Modeling*!" Then, to the rest of the class, she says, "I'm tired of it, now—all this foolishness. It's high time all you 8th graders start *behaving* like 8th graders. Not like a roomful of nursery-schoolers."

I want to roll my eyes—but I don't dare. Not in *this* lifetime. Instead, I console myself with the thought that like the Turtleneck, Polly-Esther and the teacher in Winston-Salem, she has now earned a most uncoveted spot—right at the very top of my 'List.'

Then there was the day she'd come into class with a whole bagload of plastic sand buckets and toy shovels. She'd presented them grandly on the table beside the podium.

"For *those* of you who think it's more interesting to watch the *construction* going on outside, you can run right along out there *with* them." She indicates the colorful toys with a flourish of her hand, just like she thinks she's one of Bob Barker's Beauties on 'The Price is Right' or something. "You now have your very own personal sand buckets and shovels, so anytime you're ready to join them, please feel free to *do* so. I'm quite sure they'd be glad to have you."

No one says anything. They don't dare. And needless to add, the boys who sit in the back couple of rows who'd been initially fascinated with the presence of the huge crane and cement trucks in the lot next door, now suddenly develop an intricate interest in the redemption from dangling modifiers instead.

It is a Monday morning, and Haley and I are at our lockers, side-by-side. Because our last names are only one letter apart, we are also in the same homeroom, which happens to be none other than Mrs. Waddelson's.

"Did you memorize that poem over the week-end?" Haley asks me.

Poem?

"What poem?" I ask her.

She looks at me, surprised. "You know—the one Mrs. Waddelson assigned to us last week. The one we have to get up and recite at the podium today without using any notes."

Oh my dear god!

"It's that 'Abu Ben Adem' poem," Haley continues. "The one we—" Suddenly, she breaks off, looks at me with unmasked horror. "No way! You *didn't* forget about it, did you?"

I want to cry. But there's no time for that—not now. Because the milk's already spilled, and I have to find a way to clean it up. Fast. I quickly consider my options, contemplate playing hooky first. But unfortunately, I remember that Mama has an appointment this morning and she won't be home, so that's out of the question already. Laryngitis? No—that's not any good, either. Because earlier when Mrs. Waddelson'd bid me a crisp 'good morning' in the hallway, I'd actually been dumb enough to answer her.

The five-minute warning bell rings then, and everyone begins to scatter off towards their homerooms. 'Okay, damnit! *Think*!' I panic. 'Okay, okay—this is it. *I just got a call from Mr. Nuttle who lives across the street. He called me because he couldn't find Mama since she's away on an appointment. There are burglars breaking into our house right now, at this very minute, as we speak—six of them, maybe more—Mr. Nuttle isn't sure exactly how many. But they're ransacking the whole place, and according to him, somebody needs to get over there pretty fast if we want to stop them.*'

Mrs. Waddelson will want to know why Mr. Nuttle can't go over there, himself. '*Because he doesn't have a key to our house.*' But then she'd be sure to ask why he would even need a key if the house was already broken into. '*Well, they're not exactly inside yet. They're beating on the doors, breaking out the windows, and it'll just be a matter of time now.*' But what if Mrs. Waddelson knows we have a dog? '*Oh, you mean Sam? It was the burglars—they tied him up, held him down while they put a muzzle over his mouth, then they took and threw him out in the back yard. He can't even help himself right now.*' But then she'll be sure to ask why Mr.

Nuttle hadn't called the police yet. 'He tried, Mrs. Waddelson—honestly, he did. He said he dialed 911, but the line was busy, so he was unable to get through.'

From somewhere in my locker, my literature book chooses this pristine moment to fall on my head. Just like if Mrs. Waddelson had pushed it, herself. *Get real*!

With only moments to go before the homeroom bell, I know what I've got to do—what the only answer is. Homeroom is seven whole minutes, and since I have Mrs. Waddelson for first period, too, I will have five extra minutes of travel time afterwards as well, which I will not need to use for that intended purpose. I grab the literature book, slam the locker shut, and head into homeroom, trying to figure a way to perform the tedious task of osmosis so that Mrs. Waddelson doesn't realize what I'm actually doing. Because what's the point in cramming at all if I'm going to get busted, anyway?

* * *

"Very *nice*, Haley." Mrs. Waddelson beams, her wrinkly old hands clasped on the desk in front of her. "Now, Angela—I believe it's *your* turn."

I stand up, walk to the front of the room. No one's called me 'Angela' since Robinscrest, but Mrs. Waddelson insists on the importance of calling everyone by their 'given' name.

I clear my throat. The podium comes up to my neck, and I feel like a retarded giraffe, trying to look out over the class like that. I clear it once more, then finally begin.

"Abu Ben Adem, by Leigh Hunt."

Out of the corner of my eye, I can see Mrs. Waddelson sitting at her desk, waiting expectantly.

"Abu Ben Adem, may his tribe increase, awoke one night from a deep dream of peace, and saw within the moonlight of his room, making it rich, like a lily in bloom, an angel writing in a book of gold."

I pause here, just like Mrs. Waddelson wants us to, then continue on dramatically.

"*Behold*, Ben Adem said. *What writest thou?*"

The rest of the poem is a breeze, and after I finish reciting it, Mrs. Waddelson beams, saying, "Very *good*, Angela."

On the way back to my seat, Haley sticks out her tongue at me. And though I am totally relieved, just like a big pile of rocks has been removed from my chest, I still can't decide on the outcome; whether it was Mrs. Waddelson who got played, or whether it was actually me.

Years later, I think I finally have the answer to that question, though. Because at nearly age 40, I can still recite that poem, word for word, just like somebody'd taken a permanent marker and written it right smack on the inside of my eyelids.

* * *

I cannot believe I have actually made it through another year at Carroll. But here it is, the end of 8th grade already, and we're getting ready for final exams. Since attending Carroll, I've been more or less able to pull off the 'normal' thing. Now that my teeth are straightening up and I'm dressing like everyone else, I feel like I almost fit in.

But that's the thing; *almost*. Because it seems like all of my life, I have been 'almost' everything. I've never been able to make it any further than 'almost,' and I want so much more out of life than that.

All year, I have been watching the other kids—taking note of what it is that makes them normal. For the most part, it's the way they act—or maybe I should say the way they *interact*—with their friends, with the other students, with the teachers, themselves. It seems so effortless for them; smiling, being friendly, taking things as they come. More importantly, knowing how to *handle* things as they come. Also, these kids are very dependable. They don't miss school, or come in late. And they aren't constantly missing classes because they have to go home early. This is something that I actually took notice of last year, when I first made it my ultimate goal to be 'normal' here at Carroll. And this year, in accordance with achieving that goal, I have made every effort to be present when I am supposed to, though sometimes the Fear is so bad that I can't even concentrate.

I might as well be on the moon for all the attention I am able to apply to the actual class going on around me. Sometimes I ask to go to the bathroom where I lock myself in a stall, close my eyes, try to get a hold of my shaking, of the random explosions of Fear that keep racking my body. Some days, I can actually make it, but when I get home, I am so worn out that I am usually too tired to do a good job on my homework. Other days, though, I just can't, no matter how hard I try. And it makes me angry—mostly at myself—for being a failure at such an ordinary mundane activity. Obviously, there's nothing to it. All the other kids seem to be able to do it without even thinking, so why can't I? Deep down, I know the real reason for this, though. It's because I am *not* 'normal.' And no matter how many preppy clothes I wear or how hard I try to act like them, I can never be like the other kids. Still, the alternative is simply not an option, and I know that somehow, I have to maintain this façade—*appearing* normal even if I can't *be* normal. Because this is the first time in my life I have ever really been accepted anywhere, and I don't want to screw that up now, not for anything. And if the Fear ends up winning, ends up killing me over this, then so what? I'll just take the ugly secret to my grave with me. Because returning to 'weirdo land' is so *not* an option, is so totally out of the question, and I'll do anything I have to, anything it takes, to keep from going back there.

    Another important thing that these 'normal' kids do is that they participate in a lot of school activities, like student council, advisory council, chorus, especially sports. The guys play soccer, football or basketball. Some even play more than one of these sports. And like the guys, the girls, too, play soccer, basketball and even softball. In all my life, I have never been very athletically inclined. Sure, I'd always taken ballet lessons, things like that, but I have always been very awkward and uncoordinated when it comes right down to it. And for this reason, Drake spends numerous afternoons with me on the empty playground of the neighborhood elementary school, trying to teach me how to toss a softball, how to catch one, even how to bat. And I have to say I have greatly improved, at least over my previous abilities. But still, I am disappointed to learn that after all that work, I still did not make final cuts for the softball team. Haley does, but she tells me not to give up, that there are plenty of other activities I can try out for.

Probably the most popular of all these other activities—the most coveted—is a spot on the cheerleading squad. And with tryouts for the upcoming year just weeks away, I allow myself to dream of the possibility that I could actually make the team. Because that would be the ultimate declaration of normalcy. Anyone who actually has the ability to make the cheerleading squad has no chance of being a weirdo. No, each and every one of the cheerleaders is readily accepted into junior high society, no questions asked. It is a far-fetched idea, especially given my athletic ability, but this is what I decide I will do. Not just try out for, but actually *make* the squad. I spend the next few weeks practicing the jumps I will have to do out on the patio, using the sliding glass doors as mirrors to assess my improvement. Because if I want to do this—to make the squad—then I can afford to have nothing wrong. Nothing at all. Toes must always be pointed, hands always cupped and kept in the 'box space' right in front of me. When I land from a jump, both of my feet have to return to the ground together, in the exact same spot from which I started. There is absolutely no room for error, whatsoever, and I will make sure ahead of time that there won't be any. Maybe I can't control the other areas in my life, but damnit, this is one area that I *can*. I vow to myself here and now, that I will never be 'almost' again. I will overwork myself, outdo everyone else—whatever it takes to get what I want. Because somewhere in this world, I will be successful at something. Come hell or high water, I swear it. And this is a promise—a pact that I make with myself—which will never be broken.

I get my spot on the cheerleading squad—along with ten other girls. Together, we all make up this loud, obnoxious group, and none of us can wait for next year. The coach schedules practices that will go on throughout the summer, and in late July, we will attend cheerleading camp together. It is more than I could've dreamed of—having this much fun *and* becoming normal, all at the same time.

Haley and I have studied together really hard for our English exam. Because in the entire world, we can imagine no scarier thought than winding up back here next year—right back in Mrs. Waddelson's 8th grade English class, all over again.

Drake is angry at the way Mrs. Waddelson has treated us all year, and he vows to get revenge.

"What're you going to do?" Haley asks.

"I'll let you know when I figure it out," he tells her.

Most times when someone says that, 'I'll let you know,' it really means they're just going to blow it off. But not Drake. No, you can rest assured that when Drake says those words, the gears in his brain will be grinding away, trying to find the best method of torture for each given situation as it comes. And when he'd asked what Mrs. Waddelson hated the most, Haley and I hadn't hesitated as we'd told him, "Having her class interrupted." To which Haley adds, "Especially when it's like all of a sudden or something."

On the morning of our final exam, we are heading towards the stairs that lead to the 8th grade hall when we see him—Drake, standing just under the 'Exit' sign of the back door. He is holding a ski mask and smiling.

"Drake!" Haley says, surprised.

He motions for her to be quiet.

We walk over to where he is standing.

"Are you skipping school?" Haley asks him. Because he is supposed to be over at Sanderson right now—at the high school.

"No, I had an *appointment* I had to go to, that's all," he tells her.

"Drake, does Mom know where you are?"

"Yeah, sure. I'm taking my math exam."

"You're not missing your math exam, are you?" Haley asks.

"No, of course not. I'm just going to be late since I have this *appointment* and all."

He motions for us to go away then so that we won't call attention to him. Because if any of the teachers see him standing there, they'll be sure to remember that he finished the 9th over three years ago. And then they'll want to know what he's up to, hanging out here on the junior high campus.

Mrs. Waddelson's exam is not a hard one; at least not if you've read all the literature she has assigned this year, and if you've paid undivided attention to all of her Puritan sermons regarding the proper use of established grammar. Because Hell hath no fury equal to that of proper society when it either hears or witnesses such an unredeemable sin, like—God forbid—the use of a dangling modifier.

We are almost through the exam, have totally forgotten about Drake, when it happens—when we are suddenly jolted out of the complete silence that only a final exam has the power to create.

"YeeeeEEEEEEE—*HAAAAaaaaaw! Ha ha ha ha ha ha!* Wo-*HOOOOOOOOO! Ha ha ha! Yeeeeaaaaah!*"

It is at this precise moment—in the ungodly silence that follows—that I learn exactly how a dropped pin sounds—when it hits the floor somewhere over in a remote corner of China. But it isn't long before the initial shock wears off, and up and down the hall, you can hear random bursts of laughter breaking out. Mrs. Waddelson, beside herself, adjusts her sweater, stands up, clumps purposefully out into the hallway. But Drake is long gone—the only clue to his having been there at all possibly some left over Nike prints—still steaming and beating a hard path to the back door. Mrs. Waddelson returns huffily to her desk, plucking and preening at her ruffled feathers. And though she doesn't say anything, it is enough to simply know that for the rest of the day—probably a whole lot longer, if the truth be known—her whole attitude will be changed. In fact, it is probably safe to say that she will never be the same again.

Me, in 'prep-mode' (On the bed behind me is the 'cool Hollie Hobbie pillow' that Uncle Jimmy's then-girlfriend, now-wife made for me.)

*At a junior high basketball game
(Cheer your heart out!)*

I KNOW WHAT YOU DID THAT SUMMER

"No more pen-*cils*, no more bo-*oks*, No more teacher's dirty lo-*oks*!"

I reach to turn up the radio in the Impala. This is not a problem because Kay is driving. And though we'd rather have a smaller, much sportier car to zip around in, at least this is an improvement over the Buick since we've actually downsized from a back seat capacity of 8 to a more modest one of 4.

"School's out for the summer! School's out forever! School's been blown to *pieces*!"

This is my favorite part of the song; where it dries up and evaporates into the sound of a school bell winding down. They play this song every year on the last day of school, always at 3:00 sharp; 'School's Out,' by Alice Cooper. And when you hear it, you know it's finally official; you can forget everything you've learned until next year. For three whole months. Until the Tuesday after Labor Day, which is when we always have to go back. I look over at Kay then, wondering how it must feel to know you never have to go back—that in a few days, you'll graduate, and that'll be it. It's a concept I simply cannot fathom. She'll be leaving for college sometime late in the summer, but that's a long ways off, and there's plenty to do until then. I suddenly wonder about after she's gone; who'll be here to drive me around, listening to loud music. Not even Drake because he is graduating, too. Haley says he is thinking of going into the Service, so there's no telling how long it'll be before we see him again. It feels kind of strange, imagining life without all the people I'm used to having around. But that's a whole summer away, and I push the thought out of my mind, choosing not to go there yet.

Kay has changed this year. For one thing, she has traded in all her preppy clothes for faded jeans, lumberjack shirts and thermals.

"Are you turning into a freak?" I ask her.

She gives me this look that says '*what's wrong with you,*' then says, "No."

"Then why're you dressing like one?" I ask.

She sighs, rolls her eyes. "Just because I don't wear pink and green like you and all your plastic *friends* does *not* mean that I am turning into a freak."

I don't get it. Still, this opens new avenues for me, and instead I choose to ask another question, in a sort of roundabout way. "*Sooo*—what're you planning to do with all your preppy clothes?"

She grabs her pocketbook, heading out. "I dunno. Probably burn them."

"Well, can I wear them instead?" I call after her.

"I don't care." She lets the storm door slam behind her.

Cool! Totally *cool*!

* * *

"*Angela*, what is wrong with your *clothes*?"

I look down at the bright wrap-around skirt that I confiscated from Kay's closet. Sure, it's a little long, but then Kay *is* taller than me. Like me, she's always been painfully thin, probably even more so than me. But still, that didn't stop her from reaching model-height. Or growing boobs, either, for that matter.

"What do you mean 'what's wrong with my clothes?" I ask, a little hurt.

Mrs. Waddelson crosses her arms, looking down at me. "Well, they're so *big*. Why are you wearing clothes that are too big for you?"

Outwardly, I shrug. But inside, I wonder if it's really that obvious. Because I'd had no idea. Suddenly, I feel a little demon rear its ugly head in protest, though, and I want to retaliate, to ask what's wrong with *her* clothes? Why it is that the pot's calling the kettle black? Because at least I'm in style. Afterall, I'm not the one who's coming in here everyday wearing left-over wardrobe rejects from 'Little House On the Prairie.'

"Doesn't your mother buy clothes for you that fit?"

"I guess, but . . . ."

"Maybe I should call her. Have a talk with her."

I don't know if Mama's aware that I'm wearing Kay's clothes. But even if she is, I don't think she'd care. Not as long as it makes me happy.

I shrug again. "If you want," I answer.

"That's a form of 'child abuse,' you know," Mrs. Waddelson informs me.

What? I look at her. Is she totally whacked? Because I've never heard anything so stupid. How does she figure that clothes— regardless of *how* big they may or may not be—are a sign of child abuse? Especially ones that so obviously were exclusives that came from Mimi's very expensive boutique? I remember the day she bought this skirt for Kay. It'd been on a Sunday when we were visiting Wendell for lunch, and at Mimi's request, the store owner'd met us downtown and opened her doors that afternoon, just for us, so that Mimi could take us shopping. And this skirt alone had cost nearly one-hundred dollars. I still remember it—how we'd freaked out over the price tags when we were alone in the dressing room. I mean, if I was coming to school, wearing burlap sacks or wooden barrels held up with suspenders, I could probably see it. Then maybe she'd have a point. But as it stands now, it's just a given fact. She is totally clueless.

One other thing that's different about Kay this year is that she has a serious boyfriend. Sure, she's had boyfriends before, but this one's different. You can just tell. I remember the one she'd had in Winston-Salem. He'd been very possessive, and if she simply wanted to go out with her friends one night instead of with him, then he'd just sit there and pout, trying to make her feel bad or something. For this reason, I'd re-named him 'Cry Baby.' But I'd ended up called him 'CB' for short since Kay told me it'd probably piss him off pretty bad if he knew what it really meant. She told me that he was constantly asking her what 'CB' meant—demand that she tell him what it stood for—but she'd never give in. And to get back at me, he'd given me a name, too. 'PW.' But later, Kay'd confided to me that this only meant 'prep woman,' something which I'd actually found pretty flattering.

But right from the start Merle is different. For one thing, he has this air about him that wherever he is, that is definitely the place to be. He is constantly saying these funny things, that even if I try not to, still make me laugh. He keeps his hair long and carries his wallet on a chain. And he wears a leather vest with motorcycle boots—the kind of boots with clunky metal rings on the sides and wide square toes. But he usually refers to them affectionately as his 'shit kickers' instead. He likes to listen to the radio loud, too, and he blasts all these seriously cool bands through the homemade box speakers he's built for his car; like Judas Priest, Led Zeppelin, Aerosmith and Black Sabbath. The type of music they play on WKNC. Overall, he is the coolest person I have ever met. But I'd never tell this to Kay, though. Because then she might go thinking it's a compliment or something.

Merle calls her at the same time everyday; 4:00 sharp. They talk, decide what they're going to do for the evening, then hang up.

The whole process only takes about five minutes. But still, I decide this is a major inconvenience for me. I mean, what if I get a boyfriend, too, and what if *he* decides that he wants to call everyday at 4:00, too, like Merle does? He'd never be able to get through. Or another scenario I have to consider that's even closer to immediate hand, suppose Haley decides *she* needs to call me for something very important? And what if it just so happens that this is the only time she can get to a phone? Then the line would be all busy, and I'd never be able to find out what information she had.

I pick up the extension in my room, expecting them to be talking all hoochie and stupid, but they aren't. Instead, they are just having a normal conversation.

"Get off the phone!" I suddenly interrupt.

They both stop talking. "Angie? What do you need?"

"I said 'get off the phone!'" I repeat.

"What for?" Kay asks.

"Because Haley's trying to call me!"

"How do you know?" she asks, then adds, "Besides, I just got on."

"I don't care!" I tell her. "You do this every single day!"

"I'll be off in a minute." Now she sounds irritated.

"No, you need to get off *now*!" I demand. "You don't need to be talking to that long-haired, boot-wearing, shit-kicking *freak*, anyway!"

"Merle is *not* a freak!"

"Yeah, *right*!"

Now Merle speaks up. "Get off the phone, you damn little pink-and-green polka-dotted *bitch*!"

"Well, at least I'm in *style*!" I inform him hotly.

He laughs. "Yeah, that's exactly what I want, alright. Some pink and green shit to wear, just like *yours*!"

"*Why* do you keep calling here?" I demand.

"I'm not calling *you*, you little brat-shit!"

"Well, you're calling *my* house, and that means you're calling me, too. Since I *do* live here and all!"

"Yeah, it sure is a damn shame!" he tells me. "But I guess they've got to keep you *somewhere*."

"Go to hell!" I retort.

"Only if you're not going to be there."

"Don't *worry!*" I slam the phone down. Hard. I hope it's enough to bust both of their eardrums. They so totally deserve each other! Still, though I'd never admit it out loud—not in a million years—I hope one day I have a boyfriend as cool as him.

* * *

The summer is a whirlwind of fun. But it rains more this summer than I've ever seen it rain before. And since humidity wreaks such havoc on my hair, this truly puts a cramp in my style. I have to keep it in a ponytail most days instead of loose and feathered back, like I want. I am afraid that this will ruin the image I've so carefully tried to create.

If I'm not at cheerleading practice and it happens to be sunny, then I am at the neighborhood pool, working on my summer tan. Because I don't want to attend the first football game with white, marshmallowish-looking legs. Brown is definitely 'in,' and if you start back to school in the fall all pale like that, people will wonder what it is that you did all summer.

I end up with a boyfriend of sorts this summer, but we are more or less ill-matched. Still, no one can tell me this, and I go out with him every night, anyway. I don't come in until my 10:00 curfew, and then I am usually pushing it. After I get home, I sneak back to my room and call him. He would call me, but it's so late I'm afraid Mama and Daddy'd say something, and besides, he has his own phone—extension *and* line, right in his bedroom. So it's just easier for me to call him. Besides, if the 'parental units' (better known as 'Ward and June Cleaver') found out I was actually calling a guy in the first place, they'd absolutely have identical freakin' birds! Because Mama's constantly reminding me how it is in 'Leave It to Beaver Land,' how 'nice girls' don't *call* boys; they sit back and wait for the boys to call *them*. Okay—sorry June. I hate to be the one to break the morbid news to you, but it'll be a cold day in *Hell* before I ever go out with the likes of a Wally-Cleaver-Wannabe. A *freezing* cold day!

A couple of times, we've actually talked on the phone all night, though I've always got the fear that Ward and June will hear me and pick up the extension in their room. Then I'll lose my phone privilege in here for sure. I'll wind up without any privacy at all, which will totally not work. Still, it's a risk I feel I have to take.

Kay and I don't see much of each other this summer, besides fighting over the bathroom—that and the phone. And throughout the process, Merle and I have managed to come up with some pretty exotic names for each other. On the flip side, Merle and Trinket have become pretty close though, and this really bothers me. Because I can't figure out why it is that he likes her and doesn't like me. I mention it to Kay one time, just in the passing. Certainly not for any level of importance it holds on its own.

"Maybe it's because you're a brat," she surmises. "Or maybe it's because you always call him a freak."

"Well, isn't he?" I ask.

"No!" she tells me. "But even if he was, it would be none of *your* business!"

Sweet.

It's late summer, and Kay has been packing her things up for awhile, getting ready to move into the dorm at UNC Wilmington. She chose Wilmington because she loves the beach. And wouldn't you know it? Merle's going there, with her. It so figures it pure stinks! Still, he hasn't cut his hair yet, and I enjoy listening to Mimi's ranting—about how she's going to tie pink ribbons all in it if he ever comes over to her house with his hair long like that again. That'd be a sight! I'd definitely have to have a camera on hand, be ready for the moment when it actually happened.

Kay's also packed up all her clothes—everything except the preppy ones, which she leaves hanging in the closet.

"You can wear them if you want," she offers.

"Okay." I don't tell her that's what I'd planned on doing all along, anyway. It's not like she'll be there to tell me 'no' or anything.

They are leaving this morning. The day has finally arrived. Mama's driving the Impala, and Daddy's following in one of Granddaddy's trucks so that he can carry her furniture and boxes. I cannot believe the good fortune that has actually befallen me. Now, not only can I have the whole bathroom to myself anytime I want it, but never will I ever have to fight her over the phone again, either. I cannot fathom the idea. It is simply too much.

We are having a morning cheerleading practice today, and I am looking around feverishly for my saddle oxfords. I can't imagine what I've done with them, and Mary's mother will be here to pick me up any minute. I am riding with them today because Mama and Daddy are getting ready to leave for Wilmington. I'm glad Mary was willing to work with me this year before try-outs because she'd been a cheerleader last year, too, and knew the ropes. She'd helped me out in a lot of ways; from learning what to expect, to getting over my athletic awkwardness whenever I practiced a jump or cheer.

I finally manage to locate my shoes, under the couch in the living room. But the socks I find there with them are way too dirty to even think about wearing again. And as I am on the way back to my room for a clean pair, I glance quickly into Kay's in the passing, which is now all but bare. Something makes me pause there in the doorway for a moment. All of the familiar pictures she'd had sitting around, all of her records, even her stereo, are missing from their usual spots. And the absence of these ordinary items makes everything seem large and empty. Only her queen-sized bed remains because it is too big for the dorm room.

She is sitting there, in the middle of her bed, waiting. Beside her, there is an overstuffed duffel bag, and in her hands, she is holding her favorite towel, which miraculously, has not rotted yet. Her clenched knuckles are totally white, and she seems so small and lost there among the unfamiliar surroundings. I've never seen my sister like this before—almost like she's really human or something—like she's actually a real person. And seeing her that way—so quiet and terrified, like she's somebody else—is the strangest phenomena I have ever experienced before in my whole life. An unexpected awareness rises from the pit of my stomach, kind of painful, like when you get hit with a sudden bout of homesickness. For some reason, all these foreign and repressed thoughts flood my head at once, like a dam has just broken; things

I should've said, things I should've told her—way before now—before it'd gotten too late. But in retrospect, I don't think I ever really believed this day would actually get here. It just seemed too far-fetched to be real.

Kay looks up then, catching me standing in her doorway.

I straighten up, manage a quick scowl instead, asking, "What're *you* looking at, *dig-a-dig*?" And as I continue on to my own room to retrieve the socks I'd originally been after, I wonder why it is that it suddenly hurts to swallow, that it feels like I'm going to break down crying any second now?

Kay and Merle
*(Just say **'NO'** to preppy clothes.)*

An 'updated' family portrait

ON THE OUTSKIRTS OF SOCIETY

    9th grade is a whole new experience for me; a whirlwind of new and challenging activities like nothing I have ever experienced before. I run for student council and then for class advisory council, and in between those meetings, cheerleading practice and performing at the actual games, themselves, I manage to spend every other waking minute with my boyfriend. Socially, I appear to be quite polished, like I've got it all together. In fact, if the truth be known, I am probably the only one who even has a remote clue about the reality; about what actually goes on inside this inexplicable complication that is otherwise known as my head. But as long as no one else is aware, then I have attained my goal; I have successfully become 'normal,' and that should be the end of it. Everyone should live happily ever after now. Unfortunately, I am learning that this is not always the case. Because the part that still remains to confuse me is why I don't *feel* like I belong. I mean, I'm wearing all the right clothes, participating in all the right activities, doing all the right things. But regardless of all that effort, deep down inside, I still know who I am—and there's just nothing to change that. You can't run from yourself, no matter how fast you are.

I am constantly repressing infinite rituals; the ones that I can't, I try to camouflage as part of the activity I am engaged in. And the frustration is becoming all-consuming since the little bit of leftover time I actually have alone, I am forced to perform endless tasks to make up for lost opportunities. There are many days I simply can't get out the door in the mornings due to the overwhelming panic attacks that suddenly strike. And on the occasions that I *do* manage to make it out the door, there are still days that I end up having to leave school early anyway, due to the unbearable onslaught of ruthless attacks. I would not wish this torture on my worst enemy.

Mama and Daddy know that I can't help it, but still they are afraid I won't graduate on time.

"You have to attend school a certain number of days every year," Mama explains. "Or else they'll end up holding you back a grade."

"You mean I'd fail?" I ask.

"Yes," Daddy confirms.

"But not because you're not smart enough to do the work," Mama adds. "Just because you haven't been there enough days to justify going up to the next grade."

"But that's not fair!" I tell her.

"It has nothing to do with being fair," Mama explains. "It's just that the state has a certain number of rules and regulations it has to follow, and you have to meet those requirements in order to pass your grade."

I can think of nothing more humiliating that being held back a grade. Everyone would point at me and laugh, even my friends, when they found out what a fraud I was. Suddenly, it's official all over again, and the dreaded nightmare is reborn; "Look—Angela's *retarded*!" I mean, sure, I'd stayed back a grade at Robinscrest, but that had been *my* choice. Not the school's, or even the state's for that matter. This is a totally different ball game though, something that cannot happen, no matter what. It's like being in prison—maybe even on death row—and finally the officials find out what you knew all along—that you're innocent, and they acquit you—only to find out later that your newfound freedom is short-lived. Because regardless of all the progress you've made, your worst fears are confirmed when they come for you again with what they consider to be new evidence. And this time, there is no escaping. Because in junior high school society, not only is Habeas Corpus very much alive and well, but it's also perfectly legal.

I try my best to stay at school, even when the Fear is completely strangling me. Sometimes it is so bad that I end up hyperventilating in the bathroom instead of sitting in class, toughing it out like I'm supposed to be doing. And as far as I'm concerned, no matter what façade I am able to present to the public, privately, I am extremely aware of the cold, hard truth; that I have got to be the weirdest, most screwed-up individual who has ever walked across the face of this earth. And unfortunately, there's just no amount of eyeshadow, preppy clothes, hairspray or even coveted positions on popular school teams to change who I am. The realization makes me angry. How can it be that I've worked so hard to achieve the one thing I've always wanted the most, the one thing that has driven me to achieve all that I have—simple normalcy—only to discover that this, too, is just an illusion, that in reality, I have become a failure at this as well? I have actually become a failure at something so common and mundane that most people aren't even aware of its simple existence. The only time anyone even becomes remotely aware of the concept of normalcy is when it manifests itself as *ab*-normalcy, and then it glares out at you, just as intensely as a mirror reflecting off direct sunlight would.

I am still not getting along with my boyfriend. Not that we ever really did to begin with. But lately, it seems to be getting much worse. I try to talk to Mama about it, but she thinks it's ridiculous. "Why would you want to waste time with someone who makes you unhappy? Besides, you're too young to be going steady, anyway.

You've got your whole life ahead of you. Right now, you should just be concentrating on having fun, enjoy being young. Because you won't be young forever, you know."

I want to roll my eyes. I'm so sick of hearing about this 'young' stuff, like nothing I feel is important, how everything gets trivialized simply because I'm 'young.' Overall, I decide for about the hundredth time it's just not worth arguing about. And exactly why it is I can't seem to remember this before I get started with her each time remains a mystery to me. You'd think it'd be something that'd stick in my mind since it's so completely obvious she has no clue. Because you just can't turn your feelings on and off like that, like they're a spicket or something.

"I was young once, too, you know," she reminds me. But I don't buy it. Because there's no way she ever felt what I'm feeling right now. No way at all. If she had, then she'd understand what I'm going through. I mean, get real. The '50's have absolutely nothing to do with today at all. Think about it—how can you possibly understand real life when you've grown up wearing these stupid-looking poodle skirts because jeans weren't allowed in school, when everyone belonged to the glee club, when the Saturday night sock-hop was the highlight of your entire week, and your graduating class maxed out at a staggering 20 members—all of whom just happened coincidentally to live on your same street? *Puh*-leez! Like I've said before, it's 'Leave It to Beaver,' come to life. More than likely, it's probably safer to assume she'd just hatched full-blown from an ostrich egg—right about the same time Daddy came along.

I go into my room, open my junk drawer. I pilfer through it until I come across a left-over box of greeting cards; the ones with the stupid-looking squirrels and chipmunks on them that we had to sell last spring in order to raise enough money for new cheerleading uniforms. I flop across my bed, start a letter to Kay. Sure, it's a far-fetched idea. But at least I know we both exist on the same plane, and that at least *one* of our parents definitely has to be a full-blooded mammal, seeing as the two of us had to inherit it from *somebody*. It's totally ironic how it took her actually leaving home—actually going away like this—before I could see that we *do* at least have some things in common.

* * *

If junior high's like being a big fish in a little pond, then high school is akin to being a small, easily digestible rodent in a larger-than-life alligator pit. For one thing, I do not make the cheerleading squad this year, and to make matters worse, the coach takes me aside right after tryouts have concluded and says, "You're very good, you know. Your scores were definitely high enough up there to make the team. It's just your absences last year that had us concerned."

I don't know what to say, and I'm too disappointed to care, anyway.

"At any rate," she goes on briskly, "I'd love to see you right back here, next spring—same place, same time. Just work on that attendance this year, and you'll have no problem. We'd really consider you an asset to the team."

Next spring? A whole *year* from now? That's like trying to imagine the ends of the universe or something. It's way too far off—and just not worth it.

Another thing about Sanderson High School—probably one of the more important ones, too—is that you could practically fit three Carroll Junior Highs right into its cavernous vastness. I know I will never find my way around here, especially since all the hallways look exactly alike. And I know, too, that they probably did this on purpose—back when they originally built the school. I'm willing to bet that the architects are still lurking around here, somewhere back in the shadows, laughing hysterically at all the new kids each season. I might as well be feeling my way through a maze, the promise of an obligatory slab of cheese waiting at the end for me, should I ever happen to get there.

My first period class is art. An interesting class for me to take since I can't even draw a ball so that it looks like one. Still, I figure there's probably no better reason to take the class than this—because if I *could* already draw, it'd just be a waste of time.

I stand in the doorway of the new classroom, trying not to seem conspicuous. Not everyone is here yet, and among those who are, there is no one that I know. There are four large tables around which are placed unmatched plastic chairs, about half of them already occupied, and I quickly weigh the options, size everything up, as I try to decide where I should take root. The room, itself, is cluttered. All kinds of objects—from things as basic as fake roses, building blocks, and empty egg cartons, all the way to the totally unidentifiable—of which I will not even venture to guess.

"Don't just stand there in the doorway, blocking traffic!" a loud voice booms. "How do you 'spect anybody else to get in here with you standing all up there, right in the way?"

I turn quickly to find who I suspect to be the teacher. And just by the looks of her, I can tell that her bark is far worse than her bite will ever be. Still, I don't want to call any more attention to myself since I already look like a goober as it is. I head over towards the table by the windows. I take a seat next to a totally interesting girl; she is probably the prettiest one I've ever seen, and I am intrigued. Maybe I am subconsciously hoping that by sitting beside her, some of it'll rub off on me.

She has a fantastic tan, the deep kind you can only achieve if you have that nice, naturally olive-toned skin. The kind I don't have. And her hair—*ohmigod*—it's absolutely perfect. It is long, honey-colored—brown, with just the right amount of natural blond in it—and it feathers back absolutely perfect. The way I wish mine would. And though it is humid outside, a typical morning in early September, her hair is shiny and sleek, not frizzy and limp. I am impressed, and I wonder how she gets it to do that. She is wearing a summer shirt with one of those zip-up, gray hooded jackets over it.

And on her long, thin legs, these perfectly faded jeans. I wonder if I wash a pair of my own jeans enough times, if I could make them look like that, too.

The girl looks up, notices me studying her, and embarrassed, I quickly smile, say 'hello.' She smiles back, seems friendly enough, if maybe even a little shy. I tell her I really like her hair. She tells me that it's all broken off in the back, she thinks from her blow dryer.

And then she turns around so that I can see. But the only thing I can see is that I wish she knew what it was *really* like to have your hair broken off, like mine had been one time after I'd over-colored it. I'd wound up looking like a rooster with a half-yellow Mohawk, and I'd cried for a whole week, which hadn't made it grow back any faster. Hers, on the other hand, is only slightly shorter at one point in the back, and looks instead just like she's had it cut in intentional layers. I would absolutely kill to have my hair break off like that, too—if I could be assured it'd look like hers.

During the course of the period, I learn that her name is Regina and that she is also in 10th grade. She has come to Sanderson from West Millbrook Junior High, the same school Kay'd attended before we'd moved to Winston-Salem. Like me, she has a boyfriend with whom she is thinking of breaking things off. His name is Tommy, and she has a feeling that he is cheating on her. Though I don't say anything, for the life of me, I can't figure out why.

Lunchtime is absolutely crazy here. There are actually two cafeterias, right side-by-side, and I stand in the heated doorway of each, overwhelmed by the chaos, searching amidst the confusion for at least one familiar face. Haley and I do not have the same lunch period this year. We discovered that last summer when we compared our newly received class schedules. In fact, we went on to discover that we shared no classes together at all. How nice. So far, high school really rots. I can't believe Kay actually elected to go here, and on her own accord at that. Things must've been way different back then.

My last class of the day is also my favorite subject; English. The class, itself is a complete melting pot, made up of a variety of different students converging from each of the surrounding junior high schools. Unlike my World Civ class, which is dominated by the prep group from West Millbrook, everyone here is pretty much on equal footing since other than a few acquaintances, no one really knows anyone else in the class. I *do* recognize a girl I know from Carroll, though; a tiny blond named Jody who is sitting in the back row. I wish I'd known she would be in the class, too, because then I'd have chosen a desk closer to hers, instead of the one up here, midway to the front.

The teacher is young, laid back. He is fresh out of college, and we learn through the grapevine that he is also the swim coach for the high school team. Because he is so new, he doesn't even have a classroom of his own yet. Instead, he is considered by the staff and administration to be a 'traveling teacher,' which in reality translates into his rolling everything he possess around on a gray metal projector cart from one class to the next. He *does*, however, have an office where he can spend his planning period, and where we can schedule appointments with him if we need extra help on assignments. It is located in the utility closet next to the teacher's lounge, and you can always find him there among all the left-over and out-dated text books, sitting at his 'desk,' which is actually an ex-cafeteria table (wounded in some form of combat), on which he has temporarily piled all his supplies, lesson plans, and stacks of ungraded papers. Overall, he is the best English teacher I've ever had, and I look forward to his class every afternoon. He is definitely a far cry from Mrs. Waddelson. In fact, there is simply no comparison at all. He actually makes the learning of such mundane things as dangling modifiers interesting, not as a communal necessity to avoid the unthinkable brimstone tortures of Hellfire.

Within the first few days, I have actually managed to find my way around this monstrosity, more commonly known as a 'high school.' Well, sort of, anyway. I mean, as long as I enter the same door every morning and follow the exact same path throughout the entire day, I usually don't have too much problem. Things start to seem more familiar, less intimidating.

Still, I just can't seem to find my niche here, and I feel like a total outcast most of the time. To top it all off, there is 'Janey,' with whom I used to be friends at Carroll. But Janey has changed now. She hangs with a whole different group of people in high school, and for some unknown reason, she has decided that she hates me. Not just dislikes me—I mean, totally *despises* me, and with a passion at that. I rack my brains, trying to figure out what I could've possibly done to her, but other than one small disagreement, I can think of nothing. Still, she follows me around, trailed by her new group of friends, squirting a high-powered water gun into my hair, sticking out her foot and trying to trip me. Anything at all she can do to bully me. Unfortunately, she even lives in my neighborhood, and when I get on the bus, she is always there in the front seat, waiting to whop me on the back of the head when I walk past. She doesn't do it hard enough to hurt, just hard enough to piss me off, and one morning I decide I've totally had enough of it. I turn back around, holding my books in front of me, and it's all I can do not to whop her back. I grit my teeth instead, telling her, "Keep your damn hands to yourself!" She laughs, tries to whop me again, but I back up, swing wildly at her with my books. Of course, I miss. I don't know why I do it, anyway. I realize I am way out of my league. If not only because she always has a whole posse of friends around her, then definitely because of the fact that I am still roughly about the size of a 5th grader. And a *small* one, at that. Besides, the only formal training I have in fighting is with Kay, anyway. The combination of these things, I know, should play a strong key factor in determining my vulnerability here. Because in *actual* reality, I am truly scared of Janey. But in *virtual* reality, I can never let her, or anyone else for that matter, know this. Because whenever a bully finds out you are really scared of her, it's definitely downhill from there. Things can only get worse. And since I realize this, I know I have got to stand up for myself, regardless of the result. Otherwise, this situation could very easily turn into Robinscrest, the Second Episode—the sequel we've all been waiting for. I tried to tell Mama about Janey torturing me on the bus, hoping that she'd give in and drive me to school every day. But she'd only said, "A *fight* on the school bus? Between *girls*? You'd better not *ever* let me get that phone call! You weren't brought up that way, and I never expect to hear anything like that from you ever again!"

"But Mama—she's going to beat me up! Should I just stand there and let her?"

"Yes! If that's what she plans to do. Then we'll deal with that later. *Girls* just don't *fight!*"

"But Mama—"

"*Ignore* her!"

"Couldn't you just—you know—like *drive* me to school for a few days or something? In the car?"

"Now what would that solve?" Mama asks. "You have to learn to fight your own battles. Daddy and I won't be around to do it forever, you know. It's all part of growing up."

"But I thought you didn't want me fighting *any* battles!" I tell her angrily.

"*You* know what I mean! So quit trying to turn words around on me!"

I am jolted back to reality as the driver suddenly jerks the bus into gear, yelling irritatedly, "Se—DOOOOOOOWWWWN!!!" I grab the back of a seat just in time, almost losing my footing. But I still manage to peel off a menacing glare at Janey, saying, "Go to Hell!"

She laughs. "No, *you* go to Hell!"

"*You* go to Hell!"

"No, *you* go to Hell!"

The bus lurches forward then, and I can see the driver's disgusted eyes reflected in the huge rearview mirror as she yells, "Yer *both* goin' to Hell if you don't *se-down* and *shuddup!*"

I find a seat near the back, angrily wondering exactly when it was that this shoeless-redneck-incestuous-Skoal-chewing-bus-driving-*bitty* suddenly became God, anyway. I blow my breath out, let my books drop hard on the floor in front of me. Across the aisle, Haley is laughing.

"What?" I say, exasperated.

She just shakes her head, repeating, "No, *you* go to Hell!"

Yeah, it's funny alright. Especially when it's not happening to *her*.

* * *

If I thought high school couldn't get any worse, that things could absolutely do nothing else but rise from this low point in my life, then I was only kidding myself—I'd been sadly mistaken. Because like the lower-than-rock-bottom discovery of the mushrooms growing in the Winston-Salem bathroom, the mushrooms of Sanderson High School were only now just beginning to rear the total ugliness of their heads.

* * *

Though it's hard to believe, I actually make it through my sophomore year of high school. In fact, I have actually survived to begin my junior one. My homeroom teacher is this total dork-woman, who says that she, herself, attended Sanderson High School in her day, and that there's no other place she'd rather teach than at her own 'alma mater.' I can't help but wonder why it always turns out to be the most extreme dorks who have absolutely no clue that they even *are* dorks. Any rational sense it might hold has completely eluded me.

My English teacher this year hates me, and her grading reflects that fact. She tells me that she had my sister in her class several years ago, and not to even bother to think that I'll get away with trying to pull all the stunts *she* did. This surprises me since Kay was always a strong A—B student. Stupidity was never one of her assets. I mean, true—Kay was always a different bird and all, but never a trouble-causer. Nothing like that. I write her a letter, asking about it. She writes back telling me that this particular teacher is crazy, absolutely nuts—that she once came in to class and taught the whole period with a brown paper bag over her head, just to see if anyone would notice. And when no one said anything about it, she'd gotten really pissed off at all of them. In retrospect, Kay feels really sorry for me to have gained the misfortune of landing in her English class, too. But that's not the worst of it. Because not only do I have her for English, but I also have her for my elective, Creative Writing, and this fact totally rots, completely rains on my parade. Because any of the fun or pleasurable experiences I'd hoped to derive from this class have now become null and void.

Mama and Daddy remember Mrs. Sutton all-too-well from Kay's high school days, so when she begins calling the house every night about the same time—right in the middle of supper—to complain about my 'atrocious' behavior, Daddy, having heard enough, finally loses it.

"Angie has straight 'ones' in conduct in all of her other classes. In fact, she always has. So what the hell's wrong with *you*? Quit *calling* here every night with that crap, ruining *my* dinner!"

I can hear Mrs. Sutton sputtering angrily on the other end of the line as Daddy slams the receiver back into its cradle, and I fight hard to stifle a laugh. Because if it isn't funny enough that Daddy just told her off in the first place, it's totally hilarious that he did it, using his 'movie star' voice.

Daddy looks across the table at me then. "Don't think you can start getting away with things now. It's only because I know her. And I know you. And I know you don't behave that way in classrooms. But don't start getting any ideas. I might've been born at night, but it wasn't *last* night!" He waves his fork at me. "Don't forget I've been in high school, too, you know."

I roll my eyes. "Yeah, right. In '*Leave-it-to-Beaver*' land. Come on, Daddy. That's like comparing 'Barry Manilow' to 'Black Sabbath' or something stupid like that."

"Not necessarily," he tells me. "You'd be surprised. Kids haven't really changed that much over the years. I've gotten in trouble for little things I've done, too, you know."

I stare at him. "I don't believe you. It'd never happen. Because Mimi would've killed you first."

"You'd be surprised," he repeats.

"So what'd you do?" I ask, uninvited images of Peewee Herman pranks suddenly invading my thoughts. "Wear Bubba teeth to school? Play keep-away with Ernest-the-Dork's glasses? Or did you just bring your teacher a wormy apple?"

Daddy looks off across the table in recollection then. "No," he says. "We didn't do things like that. We did things more like putting dry ice in Mr. Murphy's desk. And then there was the time we flushed the cherry bomb down the toilet in the men's bathroom." He laughs. "That was some kind of mess! Oh, and there was also the time when our social studies teacher brought us back the 'Turkish cigarettes' when she came home from a trip. We sat right there and smoked them in class. Only they weren't really cigarettes. They were much too sweet to be that."

From the other side of the table, Trinket pipes up. "What's a cherry bomb, Daddy?"

"Never mind," Mama tells her, then adds, nodding in my direction, "John, don't encourage her. That's all we need."

She stands up, reaching for the empty dishes on the table.

When she's gone, Daddy looks over at me. Finally, he asks, "So tell me this . . . . when you and your friend—uh, Katie, I think she said it was—were sitting there in Mrs. Sutton's class the other day—was there *really*—you know—was there really a *cow* standing there—*right* outside the *window*?"

* * *

Miss Dork, my homeroom teacher, tells me she needs to speak with me alone in the hallway. I feel my stomach suddenly knot up, and I can't imagine what I could've possibly done wrong. I follow her out of the room, feeling completely hollow inside.

She shuts the door against all the prying eyes, crosses her arms over her chest.

"Last week, when you had that big radio here, where did you get it?"

What? She might as well've punched me in the gut. "From my granddaddy's store," I tell her.

"And why did you have it here?"

"It was for a project we were doing in first period—in drama class. You can ask Miss Stokes."

Was she serious? Was she actually going there? To try to take a radio away that I'd had here nearly a week ago, and for a school project at that?

"Why did you have it in plastic bags?" she continues.

"So no one would see it. You know, so I wouldn't get in trouble."

"Why didn't you just leave it in your locker?"

"Because I didn't want anything to happen to it," I tell her, still trying to figure out where all this is going. "And why're you asking me all this stuff?"

"Because Lin Tran had her radio stolen last week, and she thinks the one you had was hers."

What? "You have *got* to be kidding!"

Imagine *me*, with my nervous stomach, *me*, who can't even tell a good lie without feeling a totally overwhelming tsunami of guilt. *Me*, who'd actually witnessed my very own mother drive back to the gas station and argue with the attendant for ten whole minutes— over the extra dollar in change he'd accidentally given her. She'd ended up just leaving it on the counter when he wouldn't take it back, claiming that she wouldn't spend any dollar that she didn't come by honestly. And the thing was, she didn't do this for my sake. She did it because she really *believed* it. And if there's one thing I can say about both Mama and Daddy, it's that they definitely lived by their beliefs, definitely placed a very high value on morals and standards. According to them, without honesty, how could you ever hope to aspire to those morals—the ones that should govern our lives, the ones that God has created, so that we, the imperfect mortals, can live in His image? I mean, with parents like that, how could you even consider the possibly of their spawning thieving off-spring? It just doesn't make sense. It's ludicrous.

Still, Miss Dork is unfazed. "Well, Lin Tran claims it was *hers*."

I cannot believe this! Lin Tran and her twin brother are exchange students here, and neither she nor her brother has ever said two words to me. Or to anyone else I know, for that matter.

"That's totally crazy!" I tell her. "My granddaddy has an electric store, and he always gives us radios and tape recorders. Curling irons and things like that."

She looks at me, and I can tell she doesn't believe me.

"So there's no receipt for when you bought it?"

"No!" I tell her. "I didn't *buy* it! My granddaddy *gave* it to me! If you don't believe *me*, why don't you simply call *him*?"

Instead, she calls Lin Tran and her twin brother out into the hall, too, shutting the door behind them as well.

"It's *my* radio!" I tell Lin Tran loudly. Like there's something wrong with her hearing, not her English.

She begins to jabber away with her brother in Vietnamese, and I have no idea what they're saying to each other. Then, turning to Miss Dork, says, "She needs to bring back radio that she have here other day. So I can see it." She says this like I'm not even standing there or something.

Miss Dork looks at me again. "Would you bring the radio back, please? So that we can settle this?"

I am livid. "There's nothing to settle! It's *my* radio! But I'll be glad to bring it again tomorrow—so she can *look* at it! Then she'll see she's made a mistake!"

None of them thank me for offering to do this voluntarily. Instead, Miss Dork just opens the classroom door, and we all walk back in. I can feel my face burning with anger as well as embarrassment. Because in all my life, I have never been treated like, or even felt like, such a scumbag. And the ironic thing is, I haven't even done anything wrong.

"I can't *believe* this!" I rant to Regina. We are in the bathroom, and I am watching her brush her perfect hair. Actually, it's during second period, and I am supposed to be an office assistant, but when the secretary sent me out on an errand, I'd gone to Regina's class instead, acted like I didn't know her, told the teacher that the office needed to see 'Regina' for a minute. Since I've got the 'office assistant' pass in my hand, no one questions me. We'd just seen each other before school—in the student lounge—but since homeroom comes between first and second periods, I'd just been hit over the head with this wonderful tidbit of news.

"That *is* pretty bogus," she agrees. "I guess all you can do is stick to your story—tell the truth. Because in the end, they'll figure out *she's* wrong." Regina puts her brush away then. "Remember last year in art class, when Miss Bullard lost my 'apple fantasy' picture? How she swore I never turned it in?"

"Yeah," I tell her. "I remember that. Because we spent the whole week-end at your house, working on those pictures together, so I knew you'd done it."

"Remember when she found it, though?" Regina laughs. "And she had to erase the zero and give me a grade instead?"

"Yeah, I remember. But she never even attempted to say she was sorry or anything like that."

Regina shrugs. "What can you expect?"

And I know she's right. Because if *we* do something wrong, we never hear the end of it. But if a *teacher* does something wrong, then it doesn't count. It all turns out to be nothing more than just a little mistake. A forgivable one that can easily be overlooked.

We part, heading our separate ways, me leaving the bathroom a little before Regina so no one will see us coming out together. Especially not Mrs. Morris who'll swear we've been in there, for the sole purpose of smoking. Forget the fact that neither one of us even has soot-breath. Because it won't matter. She'll swear she smells it, anyway.

* * *

"This is not same radio she have here other day," Lin Tran says to Miss Dork. We are standing out in the hallway again, just like yesterday, and I am holding the huge boom box so that both Lin Tran and her brother can inspect it. Like I'm a common crook or something. What she doesn't get is that I did this simply as a favor to her; to put her mind at ease. Because now I'll end up having to carry the gargantuous thing around with me all day again, and needless to say, it isn't exactly porter-friendly.

Now Lin Tran is speaking rapidly to her brother in Vietnamese again, and he, too, shakes his head. She looks at Miss Dork with finality, stating, "This is not same radio she have with her other day."

Miss Dork looks at me then. "Is that true? Is this a different radio that you've brought in this time?"

Like I have forty boom boxes at my disposal or something.

"Of *course* it's the same radio!" I exclaim. "Where d'you think I'd've gotten another one so soon? And just overnight at that?"

Lin Tran shakes her head with conviction. "This is not same radio." She turns back to Miss Dork then, saying, "She need to bring back same radio she have with her other day."

"It's the only radio I've got!" I tell her, exasperated, then add as an afterthought more to myself, "I cannot *believe* this!"

"You don't have another one at home that you can bring in for her to look at?" Miss Dork asks.

I just stare at her. Because like I said, I absolutely cannot *believe* this!

"Yeah, *sure*," I tell her, sarcastically. "I've got forty more stashed away in my closet! Which one do you want?"

"Only the one that belongs to Lin Tran," she tells me.

I am almost too livid to speak. "Well, I'm very sorry to inform you that I can't help you out there!"

I turn to walk away. I refuse to entertain this conversation any further. Let *them* figure it out! But right then, a new thought strikes, and I turn back around.

"Just for the record," I begin. "Ask Lin Tran how it feels to have x-ray vision!"

Miss Dork looks at me, like she doesn't get it.

"Because since the so-called 'first' radio was wrapped up in *bags*—which she clearly recalls and admits that it was—then how can she identify *this* radio—or any *other* radio for that matter—as *not* being the same one I had the other day? In fact, since she never really saw it, how can she even claim it was her radio in the first place?"

None of them seems to have a good answer to that. I shrug, adding, "Just some food for thought—that's all."

But I turn back around one more time. "By the way, if there are further questions regarding the ownership of this radio, then you can verify those with Miss Stokes. I told her what was going on yesterday, and she looked at the radio again this morning. She can verify that it's one and the same radio."

The bell rings then. I had no idea how wonderful insolence could actually feel—how empowering it really is. Still, I figure they deserve it. But even with that fact—knowing I'd won the battle this time—there was still the overall war to consider, and right now, the odds aren't looking too good for me. All the bullying, and now these accusations—the only thing I can figure is that they've finally noticed. They see that there is something different about me—about the way I move, the way I interact, the bouts of terror that I can't always hide mixed with the frantic barrage of compulsions I am constantly trying to mask—and this is how they respond to it, how they translate that difference. What other reason could anybody possibly have for singling me out? Even Haley realizes something is askew with me. Several times in the past, she has asked me about this particular compulsion or that obvious anxiety attack. I'd always tried to rationalize those things away, but you can only do that so many times before people become suspicious of you. It's only human nature.

Haley has a new group of friends this year, anyway—a new boyfriend, too—and that group does not include me. I am not of the same 'caliber' that these people are, and trying to mix with them is painfully uncomfortable. I am thankful that I've had the opportunity to meet Regina. Because no matter what—no matter how weirded out I manage to get—she always treats me the same. I know she probably notices my repetitious behavior, too, but still she never asks any questions about it. It doesn't seem to matter to her. She is definitely a breath of fresh air. And though I still haven't been able to get my hair to do like hers, I am constantly trying anyway, hoping that one day, I'll hit it just right.

* * *

The secretary has sent me down the hall to pull this kid, Justin, whom I know from my other neighborhood—the one we lived in before we moved to Winston-Salem—out of his second-period class.

"I don't know what you did," I joke. "But it must be something pretty bad because they said your mother's on her way over here now."

He gives a half-hearted laugh. Still, I can tell he's very preoccupied about something or another.

Later, I learn that when he and his sister, Donna, were walking from the student parking lot towards the school this morning, Donna had suddenly collapsed, and no one knew why. She'd been taken to the hospital by ambulance where her mother and Justin had rushed to meet her there. It was rumored by the afternoon that she still hadn't regained consciousness, and there was talk about a blood clot having made its way to her brain.

From the payphones in the student lounge, I call Mama.

"She's probably had an aneurysm," Mama tells me. "Is she still alive?"

I am shocked. "Yes. Why wouldn't she be?"

"Because when aneurysms happen, they usually kill people instantly. Daddy had a friend in high school who died like that. But maybe they caught Donna's in time. Maybe they've been able to go in and fix it."

"They say she's still unconscious."

"But at least she's alive," Mama reassures me.

It's hard to imagine Donna, who's a year younger than me, lying motionless in a remote hospital bed somewhere. I think back to junior high, how she tried to help me learn to do a back handspring. Since she'd been in gymnastics for a pretty long time, she knew the ropes.

"Make like you're going to sit in a chair," she suggests. "Then just before you sit down, jump back like this." And she demonstrates, making it look all-too-easy.

I remember the day we moved to Winston-Salem, too, seeing her riding her bike home from a friend's house, despite the bone-chilling cold. I'd waved to her then, just like it was any other day. Not like the day we were up and moving to the absolute other end of the universe. Donna and I hadn't really been friends, only acquaintances. But since we'd lived in the same neighborhood and only a few houses away from each other at that, and because we'd been in school together since elementary, we still knew one another.

In the morning, we are sitting in our first period classes when the principal comes over the intercom. Usually, announcements are saved for homeroom, but the one he has this morning is too important to wait.

"Many of you know Donna from school or other outside activities. And it is with pain and deep regret that I make this announcement to you. Donna . . . . *died* yesterday—after she was taken to the hospital."

The rest of the announcement is a blur, something about keeping the family in mind during this terrible time, and that as soon as the information is available, he'll give us the details regarding the funeral service.

I feel trance-like, almost comatose, like nothing's real, like I'm not actually here. I feel like I'm drowning in a sea of my own invisibility. I scratch the inside of my arm to make sure I'm awake, that I'm really here. Maybe subconsciously, I'd kind of been fearing to receive this news anyway, but actually hearing it—having Mr. Murray say it out loud over the intercom like that—makes it real, makes it official. It totally obliterates any possibility that maybe this has all been nothing but a bad dream. And suddenly, an image of Justin comes floating back to my mind, his preoccupation yesterday when they'd sent me to his second period class to get him. My God! And what was it that I'd said to him? '*I don't know what you did. But it must be something pretty bad because they said your mother's on her way over here now.*' I cannot believe I said something so crass, so unfeeling, like that. Why hadn't I thought before I'd teased him? I feel worse now than I've ever felt before in my life, and there's nothing I can do to make it go away, to take back what I said to him.

"Honey, you didn't know," Mama tells me. I am standing in the student lounge again, trying to wrap the silver phone cord around my wrist, but it doesn't bend.

"Why don't you send him a card?" Mama suggests. "It would be a nice thing to do, and I'm sure he knows you didn't mean it like that, anyway."

After school, I go to pick one out. Though I'm not a very experienced driver yet, having just recently gotten my license, Mama still lets me take the Impala up to the shopping center, to the drug store where I also have an after school job, though I'm off today. She doesn't even make me put 'gas money' in the mayonnaise jar this time. That had been her's and Daddy's wonderful idea in the first place—to have a gas jar that we have to put money in before we could just jump in the car and go wherever we wanted. The idea is to teach us about the expenses of a car, to make us understand that they require constant money for maintenance and upkeep. They feel this is very important since we will have our own cars one day. In reality, the jar is a pain in the butt, and it is nickel and diming us to pieces. She has even made a label for us, which is taped right to the front. It tells us the cost for each destination we might take; like, for instance, Eastgate Shopping Center is 25 cents. And so is North Hills Mall, since they are both roughly about the same distance from the house. But if we want to go to Crabtree Valley Mall though, that's a 35-cent trip because it's further down, a whole other exit past North Hills. And if we want to go somewhere that is not already posted on the jar? Then we have to ask Mama, who will then calculate the mileage, thus be able to give us an accurate quote beforehand of what we will owe for the destination. Across the bottom of the jar, there is a handwritten addendum that clearly reads, '*No pennies, and no IOU's accepted.*' Unfortunately, she knows us all-too well.

I look for a very long time before I find a card that says how I feel; one that's not cheesy, and I know when I find it that this is the one; '*Sometimes it's important to know that others truly care.*' It's very simple, but it's exactly what I want. I take it to the cash register and pay for it, then home, where I sign it and put it in the matching envelope, addressing it to Justin.

"Why don't you go back and put 'and family' after his name?" Mama suggests.

I grimace from the sour taste of the stamp, and as I stick it to the corner, I say, "Because I want him to know that I'm thinking about *him*. That I didn't mean what I said the other day."

"Well, I'm sure he knows that," Mama tells me. "But don't you want to include the whole family at a time like this?"

I shrug, then pick up my pen, writing in the words as neatly as I can in the space that's left over. But then I sit back, looking disgustedly at my handiwork.

"See, now it looks like I just squeezed them in, anyway. Like they didn't really matter in the first place."

"No, it doesn't," she tells me. "It looks like maybe you just misjudged the amount of room you had to write in, that's all. Now go put it in the mailbox and quit worrying. It's the thought that counts, anyway."

* * *

Donna's wake is the first one I've ever been to. I am afraid to go by myself, so my new boyfriend offers to go with me. When he arrives to pick me up, he is wearing an outdated tie and sports coat with khaki pants—probably the only dress pants he has. We both look at the tie, grinning.

He shrugs. "It's my father's."

Still, I reach up and hug him, anyway because it's all very special. It's like Mama said; it's the though that counts.

We drive to the funeral home in his old mufflerless Nova, and I hold my breath as we pull into the meticulously kept parking lot, praying earnestly that it won't backfire this time when he turns off the ignition. And though it does sputter and cough a little, overall, my prayers are pretty much answered.

At the front of the chapel, there is a carefully poised casket, and I know instinctively that Donna is placed there. Her best friend, Sharon, is kneeling in front of the casket, and she appears to be saying some last words—words of consolation—to her friend. Whether this is for Donna's sake or for Sharon's I'm not sure. All I know is that it makes this terrible lump come up in my throat, and I can't figure out why I ever came here to begin with. There's no way I can walk up that aisle, no way I can look at her. I turn away from Sharon, from Donna, and in the front row of pews, I catch the distraught eyes of her mother. And seeing her mother that way, in so much pain, it makes me realize that I have no right to feel the way I do. Because other than just knowing Donna from the neighborhood and from school, I have no ties with her at all. Not like these people do, not like her friends and family. I am suddenly terribly embarrassed, hoping fervently that her mother doesn't think I'm here simply to gawk, and knowing I can't go through with this, I quickly grab my boyfriend's hand, saying, "Let's get out of here!"

Back in the car, I reach to turn on the radio, trying to distract myself from the terrible feeling—from images of black holes, infinity and non-existence. There is something new by Sting playing; a cut off his latest album, 'Dream of the Blue Turtles.' I think its called 'Fortress Around Your Heart.' Something like that. Though I've heard it several times before, this time the experience is somehow different. And I realize that from now on, every time I hear this song, I will think of Donna, I will remember the way her mother's eyes looked in the chapel tonight.

* * *

Now today, after more than two decades have passed, I still know how truly right I was.

At Fort Macon, Atlantic Beach—a family trip while Kay is home from college (Kay is wearing a T-shirt sporting the logo of the coolest radio station around— WKNC, Rock 88)

ISLAND OF THE MISFITS

The anxiety attacks are coming harder, faster. I can barely manage to pull off a whole day at school anymore. I feel like I'm constantly walking across a minefield, and I don't know if the next step I take will be the last. Nothing seems to matter anymore, not if this is what it's all coming to. I mean, what's the point in life at all if its sole purpose is simply to lead you to death?

I write Kay a letter, telling her about what happened. She writes back, saying she knows exactly how I feel because when she'd been at Robinscrest, two girls that she'd known there—they were sisters—had been killed, too, on their way to school one morning. It was right after a big snowstorm, on the very morning, in fact, that the schools were scheduled to re-open, and the older of the two sisters was driving them both to school. They'd hit an icy patch on a small bridge, just feet away from the school's back entrance gates.

The car had slid over the edge into the half-frozen creek below, and trapped inside, the two injured sisters had ended up ultimately drowning. Kay says at their daughters' funeral, the parents had insisted that 'Stairway to Heaven' be played because the girls had loved that song so much. She remembers that right afterwards, there was an article in the paper about the accident, how it said the girls had done nothing wrong at all—how they hadn't been speeding, or driving carelessly, nothing like that—it was just one of those terrible tragedies that sometimes happen for reasons we can't always know, and that for the first time the media's been aware of, rock music had been included as an integral part of the funeral service.

I think of Donna constantly now, the irony eating away at my insides; the fact that it actually took her death to make me finally realize her worth. Why do we all take each other for granted like that?

It's a Thursday, and I am enduring second period. Though the Fear has me utterly shaking clear down to the bone, I am determined to make it through the day. And I sit there in the confining desk, sweating, until the intenseness absolutely becomes more than I can bear. Then, with nothing else to do, I ask to go to the bathroom.

In the empty hallway, my legs feel like rubber underneath me, like maybe they aren't really there. Still, I continue to walk on, to push forward out of desperate necessity, and as I pass by classrooms in session, I catch bits and pieces of the lessons going on in each one.

I manage to make it as far as the bathroom door, where I sink down to the floor instead. I am hyperventilating again, and my ears are ringing so loudly I can barely hear outside my own consciousness. My hands are drawn up so tight that I can't even open my fingers anymore. I am only vaguely aware of the two teachers who come out into the hall to try to help me. Finally, as my senses begin to return, the principal comes rushing down the corridor. He takes my arm, stands me up, then escorts me to the office, himself, where he wastes no time at all calling my mother. I guess after having another student die so suddenly—after losing Donna just a week ago—he is still pretty much freaked out over the situation. I mean, who wouldn't be? I want to tell him not to worry, that this is how I live, that it's very much an inclusion in my day-to-day activities, that this is completely normal for me. But I am too embarrassed to utter a word. How could I have let this happen again? It's like I have no control over myself or something, and for the life of me, I can't understand why I can't simply just *do* the normal things that other people can? It can't be that hard.

When Mama gets to school to pick me up, I feel like an absolute neon failure.

"I'm sorry," I tell her defeatedly, dropping my books on the seat beside me. I lean back against the headrest, closing my eyes as she pulls out of the parking lot. This morning's episode has left me completely drained, and I simply don't have the energy to try to explain things any further. Mama seems to sense my level of stress, and though she doesn't understand it, she still tries to do things that'll take my mind off it, that'll make me feel better.

"You want to stop at McDonald's and get a biscuit?" she suggests. "It's early enough that they'll still be serving breakfast."

"Sure," I tell her. But I don't know if I'll be able to eat it or not.

After we pull through the drive-thru, we go home, and I take my biscuit and Coke back to my room. I feel better after eating, but suddenly very tired, so I lie down on my bed to take a nap.

It is late afternoon when I finally wake up, and I stumble into the bathroom to brush my teeth, try to straighten out my hair. I've had it permed a few weeks ago, which is really 'in' this year, but after sleeping on it, it always looks like a mop. Right then, I decide that there are only two things I'd want to change if I had the opportunity to come back reincarnated; first, I'd be normal and not have all these irrational fears and compulsions going on all the time. I'd be just like everyone else. And secondly, I'd definitely have good hair this time around.

In the kitchen, I sit down at the table. Mama is cooking supper, and looks up to find me there.

"You must've been more tired than you thought," she tells me.

I stifle a yawn, saying, "I guess."

"I know you've been under a lot of stress lately, and Daddy and I discussed it. We've decided to let you take the karate classes you've been asking about."

I look up at her, surprised. "You *have*?" Because I never thought they'd go for it, that they'd say it was too dangerous. But ever since I've known my boyfriend, his younger brother has been a member of their family's local karate class, and I'd absolutely fallen in love with the concept of Martial Arts.

"Yes," she nods. "We both think it would actually be good for you to get some of that energy out. Then maybe you won't feel so stressed all the time."

I have only one question. "When can I start?"

Mama puts the lid back on the potatoes she's been stirring. "Well, I've done some calling around to see what's available, and there's a class at the Exchange Park—the same place you and Kay took baton lessons—every Tuesday and Thursday night, from 7:30 to 9:00. They say the teacher's pretty good, and he also has a children's class on Saturday mornings, but I figured you'd probably like the adult class better."

Who was she kidding? I'd absolutely turn into the next Bruce Lee! I'd be so good they'd end up putting me in all the up and coming new movies. Maybe I'd even get a starring role in the next James Bond flick. And, of course, since everyone would know about my karate expertise, about how lethally dangerous I could be, Janey would never ever try to pick on me again.

"So when can I start?" I repeat excitedly.

"Well, I think you have to sign up first. But if you want, you can go and watch tonight."

I jump up from the table.

"*After* supper," Mama tells me. "They're going to be there until 9:00."

Before supper though, Mama *does* let me take the car up to North Hills Mall to buy a pair of shoes I'd been saving up my paychecks for; these radical all-black, high-top tennis shoes, made by this company, Ciao, who carried a really cool line of new-wave-looking shoes. Daddy'd first thought the price was completely ridiculous just for a pair of tennis shoes, but Mama reminds him that this is why I have an after-school job—so I can afford to buy the trendy new clothes all the kids are wearing now.

"What's wrong with a pair of tennis shoes from K-Mart?" he'd asked. "They do the same thing, cover your feet the same way."

"Dad-*dy!*" I moan. "You just don't *do* that!"

"Why not?" he continues. "If you wear your pants long enough, they're going to cover up your shoes, anyway, and then no one will even see them. They won't have any idea how much you spent."

"That's not the point!" I argue. "The ones from K-Mart are only *copies*! And you can tell a difference! Just ask anyone! Besides, they don't say 'Ciao' on the back heel like the *real* ones do."

"Can't you just put it on there, yourself? I've got any color of Testor's model paint out in the train room that you could possibly want."

Though I know he's pretty much kidding, it is still insight into the fact that he has absolutely no clue how you're supposed to do things today, especially in fashion—that he grew up in 'Leave It to Beaver Land,' too, just like Mama. But when I point this out to him, he says, "How can you say I don't know about fashion? I've got a whole closet full of blue oxford shirts and khaki pants."

"Daddy—"

"Seriously, think about it," Daddy tells me, matter-of-factly. "It makes a lot of sense. If you wear the same thing everyday, you don't have to waste all that time in the mornings, trying to make decisions. Or worrying about whether or not something matches."

I roll my eyes, deciding it's completely pointless—not to mention totally hopeless. Because no matter how you cut it, Daddy just doesn't see things the way the real world does, the sad part being that he probably never will. Nor does he see anything wrong with this. And I can only imagine how much worse it'd actually get if I started doing that crap—wearing the same stupid outfit to school every day. It'd be something akin to pulling out the 'Bobby Sherman' lunchbox again. It never ceases to amaze me how it's possible that two complete *dorks* like them could actually produce a kid as normal as me. I mean, sure, I have my weirdness going on—the anxiety attacks and all—but at least I can honestly say I'm not a *dork*.

After supper, Mama lets me take the car to the Exchange Park. But before I leave, she hands me a five-dollar bill, telling me to stop by the corner service station first and put some gas in it. I hate to pump gas worse than anything, but I don't argue with her because she is letting me do something I've been absolutely dying to do for over a year now, and that doesn't usually happen.

In the Exchange Park's office, the lady behind the desk directs me to the large classroom at the end of the hall—the same one where Kay and I had taken baton lessons, just like Mama'd said. I don't find the class there, though. Instead, they are in the window-lined room off the hallway. I watch warily through the glass. Though I am intrigued, I am also a little put off. I didn't expect them to look so vicious or to sound so mean. I begin to think that maybe I can't handle this after all, that maybe it's a big mistake, coming here. Maybe I should go home. Just then, the instructor notices me standing there in the hallway, watching, and he opens the door, invites me in. He is nice-looking, energetic. I figure he is probably in his late 20's, and his confidence is contagious.

"We normally work out in the back," he tells me pointing in the direction of the baton room. "But once a month, the bridge club has its tournament here, and they use that room, too. Usually, it runs over, and it's about 8:00 or so before we can get in the big room."

I study the other students in the class, some wearing black outfits, others wearing white, varying colors of belts tied around their waists. There is one other girl in the class whom I notice right away, and immediately, I am intimidated.

The instructor introduces himself as Jamey Everett, and he asks my name in return. I tell him, still preoccupied with the loud explosive voices and the vicious kicks going on in the room all around me.

"So what do you think?" Jamey asks me.

I like the way he looks at me when he talks—very directly, right into my eyes—like I am this important individual, not just some stupid high school kid.

I shrug. "I dunno. They sound kinda mean to me."

He laughs. "They're not really that mean. Only when I first let them out of the closet. They generally calm down a little while after that."

"Hey, you wanna work out with us?" he suddenly suggests.

The idea frightens me, and I quickly decline, pointing out that I don't have a suit to wear. "And besides," I add. "I'm afraid I might get hurt since I don't know what to do yet."

He shakes his head, telling me matter-of-factly, "That's not going to happen in here. *Nobody* is going to hurt you. Believe me—they *know* how to pull their punches, how to control their power. And if they *don't* know that by now, then they can fall out and do push-ups on their knuckles until they *do*—until they *learn* how."

The bridge club has finally let out, and the members, mostly older people, fill the hallway, laughing and talking as they leave.

"Okay guys," Jamey calls, raising his voice. "Let's go 'fall in' in the other room."

I watch the students cease their current activities, gather their belongings—gym bags, towels, shoes. They joke with each other as they file out of the room, and the girl smiles at me as she walks past.

Jamey opens the utility closet right outside the doorway of the classroom. He motions for me to come with him. Inside, he reaches up on a shelf and hands me a suit—a pair of white karate pants with black stripes down the sides, and a black jacket. I open it up, look at it, discover the most intricate and beautifully embroidered dragon I have ever seen. I raise my eyes, meet his again.

"This was my first gi," he tells me seriously. "I want you to wear it until I can get one in your size."

I back away, saying, "No, no. I couldn't—I mean, I just *couldn't*! Suppose I—"

But he places the suit in my hands, saying, "I'd be *honored* for you to wear it."

I don't know what to say, and I look up at him again.

"You can go change in the bathroom," he tells me, then adds, "By the way, most women leave their T-shirts on under their gi's."

"Okay," I tell him, then realize that I am wearing a long-sleeved blouse-type shirt. "But I only have this one," I add, looking down at the blouse.

"I'm sure I have one in here somewhere."

He goes back into the closet returning with a clean T-shirt, which he tosses at me.

"See you back in five," he tells me.

In the bathroom, I stand on the long, wooden bench, trying to view the karate suit in the mirror over the sink. It looks good on me, and I feel a shiver, a thrill of pride run through me.

Back in the hallway, Jamey holds out a folded white belt to me, saying, "This is the most important rank you will ever wear. Before you earn your way out of it, it will be full of your sweat, your hard work, your frustration, even your tears. It will become a part of you and everything you do."

I reach to take the belt from his hand.

"You must never wash your belt," he tells me. "You can wash your gi as much as you want, but never your belt. You should never wash away all that hard work. That's how black belts came about in ancient martial arts. When their belts got dirty enough to actually appear black, then that's when they knew when they'd finally gotten there—when they'd become a genuine black belt."

I never knew that.

He shows me the proper way to tie the belt around my waist, how to find its center, place it over my belly button, then wrap it around twice tying the ends in front. Still, they hang down almost to my knees.

When we walk into the classroom, he bows in the doorway, motioning for me to do the same.

"We always rey into the classroom whenever we enter or leave. It shows respect for the art, for the training ground, itself—which is correctly referred to as the *Dojo*."

I feel awkward at first, but non-conformity is never even a passing thought as I follow his lead. I have this acute feeling that I am on the verge of discovering something really great, something that will change my life forever.

When I return home after class, Mama and Daddy get this huge kick out of my karate outfit.

"Look, John! She actually looks *mean*! Look at her karate suit!"

"It's not a *karate* suit," I inform her, matter-of-factly. "It's called a '*gi*.'"

"Oh—okay," Mama says carefully.

"Did you learn anything?" Daddy asks.

"I learned how to do a round-house kick."

"Is that when you spin around backwards?" Daddy asks.

"No, *that's* a spinning back kick," I further inform him. "A round-house is when you pivot around on your *front* foot first and then kick with your *back* leg, like this." And I demonstrate for him.

Mama clasps her hands together, saying, "John, go get the camera!"

I only let them take my picture because they are allowing me to go to the class in the first place.

I can hardly wait for the following Tuesday night, and when it finally arrives, I am at karate early, stretching out on the classroom floor with the rest of the students. I have always been pretty limber, so this is something I don't have to work very hard at. I soon discover that the other girl in the class is pretty flexible, too, and we sit together on the floor in similar Chinese splits, talking. I learn that the girl's name is Ariel, that she is fourteen, and that she has a twin sister, though they are not identical. Whereas Ariel has sandy-colored naturally curly hair that hangs down to her shoulders, Mariel in contrast, is olive-completed, with straight black hair and brown eyes.

While we wait for the instructor to arrive, I study the other students in the room.

There is a guy with a mustache and a barrel-like chest who is not very tall, and he sort of reminds me of a bulldog. There is another guy who is slightly older, much taller, with sandy-colored hair down to his shoulders and a close-trimmed beard. He reminds me of a hippy, and I get the feeling he is very laid-back, very down-to-earth.

A third guy is practicing kicks on the huge bag hanging in the back corner, and I am somewhat amazed at his strength, at the ability he has to move the bag, especially since he isn't much taller than the bulldog. At first, I'd thought he was foreign—Saudi-Arabian or something like that because he has very dark skin and strongly defined features. But when Jamey'd addressed him last week, asking him to take me to the back of the room and teach me the beginning basic blocks, he'd called him by 'Jim,' a totally American name, and the guy'd ended up having no accent at all.

Of the other students who have arrived so far, there is another long-haired guy who is wearing a bandana tied around his forehead. He is practicing these dance-like routines which Ariel tells me are called 'katas.' She goes on to explain that there is a series of related katas that I will have to learn in order to earn my next rank. I mark this in my mental notebook.

When Jamey arrives, he acts very happy to see me again.

"But then I knew you'd come back if I loaned you my special gi," he says.

I have to laugh at that. What he doesn't know is the reality of it all; now that I've discovered karate, wild horses couldn't keep me away. Because finally, I think I have found my niche, something I can be successful at, somewhere that I can fit in.

Class, itself, is very strenuous. It's just as much mental conditioning as it is physical conditioning, and in the first few classes, I learn that yes, I *can* do 25 repetitious push-ups, and on my knuckles, too, at that. Because here, behind the closed door of the karate class, 'no' is not an option, the concept of 'can't' non-existent. It is a whole different world in here, and if Jamey'd told us to go out and walk on water, I truly believe we would've been able to do it. The power of mind-over-matter is completely extreme, and Jamey knows this, putting up with nothing at all. He pushes us to the very edge, and when we finally get there, he shoves us right over it, just so we can learn what it feels like to fall. If you got hot, felt light-headed? Get over it! Got to throw up due to the over-vigorous work-out? Swallow it. And if you happened to get thirsty? "Well, I imagine the people in Hell want ice water, too. But I'll bet your bottom dollar they aren't stupid enough to ask for it!"

We learn to conform, but not to cower. It is constantly pounded into our heads that we are important, that all people are important, that no one is ever better than anyone else. We are taught not only to show respect, but to *expect* respect. I learn to control my emotions. I learn how far I can be pushed and never lose my temper. We are conditioned not to get intimidated, never to give anyone else that kind of power over us. And when he asks me a question in class, if my voice happens to waver, to raise uncertainly at the end of my answer, he booms loudly, "Are you *asking* me or *telling* me?"

"Telling . . . . ?"

"Then *tell* me, damnit! *Tell* me! You *know* the answer to that! Don't *ever* let anyone take that away from you! You've got to remember—*always* remember—that *you* are your *own* source of power. God *gave* you that ability, that *gift*, and he *did* it with the expectation that you would use it wisely!"

I learn that not only can I hold my arms out to the side for over an hour, that the idea of 'tired' is just an illusion of the brain, that 'pain' is only a suggestion which we have the power to turn away from and ignore, but that I am also able to transfer that inner strength to other areas of my life. I learn to start controlling the anxiety attacks by not giving in to them, by realizing that I am my own strength, that I have the power to control what happens in my life. And this also helps in my incessant touching of objects and repetitive behavior. Slowly, I am doing something that I've never been able to do before— I am gaining control over my life. And it feels absolutely great to stare an anxiety attack right down in the face, tell it to go to Hell, and then do exactly what it is I want to do with no reservations, with no second thoughts. I am learning that there is nothing to be afraid of, that we create our own strength, and fear can only exist in those areas where we *allow* it to enter, when we elect to give up our power to it. I begin to feel like a new person, like the person I've always known was suppressed deep down inside of me, and as I emerge from my protective shell of Fear, I am angry—terribly, terribly angry. I want my life back—every bit of it. Every single one of the grueling years I'd been cheated out of, been forced to suffer, to endure the torture of my own mind. And this new person who is slowly emerging is out for blood, vows to avenge all the wrongs I've been dealt in life.

And come Hell or high water, I will get it—from whomever or whatever I discover has had the absolute *balls* to make me live my life in this miserable, inhumane manner. The power of my own anger is startling, and I let it take over, let it take up for me—make up for all the years that I couldn't take up for myself. It is not just an awakening, but an actual *re-birth* of sorts, and I am going to live my life to the fullest, and then some. I will find a way to take back everything that the Fear dared to take from me, even if it kills me.

Though class, itself, is thoroughly intense, *after* class is another matter. We all hang around in the hallway, talking, laughing, and when it's time for the Exchange Center to close up for the night, we simply move the party out to the parking lot where we continue our bonding process. We are a strange group of sorts, probably people who would never even choose each other's company for simple friendship had we not all been connected by this common bond, by this unidentified passion we share for the precious knowledge we simply term as 'karate.' Each of us here has our own personal issues to deal with, our own demons to defeat. Like one of the guys in class has always had trouble controlling his temper. And another one has been bullied since grammar school. Still, others here suffer from a painful level of shyness, and there are even some who've just never fit in, for whatever reason. And then, of course, there is me, having dealt with what's felt like my own prison of insanity for as far back as I can remember. It kind of reminds me of that Christmas special—the one that's come on TV every single year ever since I was a little kid—the one where all the broken toys are banished to the 'Island of the Misfits.' But once there, their deficiencies no longer matter, in fact, they end up becoming the unique qualities and characteristics that define who they ultimately are—what they will later grow to become. And like that simple story, once we enter the classroom door, once we stand on the threshold and rey in, everything else that exists out there in the real world is completely shut out. All is totally forgotten, and we allow ourselves to become the very things we've always wanted to be; brave, strong-willed, confident. And the raw truth of the matter is, as long as *we* believe it, ourselves, there is no question whatsoever of its impending reality. The self-images that we are building begin to leak from the class, to follow us, to seep into our everyday lives, and what we've wishfully created as our *perceived* realties, slowly become our *physical* realities. It's this total high in a world that for each one of us, has at times, been otherwise painful.

Mama and Daddy are amazed at my unexpected transformation. They claim I am a different person now. I no longer have the same problems with attending school anymore. Sure, I can endure it. It has nothing over me. Absolutely nothing. Instead, I have been blessed with the insight to recognize that school, itself, is just a concept—nothing more; that there are much more important things out in this world—a world where we have thus far been so limited in our ignorant existence. I feel sorry for the other students at Sanderson High School who have no idea about this, who still believe that what goes on in school determines their whole world. Sometimes, I feel like I should share that knowledge with them, but for the most part, I know it would be pointless. Because none of these people would get it—would probably not even have the ability to acquire the knowledge in the first place. I can't help but feel sorry for them. How lost they must be, yet how sad that they aren't even aware of their skewed sense of direction.

Many nights after class, Jamey asks me to stay on and perform my 'perfect' kicks for him over and over while he marvels at my uncanny ability. Sometimes we even stay later than the rest of the group, and on these nights, after the recreation center closes, Jamey and I hang around and talk in the parking lot. Later, at his suggestion, we go and sit in his car where it is warmer, where we discuss the philosophy of life, talk about how much better the world would be if everybody simply succumbed to this same philosophy. I tell him about Donna and how she died so unexpectedly, about the anxiety attacks, about the Fear. About no matter how hard I try, I never seem to fit in anywhere. He understands. He's been there. He wants to be my friend. He wants to understand all of my interests, no matter what they are. And in the warm darkness of the car, as I reveal these things to him, he asks me if I am a virgin.

Jamey thinks a lot of me, tells me that I am a very special person—tells me that this is something I just don't realize about myself yet. But when I do—when that revelation finally hits home—he says the world better watch out! And he will always be there for me—always, no matter what—because he wants to help me achieve that level of success, regardless of what it takes. His enthusiasm is infectious, and he tells me that I have the potential to become everything I want to be and then some. He is careful to point out that not only am I beautiful, but also very smart with a natural knack—a true talent to be envied—in karate. And he claims with a combination like that, you simply can't lose. It's just not a possibility. These intimate talks that we share become very important to me, and I want to thank him for everything he's done for me, to tell him how much it's truly meant to have a friend like him in my life. But unfortunately, I realize that there are simply no words to express the gratitude I feel. The only way I know to repay him is to be the best I can be, both in and out of class. I want to make him proud of me. He says he already is, that he knows I am going to be his first female black belt.

At home, I am floating around on my new-found success, even though it is shadowed by this intense anger that I can't seem to ignore, that I'm not sure what to do with.

By Christmas, I have been in class for almost two months, and I feel like I've always known these people. They are the group of friends I've always been searching for. On Christmas Eve, when I am working at my part-time job in the mall—at a trendy clothing store—Jamey shows up with a friend. I am beside myself, completely excited to see him. He saunters through the doorway, casually telling me that they've just eaten lunch upstairs at the K&W Cafeteria, and now they are getting ready to do some last-minute shopping.

"I guess you don't mind pushing it right down to the wire, huh?" I ask him as I straighten a row of hangers in a sweater display.

"You gotta do what you gotta do," he tells me. As always, he is dressed to the nines, right down to the manner in which his shirt sleeves are rolled under, just up past the wrist. Then, as if in contradiction to his immaculate appearance, he openly reaches up to switch the gnawed toothpick in his mouth from one side to the other. For some reason, this bothers me, but immediately, I choose not to study it any further. I am surprised at myself in the first place for even allowing such narrow-minded thoughts to enter my head at all.

"Hey, we're having a little get-together at my house later this evening," he suddenly says. "A Christmas party. Why don't you come?"

"I don't know. I mean, will I even know anyone there?"

"Sure, you will!" he gushes. "Everybody from karate is going to be there. And I'd really hate for you to miss it. We've got all this food, all these video games lined up—the whole nine-yards. It'll be fun."

"Sure," I hear myself saying. "But I don't get off work until 6:00, and then we always open presents after supper on Christmas Eve."

"That's great!" he gushes. "That's perfect! Because the party's not even starting till around 7:30 or so. You'll have plenty of time."

"I'll have to ask my mother," I tell him. "To see if she minds if I go somewhere on Christmas Eve. And also if I can even take the car out again, too."

He winks. "I'll see you there."

Then they are gone.

* * *

We are having record-cold temperatures tonight. Mama lets me go to the party anyway though, telling me drive carefully, to watch out for icy patches on the road, and to just be home by 11:00.

"Santa can't stay up much later than that," she explains.

I park her car in the lot outside of Jamey's townhouse. Strangely, though, I don't see any of the other students' cars here yet—only Jamey's plush El Dorado, which is hooked up on battery cables that are running through his kitchen window.

I look down, check myself one last time, before ringing his bell. Over my shoulder, I am proudly carrying the new Aigner pocketbook that Mama and Daddy gave me for Christmas. The one I've been wanting for absolute ever.

He opens the door right away, as if he's been waiting.

"I knew you'd make it!" And the size of his smile makes me forget momentarily about the other guests who have not yet arrived.

"Is your car broken?" I ask as we walk past his kitchen towards the living room.

"No," he sighs. "It's just a diesel, and whenever it gets real cold like this, I have to keep the battery on a charger. Otherwise, it won't start."

"That's not good," I tell him.

"No, I've been thinking about trading it in. On one of those new Corvettes."

"You mean the one that's shaped like a bullet?" I ask. "The one that just came out for *next* year?"

He shrugs nonchalantly. "Yeah, that's it."

"That'd be really cool!" I gush.

He winks, saying, "Only if you'd do me the honor of going for a ride in it first."

In his living room, the TV is on, and there is a bowl of popcorn waiting on the coffee table. Still, something feels out-of-place, and I suddenly remember to ask, "Where is everybody?"

"Oh, they just haven't gotten here yet," he explains, sinking down across from me on the huge couch.

"Are they coming?" I ask.

"I'm sure they will. If they can get away and all."

"But I thought—"

"So how was work?" he asks playfully.

"Okay. Boring as usual," I tell him. "So where's your wife?"

"Oh, she's gone out of town. She went home for the holidays."

"Well, I think I should probably go, too," I tell him, standing up. "My mother wouldn't want—"

"But you just got here."

"I know, but—"

"Please stay. Just for a little while."

"Let me at least call her and—"

"Look," he tells me straight-up, and I notice that he sounds kind of sad. "It's Christmas, and I'm here all by myself. My wife's gone—left me alone for the holidays, and I'm not even sure if anyone else from karate is going to be able to get here or not. I mean, they *said* they were coming, but I guess they've just gotten tied up or something. All I want—I mean, I just don't want to be alone on Christmas."

I study him for a moment.

"Please stay just a little while. You'll be with your family all night after you get home, and then all day tomorrow, too. What'll a couple of hours hurt?"

I shrug. I want to tell him that it's not about his being *lonely* at all, but instead about his being *alone* that my mother wouldn't like. Still, when I look at him, I see it in his eyes—how lonely and sad he truly feels—and I find myself putting my pocketbook back down, though it's against my better judgment. I know better than this—know how Mama'd react to this type of situation, and I don't even want to think about the fact that I'm driving *her* car while simultaneously deceiving her.

Jamey points to my new pocketbook, asking, "Did you get that for Christmas?"

I glance down at the clean new leather. "Yes. It was a gift from my parents."

"Well, somebody has good taste—either you or them."

"I picked it out," I tell him, proudly.

"I figured you did."

"How come?" I ask.

"Because I can just tell you're that kind of person—very stylish, very concerned with your appearance, very conscientious. I've always known. I can tell by the way you dress, by the way you wear your hair. You're going to make it one day. Whatever it is you end up deciding to do with your life, you're going to make it big—*real* big."

I am feeling a little entranced. "How do you know?"

"I can just tell by the way you *carry* yourself, by the person you *are*. You will always have nothing but the very finest of things in life."

He offers me some popcorn, then goes into the kitchen, returning with two stadium cups filled with Coke. I hang out until it's getting pretty close to curfew.

"I'd better be going," I finally tell him. "My mother told me to be home by 11:00."

"But it's just 10:30," he points out, indicating the stylishly thin gold watch on his wrist.

"I know, but I've still got to drive home."

"You don't live in Garner or Apex, do you?"

"No—"

"Then why is it going to take you thirty minutes to drive home?"

I stay a little longer even though it makes me nervous. I figure that since it's been pretty much dry all day, maybe there won't be any icy patches on the roads, and then I can rush home, still make it there by 11:00 if I really try.

When I finally insist that I really *do* have to leave, I am putting my coat on against his protests when the phone rings.

"She just left," I hear him say, and his voice has taken back on the tone of an authoritative, responsible adult. "She should probably be getting home in the next few minutes or so."

He hangs up the receiver, and I look at him questiongly.

"That was your parents," he tells me, winking. "They just wanted to make sure you'd left already, that everything was okay."

For some reason, this bothers me, too. Not that Mama and Daddy had felt the need to actually look up his number in the phone book and to call over here like that.

They are not invasive people and have always been very good about trusting us, about giving us the benefit of the doubt. In return, their only expectation has been that we always use our best judgment. But it's more about the fact that I worried them enough to where they felt they *had* to check up on me. I feel embarrassed, frustrated, but still, I can only be angry at myself. Because I certainly can't be mad at Jamey, especially when all he wanted was some simple company on Christmas. And all the scenarios that I manage to come up with on the drive home, all the different ways I play it out in my mind, try to explain the situation to them, claim that I was only doing what any other friend would do, I still can't hide from the fact that I am ultimately responsible for my own choices. Regardless, it's still all about me, and I feel completely torn, misunderstood. And as I turn into the driveway, I can't exactly pinpoint the thing that's really bothering me. But I feel like I have just done my very best work—finally finished an important school project—and then turned around and completely given it to someone else for the grade.

* * *

Interestingly, two of the guys in karate class have actually asked for my phone number, and I am flattered by all the attention suddenly showered on me. The fact that both of the guys vying for my attention are older than me only serves to heighten my sense of sophistication. The only thing is, these guys turn out to have the same first name, and at first when they call, I have to play it cool, to ask what they did at work today in order to figure out which one I'm actually talking to.

Jim Number One, whom I'd originally dubbed as the 'bulldog,' takes me out to a very fancy restaurant for my birthday where he's arranged to have a private waiter, a bottle of wine, which I'm still not old enough to consume, and the table decorated with just the right amount of candle-lit roses, pending our arrival. After being made comfortable at our private table, we are served an umpteen-course meal, and when we're done eating, we don't just jump up and leave. Instead, we make an entire evening of it, talking, relaxing, enjoying the chocolate cake he'd had them bring out to me when they'd sang 'Happy Birthday' in a discreet barbershop quartet set-up. Never before in my life have I ever been treated so special, and at the end of the night, when he asks me if I want to go out again sometime, all I can think is, '*Are you kidding*?'

I have already been out with Jim Number Two one time before, the one I'd originally pegged as Iranian or Saudi-Arabian, and I am rushing around the house now, getting ready to go out with him again tonight. Like me, he really gets off on James Bond flicks, and we are going to see his latest. I think it's called 'Never Say Never

Again,' or something like that. Those movies always have such weird, pun-like titles, anyway.

Daddy eyes me from behind his newspaper as I frantically search for my other shoe.

"You going out with the 'gorilla' again tonight?"

"*No*, Daddy . . . . I'm going out with the *other* one."

"Oh, you mean the 'terrorist,'" he suggests.

"Dad-*dy*! Would you stop *saying* things like that? He's *not* even from *over* there to begin with, and besides, suppose you slip up and say something like that when he comes to the door?"

"So? He probably knows he looks like a terrorist."

"*Daddy—*"

"John, stop teasing her," Mama says, coming to my rescue. "There's nothing wrong with him. He's a very *nice-looking* little boy."

"That's the whole problem right there," Daddy informs her. "He ain't no '*little boy*!'"

"Well, *I'm* not a little girl anymore, either!" I want to stomp my foot, just like I used to do when I was younger and got really frustrated, but I refrain instead.

"As long as you live under *my* roof, you are!"

"Well, maybe I need to move out!" I tell him.

"How do you plan to support yourself?" he asks. "Especially when you haven't even finished high school yet."

I snub my nose. "I'll find a way!"

"Surely you can stand it around here for a couple more years," Daddy tells me. "Then you'll be going off to college, and you can do anything you want."

I cross my arms. "I'm not *going* to college!"

"That's fine," he says. "You don't have to. But if you don't go to college, then you're going to get a job and move out of *here*. Because I'm not having a bunch of grown kids hanging around the house, sleeping till noon, with nothing to do."

I glare. "*How* do you figure that the *two* kids you actually have *left* here suddenly amount all the way up to 'a bunch?'"

"It's your choice," he tells me, refusing to acknowledge my rational question. "It's either college or job and an apartment. But the day you become of-age, you're outta here!"

I finally locate my other shoe, underneath the kitchen table, and as I shove it on my foot, I tell him, "Don't get my hopes up too early! Because believe me, if I had someplace else to go right now, I definitely wouldn't be standing *here*!"

We are interrupted by a knock at the front door, and Daddy nods in that direction, saying, "The terrorist is here."

This time I give in, and I stomp my foot at him, anyway. As I turn to leave the room, I can hear him snickering.

"I'm glad you find this so *funny*!" I retort hotly.

"Oh, come on, Angie!" Daddy says. "I'm just playing with you. He *is* a very nice-looking boy—with nice manners, too. Why've you always got your feelings on your shoulders these days, anyway? Lighten up a little, will you?"

* * *

There are no doors left in our house without gaping holes kicked right through them. In front of my bedroom now, Daddy has hung a bed sheet because my own door has been broken so many times, it is no longer fixable. He says he is not going to spend money to put up a new one, especially when the same thing's bound to happen again.

One other thing's become pretty obvious around here, too. They suddenly love to ground me. They absolutely get off on seeing me miserable—seeing me sit around the house on a perfectly good night—when everyone else is allowed to go out. Because if they didn't, they wouldn't do it every single chance they got. They wouldn't use every single excuse they could come up with as a reason to ground me.

They claim I'm not acting like myself these days, that they don't know who I am anymore. Mama says with all this new anger constantly boiling just below the surface, she is afraid that I will end up snapping and then trying to use karate on *her*. Yeah . . . . *right*. And Daddy? He's just as bad. He says it's like I've gone and joined some kind of cult. Okay . . . . so when did *he* become the expert on this topic—the one about 'cults?' I am itching so badly to remind him about *their* 'born-again' phase— when we ate nothing but health food, when the PTL Club was the only show on TV fit to be watched, when they invited that fat, sweaty preacher over—into our *house*, no less—for the olive-oil-anointed-exorcism—the one in which I'd 'coughed up' the demon. Sorry, but if you ask me, *that's* more in-line with cornering the market on 'fruity'—with being 'cultish'—than anything I've *ever* done. Still, I don't say anything about it because I know it'd only be a waste of time. They'd never get it.

The worst of the fights start when they ask me why karate is going on so late.

"I thought class was supposed to be over by 9:00," Mama tells me one night when I walk in the door, my gym bag in tow.

"Well, sometimes it just runs over."

Mama looks at her watch. "Until 11:00? The Exchange Park doesn't even stay open that late."

"Well, sometimes we stand around and talk after class," I explain.

"Aren't you the only girl in there now?" Mama asks suspiciously.

I shrug. "What's that got to do with anything?" I should've never told her when Ariel quit. Because every time I tell her anything at all, it always comes right back around to bite me in the butt.

"You don't need to be hanging out all hours of the night with a bunch of grown *men*!" Mama tells me, then adds pointedly, "You are in *high school*!"

As if I need reminding. "So? *They* sure don't think I'm a baby!"

From behind his train magazine, I hear Daddy mumble, "Yeah— I *bet* not!"

"It's not about your being a baby," Mama explains. "It's just that you should be doing *high school* things now—going to dances and parties, going to football games—doing things with your friends."

Okay, so we're back to 'Leave It to Beaver' days. Great. I feel just like I'm in one of those retro TV commercials—the one where everything around you is black and white, and I am the only thing that actually exists in full Technicolor.

"And whatever happened to cheerleading?" Mama adds.

"I didn't *make* it!" I tell her. "Or have you *forgotten* that already?"

"One year!" She holds up her index finger, emphasizing her point. "It was just *one* year that you didn't make the squad. And what was it that woman said—the advisor up at the high school? About how much they'd like to have you if you just got your attendance up?"

How could I explain to her that karate is way beyond cheerleading? That it's so far advanced from that stupid stuff, anyway? That it's like the 'forbidden fruit,' how once you'd tried it, there's simply no way you can go back? Especially not to something as naïve as cheerleading.

Still, Mama and Daddy stand their ground. They tell me that I have to be home by 10:00 on karate nights from now on. I am defiant, humiliated. How can they even think of doing this to me? Especially when they know how important karate is, how it's helped me break away from the Fear, how it has actually become my whole *life*!

"You spend way too much time with those people, anyway," Mama tells me, dismissively.

"What's *that* supposed to mean?"

"Just that I'd like to see you take on some new interests, that's all. You're making way too much out of this—this *karate* class!"

I've reached the turning point—the one that causes me to realize the hard truth; that she just doesn't get it. And I feel totally betrayed. But then again, what had I expected? Like everyone at school, she, too, is an outsider. An alien of sorts. She is the enemy, just as much as they are.

After class, I sit in Jamey's warm car, complaining about the unfairness of it all. But Jamey helps me to understand. He explains how sometimes parents can become controlling, especially when they see their children growing up. He tells me not to worry, that these things have a way of working themselves out. He assures me that everything will be alright when they finally accept that I am my own person, and that I will decide who my friends will be. He puts his arm around me, comforting me. Lately, he likes to touch me, likes to rub my shoulders, my back. He tells me that I am totally unique, that our friendship is very special. Sometimes, he lets his hand rest on my thigh, and when he does this, he tells me how he is totally amazed—simply in awe—over the tight, strong muscles I have managed to acquire, especially being such a small person. He says not everyone can do that—that most people would absolutely kill to be both small and shapely at the same time. He tells me I am lucky, that my athletic body is a gift, too, just like my beauty and my talent. He says I should not take that lightly when making any decisions that regard my body. And tonight, when he tells me this, his hands do something a little different. They begin to roam over my stomach. I am a little startled at first because I hadn't expected it. But at his firm persistence, I finally begin to relax, to decide that that this much is okay, that this much is probably normal.

But when I feel the tips of his fingers brush lightly over my breasts, all the alarms suddenly go off at once. I jump back in the seat, shove his hands away, fumble awkwardly with my T-shirt. When had he slid it up? I feel exposed, embarrassed, and I blurt out, "No! You can't *do* that!"

But I should have never lost it like that. I know instantly that I have hurt his feelings when he looks down, says that he doesn't understand, that he'd thought we were friends.

I feel absolutely terrible! All I want to do is make things right again. How could I *do* this to him?

But he helps me to understand. He explains that friendship has to express itself if it is to survive and grow. He tells me that friends always touch each other. Hadn't I ever hugged a friend before? He is not surprised when I feebly explain that my parents have always warned me, have always said that this sort of thing wasn't right.

Though he's sorry he has to be the one to do it, *someone* has to point out to me the cold, hard truth—the fact that my parents just don't want me to have any friends.

"Think about all the times they ground you," he says. "Don't believe for one minute that they aren't doing this to try to isolate you."

"Why would they do that?" I ask, genuinely surprised.

He holds his open palms out, saying, "You already know the answer to that."

But when I only continue to look baffled, he says, "*Control*. It's all about them trying to *control* you. And as long as you *let* them, they *will*."

"But they've never been like that!" I tell him. "They've always let me make my own decisions."

He smiles, looks down, then faces me again, placing one finger underneath my chin as he says, "They just don't *want* you to think they'd do that. It's all part of the game—part of the control factor."

I feel a tear slip down my cheek. But I instantly swipe it away. I don't want it messing up my make-up, which I have been applying very liberally as of late. Because I've never been called 'beautiful' before, and I want to make sure it is true, that I live up to its expectations.

Jamey reaches for me, tucks me back into the curve of his arm, saying, "I want better for you than that. You *deserve* better."

Now he is rubbing my shoulders again. "You will have it one day, too. I can *feel* it."

He turns me around in the seat, telling me, "You can't keep shutting everybody out like this, though. At some point, you're going to have to turn loose and let *somebody* be your friend."

He pulls me tighter into his arm, sighing as he says, "I want to *be* that person."

What he is saying finally hits home, and I suddenly realize that if I can't be the kind of friend he needs, then he'll quit hanging around with me. And since everyone in class is so tight—they do absolutely everything together—if I'm no longer a friend to Jamey, then the rest of the class will no longer accept me, either. And since I have learned by now to steer clear of all those other 'silly high school girls' who just don't get it, if Jamey leaves me, too, then I'll be all alone.

So after class when we go to his car, I let him touch my stomach. I close my eyes and keep quiet when I feel his hand move up under my shirt. I don't want to hurt his feelings anymore, especially after all he's done for me. For some reason, I am humiliated, and I grow to hate myself more and more for allowing these invasive feelings to even happen.

Outside the car—away from the secret, I begin to see Jim Number Two pretty steadily. First and foremost, because I really like the guy. But also with the ulterior motive that if Jamey sees me dating someone else, then maybe he'll leave me alone. We can still be friends, of course. But just not like *that* anymore.

Inside the class, I am ignored. When it is time for my rank to be earned, Jamey says nothing about it. One night after class, I catch up with him as he is getting into his car.

"Hey, what about my brown belt?" I ask breathlessly.

He looks at me seriously. "You know you never ask about rank."

"But you said a long time ago that I'd be getting my brown belt soon."

"How long is 'a long time?' How do you measure time that's passed?"

"Come on, Jamey! I've worked hard for it, and you know it!"

He turns the keys over in the palm of his hand, kind of laughing.

"Angie, the only way you're ever going to get your brown belt is if you take your clothes off!"

I look at him. Is he serious? I can't tell for sure, but he *seems* to be joking.

"You're kidding, right?"

He shrugs, putting the keys into the ignition. "You do it for Jim. What's the difference?"

He shuts the door and drives off, leaving me standing in the parking lot.

Later, still feeling crappy from the encounter, I admit to Jim what Jamey has said to me.

"I'm sure he didn't mean it," he reassures me. "He was probably just joking. You know how he is."

"I don't think so," I tell him. "It wasn't like that. You weren't there."

"Well, next week after class, I'll ask him about it. Now quit worrying. I'm sure it's nothing but a big misunderstanding, that's all."

He pops a video in the VCR, and we become more or less engrossed in the karate flick that is playing.

* * *

"Don't *ever* bite the hand that feeds you!" Jamey tells me. "Don't *ever* do that again!"

"But you *know* you said it! And I didn't know what to think!"

"It was a *joke*! Since when did you become such a prude about handling *jokes*? I thought you were a lot more *mature* than that!"

"I didn't know it was a joke!" I protest. "I mean, what am I supposed to think? Look how long it's been since you told me I was working on my brown belt test."

"You never question the Sensei about your rank. *I* will decide when you're ready—when it's time. It's not for you to ask."

"But you said I was working on my test *months* ago!"

"*I'll* decide when it's time," he repeats over my protests. "And I can tell you right now—the more you question me about it, the longer it's going to be. Now, I'm really getting fed up with your attitude. You need to go on into class and appreciate the fact that someone is giving you the *opportunity* to learn. There aren't many Sensei's out there who would put up with all this disrespect and backtalk—with such *insolence*. Now don't make me change my mind about having you in the class."

* * *

There is this huge tournament coming up—the Battle of Atlanta—which is the biggest one on the east coast. The whole class is going down to compete—making a road trip of it. I am going, too.

"Not while you're living under *my* roof!" Daddy thunders.

"Why is it always *your* roof?" I demand. "Don't the rest of us count for anything?"

"As long as I pay the bills around here, then it *is* my roof! And as long as you stay under it, you will abide by my rules!"

"You just don't know how bad I really hate living here, do you?" I yell. "Because if you had any clue whatsoever, you wouldn't make me stay here another freakin' day!"

The fight spawned tonight is the worst one we've ever had. Daddy looses his temper, Mama cries. They tell me they can't handle the intense anger anymore.

"What is it that's eating away at you?" Mama asks. "What is it that's making you act this way?"

"Well, living *here* for starters!" I tell her, jerking the sheet over my open door.

I don't go to school the next day. No one even tries to wake me up. In fact, when I get out of bed, no one is at home at all. Martie's at school, of course, but between Daddy, who's been working second shift lately, and Mama who now has a part-time job at a printing company, one of the two of them is almost always home.

I go into the kitchen, make a huge pan of cinnamon toast. I carry my plate in the den, watch game shows on TV as I wash the toast down with a big class of Coke. I can't help but wonder where everyone is. Maybe they've abandoned me. Maybe I finally drove them all away. That'd be cool.

It is late in the afternoon when they finally come home. Mama's eyes are red, and Daddy is looking all serious, almost stoic-like.

"We found you an apartment," Mama says.

What?

"Just up the street. It's in the same neighborhood. We'll be close by incase you need anything."

"This is a *joke*, right?"

Still, their poker faces don't fall.

"You went out and found me an *apartment*? How'm I supposed to live in an *apartment*?" What the hell were they thinking?

"It's what you said you wanted," Mama tells me. "And we think it would be good for you. For all of us. It'll give you room to grow and be yourself. And it will spare Martie witnessing all these terrible fights."

"What am I supposed to do for *money*?" I demand. Because this is crazy! Unfriggin' believable!

"We've been down to see Mimi and Granddaddy," Daddy tells me. "And they say there is enough money coming into your stock account through dividends to pay your rent. They offered to pay your utility bills for you if you'd just send them through the mail."

"What's a utility bill?"

"You know—your lights, your phone."

My thoughts are colliding heavily into each other, and the questions are coming faster than I can spit them out. "Am I still going to be able to eat here?"

"We thought we'd give you grocery money every week. Then you can buy your own food. The A&P's literally right next door to the apartment complex."

I shake my head, holding up my hands as I tell them, "All those times I said I wish I could move out—I wasn't really serious! I mean, I was just mad, that's all!"

They look at each other.

"Really—I was just mad!"

Still, they don't say anything.

"You're serious, aren't you?" But it's a pointless question. Because as freaky as it sounds, I already know the answer, that the decision's already been made for me.

"So when do I have to move out?" I demand.

"Daddy and I thought we could help you get settled in this weekend."

"Settled in? This *weekend*? With what?"

"Between Mimi and us, we're getting some furniture together. We'll make it real nice—just wait and see. I promise. And Daddy and I will be right around the corner if you need us. But the whole point is, we want you to be able to grow, to become all you can, and we feel like the only way to accomplish that is to let you go—to set you free. So that you can make your own decisions—grow up without feeling so confined."

Though I've never been fired from any of the little part-time jobs that I've worked, I still figure it'd probably be very similar to this— the hopeless feelings, the bottomless pit that my stomach has become, the overwhelming shame that stems from knowing that ultimately, I caused all this. As of this very moment, I have been officially excommunicated from the family.

My first night of karate (I only let them take pictures because they were allowing me to go to the class in the first place.)

Karate became a way of life for me.

Flexibility'd never really been an issue for me . . . .

. . . . which may have been one of the reasons I excelled in karate

BE CAREFUL WHAT YOU WISH FOR

I am all alone, sitting on my same bed—the one I've had since I was a little kid—which, in contrast, is itself sitting in very unfamiliar surroundings. It is so quiet here. The sound of my own thoughts echoes off the walls around me, and the walls, themselves reek of fresh paint. The odor doesn't really bother me—only manifests itself to consistently remind me that I'm definitely not in Kansas anymore. In my hand, I am holding a Bible—the one Mama'd placed on my bed the night they'd left me here, all by myself for the first time. At the moment, I'd still wondered if this was all a cruel joke aimed at an ungrateful teenager, just to teach her a lesson. But after I read the message she has written in the front, I know that it is not. I recognize the familiar handwriting right away—from notes she has written me for school, from report cards she has signed, from grocery lists left randomly around the house. Strange that I've never really given it much thought before, but now, its familiar presence is comforting, almost soothing.

I read the message she has left for me once more. I know it will be a very long time before I open the Bible to read it again—before I feel ready.

> *Dear Angie,*
>
> *Always remember no matter where you are, Daddy and I love you very much. And so does God. He has His hand on you, and we know it. You are a very special person with so many gifts and talents and now it's time to let go of you so that you can grow and be what God would have you be. But we're glad He gave you to us for the years He did, and if we've taught you one thing—to know God—I feel all right. Don't ever forget Him; He never forgets you or leaves you (Hebrews 13:5). If you're ever afraid or alone, call on Him—pray and read His word. He'll talk to you through it. He cares. And so do we.*
>
> *Love,*
> *Mama*

When they'd left me that first night, I was down on my knees, scrubbing the bathtub. I don't know why it was suddenly so important to me—having a clean bathroom like that—but for some reason, it was. I guess I just needed to be doing something with my hands—something mundane that I wouldn't have to think about. And scrubbing seemed as good a thing as any. Mama'd leaned over to kiss me as they'd left, and I'd barely turned my face towards her—not because I didn't want her touching me—only because I didn't know how to say goodbye.

After they'd gone, it'd all felt weird, like everything was totally wrong or something. I shouldn't be here like this. Instead, I should be getting ready for bed in my own room, surrounded by the familiar things that had seemed so natural I'd never really paid attention to them before; at least until they were no longer there. The sound of Martie's bath water running upstairs, the hum of Daddy's electric trains in the shed next to my room, the awkward thumping under my bed where Sam attempted to scratch his imaginary fleas. (He'd developed a skin condition in his later life, which actually prevented fleas the privilege of taking up residence there, much to Mama's delight. But regardless, you couldn't say anything to *him* about it; he had no clue that he didn't have fleas. *He* still thought he itched.) Now, without my bed there, I wonder where he'll sleep?

The nights seem so long here. Strangely, I am not scared, only lonely, and when I'm lying there, trying to fall asleep, the fact that I am alone looms really huge. I think back, try to remember a time when I'd stayed by myself before, but I couldn't remember any at all.

I am supposed to go back to school tomorrow, just like it's any other Monday. Yeah . . . . right. And tomorrow will also be the day that pigs start to fly on gilded wings, too.

* * *

I am sitting on the makeshift couch—a day bed covered with a bright flowered sham that Mama'd made—watching soap operas. My TV is the little black and white one that Mimi'd had in her kitchen for as long as I can remember. Though familiar, it, too, looks sorely out of place in this new environment. At first I'd felt bad, taking the TV she'd had for so long and that I knew she still used. But she told me not to worry about that—Granddaddy would bring her a new one home from the store. "Besides," she'd added. "It's good company. Even if you're not watching it, you can still have it on, listening to it when you're doing things around the house, like washing dishes, or straightening up.

Washing dishes? Is she kidding? I'd sure hate to break the news to her, be the one to tell her—how the chances were probably slim to none—that I'd be throwing any type of dinner parties around here in the near future. Get *real* already! I mean, who would I even invite? Mimi, herself? And Mama? So what would we do? Sit around and share culinary secrets? Or better yet, maybe they could share their experiences regarding the best methods of dish washing with me—which detergent is most economical, the best grade of towel to use for drying. Yeah, I can see that, alright. The three of us, sitting around the little fold-out card table that Mama'd given me, complete with the cloth over it she'd made to match the one on the day bed. Cozy. *Too* cozy, if you ask me. We have nothing in common, the three of us. I mean, I'm honestly still contemplating the theory that I'd been stork-delivered. Either that or I'd hatched full-blown at some earlier point in life and just couldn't remember all the details. To me, this makes a whole lot more sense than to think I'm actually *related* to these people. Thanks anyway, but I think I'll just stick with the Chinet for now.

* * *

I have been in the apartment for nearly two weeks. I can't remember feeling this lonely or misunderstood before in my whole life. I do not have a phone yet because the service technician hasn't been by to hook it up. Most nights I walk up to the shopping center, use the pay phone to call Daddy. A couple of times, he's come to visit me, but for the most part, he wants me to get used to the way things are.

I wish something would happen to me. Something really bad. I take chances now that I never would have before. I go for walks at weird hours of the night, and on my way home, I cut through the alleyway behind the A&P rather than walk around in front where it's all lit up. I even accept a ride from this dude I don't know, and we end up driving around town in his Camaro for hours, just talking. Unfortunately, he turns out to be a really nice guy. But that's the way it goes. When you *want* to get kidnapped, raped or murdered, there is never anyone around to do it.

Now that I have unofficially dropped out of school (I haven't been back to fill out any of the necessary paperwork yet), my days consist of sleeping as late as possible, getting up and dressing—full make-up and everything—so I can then lounge around on the daybed, watching soap operas for the remainder of the afternoon. I still go to karate class, and that is the highlight of my week. Usually, one of the other students will pick me up. Sometimes, Mama lets me walk up to their house and take her car. At night when I get back, though, she drives me to my apartment because she says it isn't safe for me to be out walking that late. Yeah . . . . *Right!* If only she knew!

Jamey, after learning about my situation, comes to visit me nearly every afternoon. The office where he sells insurance is right around the corner from my apartment complex, so he says it's no big deal for him to be there. He can always get back to work real quickly if something comes up. When he comes to visit, though, he doesn't use a parking space like everyone else. Instead, he pulls his new black Corvette right up in front of the building, parking it long-ways. Sometimes he brings me lunch from Wendy's or Burger King. Other times, it's house-warming gifts, like 'Emmit,' the huge bush-like plant that now sits by the sliding doors in the living room where it can get plenty of sunshine. At first, I'd been pretty skeptical because I've never been that good with plants. In fact, if the truth be known, given the opportunity, I could probably kill kudzu. But Jamey reassures me that Emmit, being a hearty type of foliage, is almost impossible to kill. (And years later, I discover he'd been right. Because Emmit will survive three grueling moves, periods of serious drought when I forget to water him or simply up and go on a spontaneous beach trip, and a whole multitude of cats who will pass through, using his dirt to their own advantage.) Jamey still likes touching me, and luckily, this is as far as it goes in the afternoons when he visits. I wish he wouldn't do it at all, but I like the company, so I give in, let him touch me, even though it humiliates me, makes me feel dirty.

One afternoon, there is a knock at my door, but this time when I open it, it is not Jamey standing there, but instead, my sister, Martie. She is holding Sam by his leash, and the dumb dog is wagging his tail so hard he's actually beating himself in his own butt with it. I open the door, let her in, and Sam immediately jumps up, licking my face.

"O-*kay! Enough* already!" I tell him, wiping the slobber off.

"I thought he just needed to see where you lived," Martie tells me. "He goes in your room every night and lays on the floor, like he doesn't know what's going on."

"He probably doesn't," I tell her.

She releases Sam from his leash, and he trots off, exploring all the new nooks and crannies. From the bathroom, we hear him lapping out of the toilet.

"So how are you?" Martie asks, dropping down onto the daybed.

"Good, I guess," I tell her. "How about you?"

She shrugs. "The same as usual. You know Mom cries every night."

Of the three of us, Martie is the only one who calls her 'Mom.'

"Well *she's* the one who threw me out."

But neither one of us can comment on that because Sam returns then, trying to lick me in the face again. This time, I back away though, because he has serious toilet breath.

"Well, I guess we'd better be going," Martie says awkwardly. "Mom doesn't know we walked over here. She's still at work."

"I'm glad you came," I tell her. "You'll have to come over again when it gets warm. Then we can go up to the pool."

She smiles. "I'd like that."

As she is walking out the door with the dog in tow, I ask, "How's Daddy? Still wearing the blue oxford shirts?"

She rolls her eyes, and I am glad to see that I have at least taught her one useful thing over the course of my years at home.

"Actually, Mom took him shopping," she informs me. "He's got some pretty cool stuff now. Even these leather suspenders. And she made him get expensive shoes this time, too."

I have to laugh at that. "No more skips from Pic 'n' Pay? So why the change?"

She shrugs. "I don't know. But he really looks good. You should tell him that when you see him."

"I will," I say, then add, "Seriously—thanks for coming by." Because her visit has really meant a lot to me. More than she'll ever know.

Mama helping me get settled in my new apartment

*(left) Kay and me, standing outside my new apartment
(right) My first Christmas in the new apartment, where we all sat around the card table and attempted to eat what I'd attempted to cook
(Daddy is having a beer first—who can blame him?)*

Dear Angie,

Always remember no matter where you are, Daddy and I love you very much. And so does God. He has His hand on you, and we know it. You are a very special person with so many gifts and talents and now it's time to let go of you so that you can grow and be what God would have you be. But we're glad He gave you to us for the years He did, and if we've taught you one thing — to know God — I feel all right. Don't ever forget Him; He never forgets you or leaves you (Hebrews 13:5). If you're ever afraid or alone, call on Him — pray and read His word. He'll talk to you through it. He cares. And so do we.

Love,
Mama

Mama's Message
(I still have the Bible she gave me the day I moved out—I always will.)

FOUR-LEGGED FRIEND

It is only after Martie's visit that I realize exactly what's missing from my new life—a pet. And even though the apartment complex has a strict 'no pet' policy, I refuse to go another day without one.

Mama lets me borrow the car, which I drive to the local SPCA. When I tell the attendant that I want to adopt a cat, she explains that since it is not really kitten-season, they only have a couple in the back at this particular time. She tells me that if I want to wait a few weeks until spring gets here, there'll literally be kittens coming out of the woodwork. Still, I tell her that among the few they have, I am sure I can find one to adopt today, since after all, *they* need homes, too.

True to her word, there are only two cats housed in the cages in back. A small gray tabby, and a black and orange tortoise-shell. I wish I could adopt them both, but I don't have enough money to cover the adoption fee for two. As I stand in front of the cage, trying to make this impossible decision, the little tortoise-shell puts her paw through the bars, touching my hand. I reach in to stroke her whiskers, and she succumbs, purring loudly.

Her name will be 'Ginger' due to her spicy color, and at the front desk, they make me fill out all kinds of papers and sign all these forms, agreeing to keep up her routine vaccinations as well as have her spayed as soon as she is old enough. Yeah . . . . *right.* The shots are fine. But spaying her? It'll never happen. Not in a million years. Because I want her to have kittens, and then *more* kittens on top of those kittens. Then we'll all be one big, happy family.

When I return the car to Mama and Daddy, I ask if they would drive me home. I am afraid if I carry the cat in my arms that far, she will scratch me and try to get away.

"Her name's Ginger," I tell them, holding the small cat up for their inspection.

"She's cute!" Mama says, reaching to scratch underneath her soft chin. Again, she succumbs, purring loudly.

Daddy shakes his head. "She looks like a harelip."

"Da-*dy! She* can't help that she has that orange patch beside her mouth. That's just the way her fur is." I mean, leave it to Daddy! Because only *he* would think of something stupid like that.

Mama drives the two of us home, and once inside, I put Ginger down where she can explore her new surroundings. While she is doing this, I walk to the A&P to buy cat food and litter. But once on the pet isle, I end up purchasing two matching bowls for her as well as a pink collar with a jingle bell on it. I've pretty much spent my grocery money for the week, but so what? She is well worth it.

That night, after I eat a TV dinner and she has filled up on an expensive can of cat tuna, we go to bed. She settles herself on the pillow beside my head, pawing herself to sleep. And I can honestly say that this is the first night I've actually slept good since moving out of the house. I need to nurture; she needs to *be* nurtured, so from the very start, we make a pretty good match, and I decide that we'll probably be okay together, that things are finally going to work out—for both of us.

My new 'roommate'—Ginger

WAKE UP AND SMELL THE COFFEE

It's kind of ironic—I even have to admit this, myself—that I end up going back to school, especially when no one's pushing me to do it. Instead, I do this out of sheer boredom because I am so tired of sitting around here day after day, doing absolutely nothing. Honestly, I'm fresh out of new ideas at this point, so it's kind of a last resort. My teachers are pretty understanding about it though, having been alerted to my situation beforehand by the guidance counselor.

But even more ironic is the fact that a couple of my friends have actually moved into the vacant apartment across the hall, the one that's kind of caddy-cornered to mine.

In the apartment directly across from me there is this totally strange couple—an unbelievably promiscuous girl, married to a much older Arabic man who beats her on a pretty regular basis. I can't say that I blame him, though. Because if I was married to her, I'd probably beat her, too. One day when her husband was at work, she'd actually done the maintenance guy and the cablevision guy, all in the same afternoon. When I expressed surprise over her crass behavior, she'd just brushed it off, saying, "Well, neither one of *them* was as good as the plumber I had *last* week."

Okay . . . . so this is just a little too much information than I need to know, and I wish she'd spare me the disgusting details. Still, she continues to behave in this way, and many times afterwards, when her humiliated husband finds out what she's done and is ranting and raving all over the apartment, she sneaks over here, knocking on *my* door (or even my window, in some extreme cases), expecting *me* to hide her from his wrath. So today, when I hear the knock, I am more or less expecting to find her standing on the doorstep—not Buddy and his girlfriend, Liz, whom I haven't seen in a long time—at least not since I've moved out. I am beside myself, happy to see them, and I readily invite them in. But when Liz says, "Hold on—let me go shut my door," I'm like, "You moved *in* here? You *live* here now?"

Buddy laughs, then says, "Hey Angie, guess what? We're gonna be like *neighbors* now!"

I have known Buddy and Liz ever since back in the 9th grade. Buddy, who works at the A&P, also used to live across the street from a guy I'd dated, and the two of us had doubled with him and Liz several times before.

Buddy's really into fast cars, especially ones with extremely loud stereos. In fact, out of the two vehicles I've known Buddy to have (a Roadrunner back in high school and now a new bright red Camaro Z28), he has not only designed, but also constructed his own audiological concept of the car stereo, to which he is constantly adding new and improved pieces as soon as they become available. I mean, if there's a new equalizer out there on the market, Buddy will have it before it even has time to hit the shelves in the audio stores. If there's this new self-feeding in-dash tape deck, complete with its own remote control, you can find that in his car as well. And in every conceivable crack of the interior, he has installed high-powered speakers. And where there aren't any ready-made spaces? He has cut them out, himself, for the sole purpose of adding even more speakers, as he deems necessary. His car doesn't have a trunk—instead, it is a compartment to house his power booster and kicker box. And when you are outside, you can always tell he's en route because you can hear his stereo from blocks away—maybe even a mile or so if the weather conditions are just right—the bass vibrating and thumping, the treble hissing—long before the car, itself ever manifests.

When Buddy goes on his break at the A&P, he doesn't sit down and eat like you're supposed to. Instead, he walks out to the parking lot, sits in his car and listens to his stereo. Realistically, you'd probably have to say that *everyone* in or around the A&P at that particular moment in time is afforded the privilege of listening to his stereo, too. And what if they didn't like 'Night Ranger,' 'Judas Priest,' 'Billy Idol,' or just happened to have an uncannily low tolerance for the musical arrangements of 'Twisted Sister?' Then as far as Buddy was concerned, they were just shit out of luck. "It's not like this is the only A&P in Raleigh," he says. "Hell, if they don't like it, they can go right around the corner to the Food Lion over there. It's a lot cheaper, anyway." But he knows, just like everyone else around here does, that it's pretty unlikely any of the older, established residents who live in the surrounding neighborhood and who have been loyally patronizing this particular A&P ever since its creation, will ever darken the modern automatic doorway of the new Food Lion. And his response to that? "Hate it *for* 'em."

At night, we all sit over at Buddy's apartment, listening to equally loud indoor music. Because even his house stereo breeds something akin to temporary deafness in whomever happens to be residing in the surrounding area or even just passing through the next city block. It is on one of these particularly loud occasions that he receives a visit from the police.

"It's no wonder you couldn't hear me knock! I can hear your *music* from over two blocks away! Turn it down some, will you?"

But the policeman hasn't even been gone five minutes before the decibels are vibrating again, just as heavily as before, probably even more so now.

Nights are really starting to pick up around here, are actually starting to be kind of fun, since Buddy and Liz moved in. And now that the strange couple across the hall has moved away, Buddy's best friend, Robert moves into *their* old apartment, complete with his new wife in tow. As the circle grows, I begin to invite my friends over, too, many of whom I haven't even seen since the karate ordeal started. And when your old high school buddies learn that you are living in an apartment, all by yourself? And then *they* go on to leak this juicy bit of information out to every single one of your classmates as well? I can honestly say that in such an untraditional situation, there's at least one thing you can count on, point blank. Nothing—and I mean absolutely *nothing*—will ever be the same again. It's guaranteed. Not after your formal introduction to four of the most simple, mundane words that exist in the English language, which somehow, when strung together, quickly manage to amass the overwhelming power to completely change life as you've always known it;

'Can *you* say *party?*'

* * *

Out on my patio, shoved under the bushes, there is a dehydrated Christmas tree. There's no telling how long it's been there, or whose it even was. But several of the guys have hauled it out, brought it inside and propped it up in the corner. They are attempting to decorate its dried out branches with beer cans, and in those spaces that are too small or weak to accommodate an empty aluminum can, they are decoratively arranging Cheetos and soggy pretzels. For the grand finale, an empty Everclear bottle is hoisted up, turned upside down, and stuck on what's left of the twigish peak.

Meanwhile, back in the bedroom, the door is shut against all the outside commotion. The bedroom, itself, has been transformed into the 'business office' where all the important transactions are completed; where quarter bags are carefully being weighed, cut and sold by none-other than one of the richest guys in school, along with a group of his cronies.

Out here in the living room, there are even more people gathered around the card table. Regina has brought her cousin over tonight, too. He is down visiting from Indiana, and is sort of the ringleader at the table where they are attempting to build this huge sculpture out of liquor bottles and paper towels. It is quickly starting to take on size rather than shape. Over by the daybed, on the makeshift coffee table which is actually fabricated from an old wooden cable spool, there are open pizza boxes, half-eaten and crust-strewn, that Buddy and Robert have had delivered. Both my front door and Buddy's are wide open, and we have our stereos set on the same station, blaring the same rock song back and forth across the echoing hallway. Liz is at work, but will be off at around 9:30 or so. And when she comes home, she'll more than likely bring more snacks with her.

The guys at the card table have run out of objects with which to build, and Regina's cousin, for lack of anything better to do, reaches into his pocket and pulls out a lighter which he then uses to set the whole monstrosity on fire. It is probably no coincidence at all that Def Leppard's 'Pyromania' is screeching from the maxed-out speakers in my living room as well as blaring from Buddy's state-of-the-art sound system across the hall.

The oversized sculpture on my table has quickly become a total inferno, and several of us run to the kitchen for water, which we toss on the open flames. But by the time we finally manage to extinguish the blaze, the whole top of the card table is melted, black, crusted over with charred soot. And all I can hope at this point is that Mama doesn't decide to host another bridge game anytime soon. I quickly toss the tablecloth, which we'd removed earlier in order to give the growing sculpture more traction, back over the charred ruins, thinking that maybe nobody'd notice it quite as bad after it was covered up.

The group of newly-inducted pyros has now zeroed in on the dried out Christmas tree, still standing over in the corner, and I am laughing so hard I almost can't get the words out, telling them to please take the tree outside first. Because I definitely don't want my carpet to end up smelling like the card table does right about now. Even the smoke alarms are bleeping loudly in protest, but the sound only manages to blend in with the blaring music. Oh well, at least now I can figure they work. And anyway, I've never been very good at remembering to check batteries, so I figure this is probably a good thing.

We open the back door to let the smoke clear out, and the guys haul the dead tree onto the patio where its tribal-like incineration continues. The Everclear bottle on top suddenly explodes, popping loudly as it sends shards of flying glass in every conceivable direction, and the guys cheer, raise their fists in testosteronic-induced victory. *Too* cool! I figure I'll just have to worry about the mess later. *Much* later.

In the morning, I step over motionless bodies on my way to the bathroom. But before turning on the shower, I decide that it's much too early to be up yet, so I trudge back to bed where I collapse for another few hours.

This time when I get up, the bodies have extracted themselves, and on my second-attempted trip to the bathroom, I end up taking a last minute detour to the kitchen first where I grab a slice of left-over pizza. Actually, I don't know why I'm bothering to get showered up now in the first place. Because the only thing we'll end up doing is lounging around the pool all day, which means I'll have to start the whole hair-washing process over again, before the evening festivities begin. When Liz's not working, she comes to the pool with us, but she always slathers on a ton of sunscreen. Not Buddy and me, though. We are having this unofficial contest to see who can get the darkest, and better yet, who can do it in the most economical amount of time. Buddy has even gone out and bought this huge silver raft. It's supposed to attract the sun, and he lies around on it in the pool most of the day, soaking up rays while he guzzles Sun Country Coolers. As for me, I'm just sticking to the baby-oil-and-iodine-thing. It's never failed me before.

"Aren't you afraid of getting wrinkles?" Liz asks me. "Or even worse, skin cancer?"

Wrinkles? Yeah . . . . *right*. That's like a million years away or something. And *cancer*? I'm not even old enough to worry about that yet.

This is pretty much how our summer goes—the summer of '84. Liz works mostly during the day, sometimes right up until closing. She is a stock person at a big warehouse-like store that's just up the street, called 'Tons of Toys.' And Buddy, no longer working part-time at the A&P, is now pulling third shift for this company called 'Data General.' He does something with computers, but I'm not sure exactly what. And me? I'm just being a total bum, preparing for my senior year of high school. I have transferred out of Sanderson to this alternative-type school with a cool new program going on. It's called the 'Magnet Program,' and there are more classes offered than you could possibly ever take. Fun classes, like pottery, ballet, modern dance, photography, acting, even Japanese. Plus, the classes there are shorter, too—like 45 minutes or something. The school, itself is an older inner-city one, and with this popular new program in place, its ultimate purpose is to attract interest in an otherwise declining area. It's a whole lot like the artsy school in that movie, 'Fame,' and students literally come out of the woodwork from all over, just to go there—Cary, Apex, Garner, Wendell, even Zebulon. It's definitely a melting pot where you are free to make your own niche, not be confined by your social standing or the neighborhood in which you happen to live. And when I learn that two of my teammates from the junior high cheerleading squad are now cheerleaders at this school, too—at Enloe—I decide to try out as well, right along with them.

The three of us end up making the varsity squad, along with seven other girls, and for me, this simply adds to the list of things that I can look forward to for next year. It'll be a whole new life, a change that I definitely need, and I can hardly wait. It'll give me a chance to start all over again. And this time I'll have to concentrate really hard, make every effort I possibly can not to let the panic attacks and the compulsions get in the way again. Because one thing I ended up learning at karate is that the level of concentration it physically takes to keep all those things under control is totally consuming. It literally eats up the rest of your conscious existence, keeps you from functioning as a regular human being. I mean, I might as well be an amoeba, for all the contribution I can make to human life when I'm struggling so hard not to give in to the Fear and the endless compulsions. And honestly, it's just not worth it. Because either way, life is going to keep passing by, and I want to have something to remember, something to take with me. I don't want to spend my whole existence in battle, in a Civil War in which one side of me is always pitted against the other. This is something I will just have to learn to live with, my 'cross to bear' in life. And though it feels like I have been dealt a very unfair hand, I still intend to make the most of it, to live life to the absolute fullest of my capabilities. Because when I get to be 80 years old, I don't want to be like the Amish woman who's never been off the farm. I mean, there's so much I want to see, so many things I want to do. It's just that I don't know where to start or even *how* to begin. But for right now, that'll all have to wait, to stay in the future where it belongs. Because at this moment, it's all about the here and now, and nothing else matters— except choosing the right pair of shorts to wear over to Buddy's tonight. The one that'll make my tan look the darkest.

Later that evening at the Fast Fare, I run into this guy who'd visited our karate class several times last year. He'd been a brown belt at the time, and very good at what he did—not to mention cute as hell. He has a baby face, long sandy-colored hair, and drives a topless Jeep, barefooted. He is wearing a ripped tank top and these perfectly tattered painter pants. Everything about his style fits together so well. He recognizes me, too, and I invite him over for the nightly party.

From the very beginning, Don and Buddy hit it off in an extreme way. They both drink Sun Country Coolers and like loud music. And when Buddy'd decided to get his ear pierced, Don had gone along with him, had actually ended up doing it, too. And they'd even saved money overall because they'd been able to split the cost of a pair of earrings between the two of them.

I manage to develop this huge crush on Don, and we go out a couple of times, though it's pretty casual. But from the very beginning, from the very first time he'd met her, I knew he had this thing for Regina, and I sensed that she kind of liked him, too.

"I don't want to go out with him if *you're* going out with him," she tells me.

"We're not going out," I explain. "We just went a few places together, that's all."

"Are you sure?" she asks skeptically.

"Sure, I'm sure. Why wouldn't I be?" I'll never admit to her about the crush I have on him, though I'm pretty sure she knows it, anyway. Otherwise, why would she be so careful not to step on my feelings? Besides, the guy she's dating now is totally abusive at times, and she really needs to get rid of him, to find someone who will treat her well. And maybe Don is that person. Who knows?

She seems to accept my simple explanation, and as we are standing in front of my vanity mirror, she begins to brush out her beautiful hair. And though I've pretty much given up on the possibility of it actually happening, I still hold out hope that one day it just will—that I'll wake up with hair exactly like hers.

The infamous 'Buddy'

The 'party shack'

A DOSE OF YOUR OWN MEDICINE

It's official. I can honestly say that if you live such an extreme existence, there's at least one thing you can count on, point blank. Nothing—and I mean absolutely *nothing*—will ever be the same again. It's guaranteed. Not after your *informal* introduction to four *more* of the most simple, mundane words in the English language, which somehow, when strung together, quickly manage to amass the overwhelming power to completely knock you on your suntanned butt;

'Can *you* say *Mono*?'

It is late August, and it feels like it's about 110 degrees—both inside *and* out. I am lying in the bed, flat on my back, begging God to please forgive me for whatever it is that I've done to deserve such a horrible punishment. I mean, I'd known for a while—maybe a couple of weeks or so—that I was sick. *Really* sick. Because this was too relentless to simply be anxiety attacks. Still, I'd hoped that's all was there was to it. But when I'd gone down to the beach on an impulse trip with my friend, Rochelle, and her sister-in-law, Melinda—for kind of a girl's week-end out—the reality had hit me. Hard. Right about the time I was walking back from the beach one afternoon, lawn chair in tow, and I suddenly didn't know if I would even make it across the street. Not a good realization when you are standing somewhere in the middle of the double yellow lines, right about possum-track position.

I call Daddy from the payphone outside of the trailer where we are staying.

"I'm *sooo* sick!" I moan pitifully into the scalding receiver. The accompanying humidity's not doing much to improve conditions, either.

"What's wrong with you?" Daddy asks.

"I don't know," I whimper.

"Well, what hurts?"

"Everything." I start to cry, but it only makes my sore throat burn even worse.

"What do you want me to do?" Daddy asks. "You're three hours away, you can't tell me specifically what it is that's hurting, and you want me to make a *diagnosis*? Over the *phone*?"

"No," I sob. "I just want to come home."

"Well how did you get down there?"

"In Melinda's car."

"Who's Melinda?"

"Rochelle's sister-in-law.

"Who's Rochelle?"

"You know Rochelle, Daddy. She's Boyd's girlfriend."

"Who's *Boyd*?"

"He's a friend of Jason's."

"I thought you guys had broken up two *years* ago."

"We *did*. But I'm still friends with *these* people."

"Well aren't they going to bring you back, then, too?"

"I guess so . . . . eventually."

"Then why are you worried?" Daddy asks me. "Are you having anxiety attacks? Is that it?"

"*No*, Daddy . . . . I am *not* having an anxiety attack. I'm sick—really, really *sick*. I'm serious. I think I might be dying or something." I pause to catch my breath, wait for the light-headedness to go away. Why hadn't I listened to Liz all those times before?

"I mean, I hate to be the one to do it—to break the news to you and all . . . . but I think I might have . . . . you know . . . . *cancer*."

"Do *what*?"

"I mean, this could be the beginning of skin cancer, something like that."

"Angie—"

"Look, Daddy . . . . I just want to come home. That's all."

He sighs. "I don't even know where you are."

"Atlantic Beach."

"I know *that* much. But I don't know where down there you actually *are*."

"We're staying in this trailer."

"Angie, do you know how many trailers there are in Atlantic Beach?"

I start to cry again. "No."

"Well, it's getting late now," Daddy tells me. "Why don't you go to bed, get some rest? Then you can call me back in the morning and we'll figure this thing out."

I am too tired, feeling much too sick to argue with him, so I finally agree.

In the morning, though, I actually feel a little better, if you overlook the fact that I also feel like I've just been mowed flat by a steam roller. Rochelle and Melinda are planning on leaving today, anyway, so there's no point in calling Daddy back and trying to explain to him how to find me. Not when I can just ride with them.

When we get back home, Rochelle asks me to spend the night with her, and at first I agree. But when the terrible sickness washes over me once again, I ask if they can just take me home instead.

I have them drop me off at Mama and Daddy's rather than my apartment, and Mama meets me at the door, car keys in hand.

"Don't bring it in here," she tells me. "What ever it is, we don't want to catch it."

Okay . . . . *Sweet.* So why don't you just give me an 'unclean' sign and a cowbell to go along with it?

She drives me home, helps me to get settled in my own bed.

"You can't keep burning the candle at both ends," she tells me. "It's going to catch up with you, just like this."

I would argue with her, but my throat feels too much like it's closing up, and besides, I am so thankful to be back in my own bed, it just isn't worth it.

Still, I wake up in the middle of the night with this horrible pain in my side.

That's it! Appendicitis! *That's* what's been wrong with me all along! I should've known! I remember a couple of years back—when Kay'd had it. How they'd rushed her to the hospital, just in the nick of time. Just before it'd ruptured. Mama'd called home, asking me to pack an overnight bag with some of her things—her gown and robe, her toothbrush. Anything else I thought she might need. Mama tells me she's really sorry, but that since they have the car with them at the hospital, I'll probably have to walk to work tonight. But still, I am much too worried about Kay to even think about that now. I tell Mama I'll pack her a bag and carry it to work with me, and then when things settle down some there, she can come pick it up. She thanks me, sounding genuinely grateful.

And after putting everything I can possibly think of that she might need into her travel case, I snap the lid shut. But just then, I happen to glance over at her nightstand, to notice the picture of Merle still sitting there—the one where he's wearing the leather vest. I reach for it, unsnapping the lock on her travel case, then put the picture on the very top, where she'll be sure to see it, first thing.

Kay'd actually been at work that afternoon, too, when it'd happened to her.

When she'd become violently ill like that. She'd been working at Wendy's that summer so she could save money to put away for next semester in school. She told her manager, Rodney, that she was sick and needed to go home, but he outright refused to let her leave, saying instead, "Go clean up that bathroom, and when you're finished doing that, then you can re-stock the salad bar!"

"But Rodney, I'm *sick*," she'd told him. "I'm throwing up. I don't think I should be handling food that's going to be used for human consumption."

"Don't tell me what you think! I don't care! Just go get busy!"

Instead, Kay'd called Mama who drove up to the restaurant to get her, and when she'd seen Kay, she'd known immediately that something was really wrong.

After I heard about that, how her boss had treated her when she'd been so sick, anytime I found even the slightest remote excuse at all to borrow Mama's car, I'd make it a regular habit to casually swing through the drive-thru at Wendy's and order a cup of water, then glare horrifically at Rodney when he'd hand it out the window to me. And to think he'd had the absolute nerve to act like he didn't know what was going on! He's right on up there—running neck and neck with Mrs. Waddelson—in hot pursuit for the top spot on my 'List.'

I don't think about it being 4:00 in the morning, only about the horrible pain in my side, and I call Mama to tell her I need to go to the hospital right away because I have appendicitis.

When she gets there, I am sitting on the edge of the bathtub, running hot water over my legs because I am having a chill. But when I show her where I am hurting, she says, "That's your *left* side."

"I know."

"Well, your appendix is on your *right* side."

"Well, why is it hurting then?"

"It's probably not your appendix," Mama tells me, then asks, "Do you have any fever?" She drops a hand across my forehead, then answers her own question. "Nope—cool as a cucumber."

"But Mama, something is *really* wrong. I can feel it."

She helps me back to bed, gives me a glass of water and some Tylenol to swallow, then says, "I'll call Dr. Pridgen in the morning. You just rest, see if you can't get feeling a little better before then."

The sun is up when she calls, and I figure it's around 9:00 or so. I get dressed, go outside to wait for her to pick me up. I'm actually feeling better again, not to mention a little guilty as well, thinking that I'm probably going to end up costing her all this money for nothing at all.

That evening, I am out on the porch, watering Emmit (who, unbelievably, is still alive), when I receive the phone call—the one from Dr. Pridgen to give me the diagnosis.

"You have Mono," she says.

"I have *what*?" I ask.

"You know—Mononucleosis."

"But isn't that that mess you have to get from like kissing somebody else who's already got it?"

"No, not necessarily," she explains. "While ultimately, it is passed orally, usually people who're very run-down have a tendency to catch it much easier than those who're healthy. And not eating right, combined with too much sun exposure, not enough sleep—all those things add up to help zap your strength."

"What about my throat and my side?" I ask her.

"Well, the lymph nodes in your throat are swollen up almost as big as golf balls," she reminds me. "And the pain in your side is actually your spleen. It's swollen up, too, due to the infection caused by the illness, and you need to be very cognizant of how dangerous that can be. You definitely don't want your spleen to rupture, and for this reason, I am recommending that you go to bed for at least two weeks. And I don't mean lounge around the house. I mean get in the bed and *stay* there. Let someone wait on you hand and foot. Then, in exactly two weeks, I want to see you back in my office to see if the swelling's gone down any."

"But I don't live at home anymore," I tell her. "There's no one here to do that for me."

"Well, I'll call your mother, too," Dr. Pridgen says. "Because I'm sure she'll understand the necessity here."

Yeah . . . . right. And *she's* the one who wouldn't even let me back in the house last night simply because she was afraid I'd spread germs. Because she thought I'd contaminate the rest of them.

Still, regardless of what I'd believed, Dr. Pridgen is right. Mama calls to tell me she will bring breakfast every day, as well as supper. She tells me she will stop by the store and get some drinks to put in my refrigerator, and for me to just stay in the bed and rest. She tells me if I need anything else I should call her and not try to get up and get it on my own.

The terrible run-down feeling comes and goes. Sometimes, when I'm feeling okay, I'll get up, walk to the bathroom. But before I can even return to my bed, I end up collapsing on the floor, out of breath and light-headed.

Buddy and Liz take turns looking after me. During the day, Buddy comes and gets me, carrying me to the couch in their living room where he tries to revive me with loud music. After about a week of this, Buddy looks over at me one morning saying, "You know what, Angie?"

"No—what, Buddy?"

"You look awful."

"Thanks . . . ."

"No, I mean you *really* look like shit."

"Okay . . . . so you wanna Twinkie?"

"No, I just think we need to wash your hair," he tells me.

"What? I can't even make it to the bathroom by myself, so how is *that* supposed to happen?"

"In the sink," Buddy informs me.

And before I know it, he has my head dunked under the faucet in the bathroom, shampooing and rinsing, like nobody else's business. Afterwards, he tries to blow it dry, to style it, but my hair, simply being what it is, does not do right. I could've told him that from the very beginning—how hard it is to style—but I'm too sick to care.

"I know," he says after studying his botched handiwork. "Let's *cut* it." He goes for the scissors. "That's what you need—a *good* hair cut! That'll fix everything!"

Before I can even protest, he has propped me up in a chair, snipping away at my shoulder-length hair until it comes to just under my chin. And as bad as I feel, I have to say the cut is pretty flattering, and it actually brings some life back to my sallow features.

"See, that's what you needed," he tells me. "Now you don't look so much like shit anymore."

"Yeah . . . . thanks."

* * *

"Ohmigod!" Liz exclaims, dropping the grocery bags she is carrying on the living room floor. "You cut your *hair!*"

I motion over in Buddy's general direction, saying, "*He* did it."

She comes closer, inspects my head from all angles. "*Buddy* did that?" She runs her fingers through the layered pieces. "I mean, it looks *good! Really* good!"

"Sure, it does, Liz!" Buddy pipes up from across the room.

"How did you learn to do that?" she asks him, incredulously.

Buddy shrugs. "You just have to look at the person, you know? See how their face is shaped, the way their hair grows and everything. Then it all just comes natural."

"I can't believe this!" Liz exclaims. "You should be cutting hair instead of working on computers." She looks at him. "Can you do mine, too?"

"Sure, Liz!"

Thus is born 'Buddy's Beauty Shop,' which is run out of the back door of his kitchen in the Montecito Apartments. He studies Liz, who is sitting in the chair, then tells her, "Nah—you need long hair. Your face is kind of heart-shaped. But still, we can give you layers, kind of lighten it up a little or something."

After several minutes of snipping and blow-drying, Liz turns out looking just like a 'Penthouse' model.

"See?" Buddy tells her, standing back. "I always *knew* you had it in you!"

"Buddy, it's great—really great. But I can't go to work like this."

"Why not?" he asks. "You look good!"

"Buddy, I work in a *toy* store—not a strip joint!"

"So? Who do you think has the money? The parents, of course. So go sell a shit-load of Barbie dolls to all the little kids' dads. And then when the managers see how much profit you're making for the company, they'll give you a huge raise!"

Robert's wife is next, followed by Robert, himself. But when Buddy summons Don over to the chair, he hangs back on the couch instead, grabbing the ends of his long, sun-bleached hair protectively with his rough hands as he stutters, "N-n-no, Man! Mine's fine, j-just the way it is!"

Don's pretty bad about that—about stuttering, I mean. But the funny thing is, he only does it when he's *not* drinking. After he gets a couple of Sun Country Coolers down, he talks just as plain as the rest of us do.

"Oh, come on, Man!" Buddy says, approaching the couch, scissors in hand. "You gotta at *least* let me trim your split ends!"

Don backs further into the upholstery, warding Buddy off. "Y-y-you better *quit*, Man!"

From back in the kitchen, Robert calls out, "Hey, somebody get that guy a *beer*, will you?"

* * *

I am slowly starting to get better. And I do mean '*slowly.*' It's been three weeks now, and school has already started. At the first football game, I have to dress out in my cheerleading uniform and sit on the bleachers because Dr. Pridgen still isn't satisfied with the progress of my un-swelling spleen yet. I can only hope that people know I'm benched because I'm sick, not because I've managed to get in trouble—especially so early in the year. I haven't even been back to karate yet, and the class has sent me a 'get well' card, signed by everyone, which helped me to feel better even more.

I make a lot of new friends at Enloe, and I can honestly say it's the first time I've felt like I fit in since junior high—at least in school, that is. Still, I don't really feel like a high school student anymore—not when I'm living such an *un*-high school lifestyle. So far this year, I've been carpooling with friends, giving who ever happens to be driving that week gas money since I cannot repay them by driving a week, myself. It is around Thanksgiving that Daddy totally floors me when he calls, saying, "I've talked to Mimi and Granddaddy about it, and they're going to let us take enough money out of your stock account to buy you a car."

What? What had he said?

"You're kidding, right?" I ask in total disbelief.

"No, you need one now. Especially with the situation you're in."

Oh my dear god!

"Can I get a Corvette?" I gush.

"I seriously doubt it."

"A Fiero?"

"Don't count on it."

"Well, what about Camaro then?"

". . . . we'll see."

* * *

We've been out car hunting all day, and nothing's panned out yet. I want something sporty; Mimi and Granddaddy say I have to buy something practical, especially since they're paying for it out of the stock money that Granddaddy himself, had put in the bank for us. On the way back to my apartment, we are driving past the K-Mart parking lot—where people sometimes use the back spaces to sell their privately owned vehicles—when I see it.

"Daddy, stop!"

"What?"

"That one!" I say, pointing. "That's the one, right there!"

Daddy pulls into the parking lot, slowing to look at the small car I've pointed out.

"I don't know, Angie. That looks brand-new. It'll probably be out of our price range."

But already I am out of the door, walking over to look in the windows. And it actually has a stereo! Speakers someone's had installed in the doors, even a friggin' equalizer. Buddy'll absolutely shit!

The price is written on the window—$1,500.00—along with a phone number.

"See, Daddy?" I gush. "It's *under* our price range! That means we can get it!"

Daddy walks up to stand beside me, inspecting the little car. "No, *that* means I wonder what's wrong with it."

"Nothing's wrong with it, Daddy! Just *look* at it!"

Daddy walks around it, thumping the tires, looking in the windows.

"Well, it's clean. I'll definitely give them that. But just because it's clean doesn't mean there aren't other things going on under the hood."

"Daddy, just *call* him!"

"We haven't even driven it yet, Angie."

"And you *won't* until you call him!"

Daddy glances back in the window, shielding his eyes.

"Got a heck of a lot of miles on it. Over a hundred-thousand."

"So? That just means it drives good! *Real* good!"

"And it's stick shift, too."

"Just what I've always wanted!"

"You don't even know how to drive a stick shift."

"You could teach me . . . ."

"I don't know . . . ."

"Daddy . . . . *Please*!"

I refuse to leave the car's side, just in case anyone else happens to pass by and decide that they, too, can't live without it. I put my hand protectively on the door handle while Daddy goes up to the service station to call the man whose name is written beneath the phone number.

"I'm not saying 'yes,'" he tells me. "I'm just going to call and *ask* about it, that's all."

I smile. "Then *ask* him if he'll let us drive it!"

It is after supper before the man can meet us back at the K-Mart, and though Mama and Daddy let me stay at their house for supper, I can barely eat anything at all.

"You know what Dr. Pridgen said," Mama reminds me. "About how you should be eating right."

"I know—but I'm just not hungry right now."

"Well you'd better *get* hungry—especially if you don't want to end up getting sick like that, all over again!"

When we return to K-Mart, the man isn't there yet, and under the windshield wiper, there is a note. I reach for it, reading it;

If car is still available, please call me. I would be very interested in finding out more about it.

Then there is the obligatory 'thanks,' followed by a phone number. I quickly slip the note into my pocketbook before Daddy can see it—and horror of horrors—get any bright ideas.

The owner of the car turns out to be a traveling salesman, thus explaining the high mileage.

"But they're *highway* miles," he explains. "Not just regular miles."

"What're highway miles?" I ask Daddy.

"It means the car's been driven straight and at a pretty consistent speed. Not constantly being stopped and started, and idling at traffic lights."

"Is that good?" I ask.

"Well, I suppose it helps," Daddy tells me. "But with that many miles, I don't think it really matters, though."

Daddy drives the car, and I sit in the passenger seat beside him. There is a small rip in the vinyl, but I figure I can patch that with matching tape or something. I reach to turn the stereo on, basking in the bass. But Daddy turns it off just as quickly, telling me, "I've got to be able to hear the engine. And besides, you don't need to be riding around with the music on loud like that. An ambulance'll run clean over you before you ever even hear it coming."

He gears down to stop for the light at the intersection. Once we are moving again, he turns to the left.

"Doesn't have power steering, either," he comments.

"Oh, Daddy! Why does everything have to be *power*? See, it doesn't even have power *windows* or power *seats*, either! So why does that matter?"

But Daddy only shakes his head, telling me, "No, no—power steering is different. Most cars come with it these days. In fact, I think they *all* do. It keeps you from having to wrestle so hard with the steering wheel."

"Dad-*dy!*"

He looks over at me again. "You really like it, don't you?"

* * *

All I can manage to do until this week-end finally rolls around is stand at Buddy's door, looking out into the parking lot where the little tan 1977 Toyota Celica ST is parked. Because that's when Daddy's coming over to teach me how to drive it. And I honestly don't think that a new mother—one who'd just spent three grueling days in labor, at that—could feel more proud at this very moment than I do. Sometimes, I just go out into the parking lot and sit in the little car, listening to it's stereo. I can hardly believe it's really mine as I rub my fingers over the dash, trace the end of the gearshift, open and close the glove compartment where the new registration is stored. Daddy's told me umpteen times how important it is to never take the registration out, how I'll need it if I ever get stopped by the police. Yeah . . . . *that'll* be the day!

And in the mornings when I get up, the first thing I do is run to the door to make sure the little car's still sitting there.

On Saturday, it takes me all of fifteen minutes in an empty parking lot to learn how to drive a stick shift. Daddy says he's never seen anyone catch on so quickly before, and this makes me proud.

"Even your mother can't drive a stick shift, and I've been trying to teach her how to do it for twenty years!"

Once by myself, it takes a little getting used to though, especially when I have to stop on a hill or something. But when my confidence finally kicks in, just like with all the other things in my life lately, I know that nothing will ever be the same again, and this time, it's a good feeling.

The 'big time'—high school varsity cheerleading

My close-knit ballet class at the magnet school (enjoying one of our 'learning experience' parties)

ANOTHER SUBURBAN FAMILY MORNING

Buddy is growing an onion. He is curious to see what'll come up, since it's officially a root and all. So far, it's been these little green sprouts, and he waters it religiously, hoping they'll grow out much fuller. The onion, itself, had been old. *Nasty* old, I mean. It'd been underneath his and Liz's kitchen cabinet for no telling how long, and the putrid smell is what actually drove its existence to the forefront.

"Buddy, why don't you just throw that disgusting thing away?" Liz asks.

"Because I think it still has a lot of life left in it," he tells her. He peels the rotten part off, plants what's left of the bulb in a green plastic flower pot, which he then places near the kitchen door.

"So it'll get *plenty* of sunshine!" he tells us.

For the first couple of weeks, he just sits around, watching it, constantly watering it, waiting to see what changes will occur. And at first, when none do, he takes a road trip up to the hardware store where he purchases a bag of this Acme-fertilizer-stuff to put in the pot along with the onion. That's when the little green sprouts finally began to appear.

"That's his name," Buddy tells us proudly. "*Sprout!*"

"Damn if *that* ain't original!" Don says.

We are all sitting around Buddy's living room, waiting for Robert to get off work and for Regina to finish at haircutting school for the afternoon. Then all of us are going to Pizza Hut for supper. Liz, who'll get off an hour later, will meet us at the restaurant.

"Okay . . . . so what the hell would *you* name it, then?" Buddy retorts, carefully replacing his potted onion on the little kitchen shelf he'd built—just for the sole purpose of having a nice place for its display. Earlier, he'd carried the onion outside on the patio so it could partake of the fresh afternoon sunshine, but now with the cool, evening breeze settling in, he doesn't want it to get too chilled.

"Well, in the first place, I-I-I wouldn't be growing a damn *o-o-onion!*"

Buddy comes into the living room then, popping the top on a fresh Sun Country Cooler, which he hands to Don. "Drink this. You'll feel better."

". . . . thanks, Man."

* * *

In the little less than a year since I have graduated from high school, I have also managed to become a certified bum. I mean, if they gave out a diploma for 'Bumville,' I'd have definitely earned it by now, with honors. I have learned exactly how tan my skin can get. I have learned how to eat frozen pizza at midnight, how to sleep until noon without feeling any guilt. I have learned not only to watch, but also to find quite educational the new concept of 'M-TV,' as well as 'Night Tracks,' which is another video show that airs on late-night.

That's how I know when it's after midnight—when 'Night Tracks' comes on. Buddy calls it 'Bat Tracks' though.

"Because it comes on really late, when the *bats* are all out, flying around." He makes these little bat-like things with his fingers, beating them together so they sound like furry little wings. Gross! One time he'd done his hands like that, making the bat noise right in Don's ear when he'd been passed out—asleep on the couch. And Don had woken up later to tell us, "You know, I-I-I just had the *weirdest* dream!"

"About bats flying around?" Buddy suggests.

He looks at Buddy. "How'd *you* know?"

Buddy is tired of having to leave the party every night, especially when it's just beginning to crank up. He has to be at his third-shift job by midnight, which means he has to leave the apartment by 11:30 or so. Every now and then, if we're having a particularly good night—like we are tonight—Buddy'll call in, ask to speak to his supervisor.

"I'm not coming in to work," he says over the blared commotion of the TV and stereo combined. "No, really. I can't tonight. See, I've got this *terrible* diarrhea . . . . I mean, it's just *unbelievable*."

We bury our heads in the couch pillows, or in the otherwise closest mufflers we can find, absolutely busting out our sides with laughter.

"No, no," Buddy is saying into the phone. "See *Imodium*—stuff like that—just doesn't work for me. It kinda makes everything back up, you know? Builds it all up till it can't take anymore—like a volcano or something. Then I'm sorry to say, but I absolutely *cannot* be held responsible for what happens to Data General's bathroom."

Now Don has fallen off the couch, is rolling around on the floor. No sound is actually coming out of his mouth, but his face is beet red and tears have started streaming down his cheeks. He looks like he's going to explode right about any second now, and just the sight of him lying there like that is enough to tear the rest of us up all over again. As soon as Buddy hangs up the phone, Don lets it fly, laughing so hysterically I'm afraid he's going to hurt himself. He ends up getting choked on his Sun Country, and Regina has to whack him on the back several times before he stops coughing.

"I can't *believe* you!" Don hoots as soon as he is able to speak. "I cannot *believe* you just called up your employer and told him you had the *shits*, Man!" Now he is laughing all over again.

"Buddy, you really shouldn't have done that," Liz chides him.

"Why not?" he asks. "I mean, who the hell's gonna argue with it?" He definitely has a point.

The guys end up playing a serious game of 'quarters,' and it is determined that the one still left standing after everything's over with will be declared the winner. Don is the first to pass out. Buddy goes over to the couch where he is slumped over and takes the Sun Country out of his limp hand. He then holds the half-empty bottle over Don's pants, draining the rest of the beer there.

"Buddy!" Liz chides again. "You're going to make him think he's had an accident!"

"I know!" he says. "That's the whole point!"

"Buddy, that's mean! When're you planning on telling him the truth?" Liz asks.

"Not till tomorrow night. Not till he spends a whole day at work, worrying about it."

She shakes her head, saying, "I can't *believe* you!"

"So? It'll sure teach him to laugh about my *diarrhea* again!"

* * *

Over the course of my senior year, I have also managed to meet 'Adrienne,' who is completely unlike anyone else I have ever known.

I first learned about her existence through Rochelle who, when she found out I was attending Enloe, asked, "Have you met my friend, Adrienne, yet? She goes there, too."

But at that point, I had not. So for weeks, I heard all these stories about the elusive Adrienne whenever Rochelle and I'd talk on the phone, and I became totally curious about this pseudo-person long before I'd ever confirmed her actual existence.

I finally meet her in the locker room, of all places. She is getting ready to dress out for gym; I have just put my clothes back on after my two-hour ballet class. (I'd needed to sign up for one of the magnet classes in order to attend Enloe, and I figured that two hours of ballet every day would eat up some serious time. And since I wasn't going to college, anyway, what difference would it make?)

"Are you Angie?" she asks me.

She is tall, thin, blond. Pixyish, but in a very sexy way.

"Yeah. How did you know?"

"Well, because Rochelle described you—and also because of that," she indicates my cheerleading uniform. "You're like the only one here I don't know, so I figured it had to be you."

Okay. So this is Adrienne.

She pulls off her shirt then and reveals the biggest, most perfect boobs I have ever seen in my life. They even put Kay's to shame. *Forget* what they do to mine. I contemplate the option of hating her, but for some reason, I just can't. Maybe because she is so down-to-earth, so open and friendly. After all, *she* can't help it if she's gorgeous—with a perfect body to go along with it. (Yeah . . . . *hmph*!)

"Hey, what're you doing this week-end?" Adrienne asks, adjusting her gym T-shirt down over her gargantually perfect breasts.

"Other than the basketball game tonight, that's it," I tell her.

"Because we really need to get together, you know? Rochelle told me all about you, so I feel like I already know you, anyway."

Before the meeting is up, her open friendliness has totally piqued my curiosity, and I have already invited her over to our week-end party shack. Rochelle'd told me that Adrienne's in the 9th grade—a freshman—but I find that hard to believe. She seems much older, much more mature. Like I'd hang out with her anytime.

She ends up coming to the party that week-end, and since she is only fifteen, her mother drives her over—right up to the apartments, at that—and drops her off.

"Jeez!" I say, unbelievingly. "Does she know what the deal is?"

Adrienne smiles. "She thinks you live here with your mother. Like I sort of told her your parents were going through this terrible divorce or something."

Oh my god! No, she *didn't!* Still, I have to laugh at the nerve of it all—at her complete openness.

"So what if your mom decides to come in?" I ask.

"She won't," Adrienne tells me.

"How can you be so sure?" I ask her.

"Trust me—you don't know my mother!"

Later, I will learn how truly right she is—and I even go so far as to imagine how things could've been different for me at home if Mama'd been like that, too—completely laid back and cool about everything, like Adrienne's mother is. I'd probably still be living there if that were the case.

The first time I go over to Adrienne's house, she leads me up the stairs to her room. Her two sisters have connecting rooms, and they all share a bathroom together. One of them has left a whole slew of make-up out on the bathroom cabinet, and there is this huge message scrawled across the mirror in bright red lipstick that reads, *'Clean up this fucking mess!'* But Adrienne just laughs, saying, "Oh, my mother probably wrote that!"

Unbelievable!

"Wrote what?"

I turn at the sound of a new voice to find Carly, Adrienne's younger sister, standing in the doorway.

Adrienne points towards the bathroom, saying, "That message on the mirror!"

From inside the bathroom, we hear Carly break out laughing. Then she says, "Here, let me make it even better!"

We stand in the doorway, watching as she wipes off the word 'mess,' leaving the rest of the message as it is. *Too* unbelievable!

It is only a few minutes later, when I am driving Adrienne up to the store, that we run into her other sister, Liza, who is 11—the same age as Martie. But she is not holding a Cabbage Patch Kid or even a Barbie doll. Instead, she is packing a box of Marlboro Regulars against the palm of her hand when she sees us.

"Whassup, Girlfriend?" She pulls out a cigarette, firing it up with a pot-leaf lighter.

"Where're you headed?" Adrienne asks her, like it's any other day.

"Over to Carl's."

"Oh, okay," Adrienne says. "Tell him I said 'hi.'"

"I'll do it! Later, dudes!"

Then she is gone.

"Who's Carl?" I ask Adrienne when we are back in the car. I am imagining an uncle or cousin, something like that.

"Oh, that's her boyfriend."

"She has a *boyfriend*?"

"Sure."

"How old is *he*?"

"Um—like sixteen, I think. He's a year ahead of me in school."

Okay . . . . too *completely* unbelievable!

BIG HAIR ROCKS ON

 I am hanging upside down in my chair, the blow dryer wide open. Just having a perm isn't enough these days. No, it's got to stand up on end. Completely. Because this is 1986—definitely the era of hair spray and shock-gel, and it's not about whether or not you should *use* it, but rather which brand you should buy. Personally, I always look for the one that's the closest to Crazy Glue. Then I know I've hit on something good.
 Adrienne is coming over shortly, and we are going out riding in her new car. Actually, she's had the car since she was fifteen—ever since she got her driving permit. Her father'd bought it for her early like that so she could get used to it before she actually got her real license—before she'd be out on the road by herself. The fun part for us had been that until she turned 16, we all got

to drive her around in it. And it wasn't just any old car, either. No, her dad wasn't like that. He'd gone all out and bought, straight off the showroom floor, a bright red IROC Z-28, complete with T-tops and all the bells and whistles you could ever want. But one thing I can honestly say is that if there was ever anyone who deserved her own car, it was definitely Adrienne. She'd always been a straight-A student, always helped her mother keep the house up, always been very dependable. She is definitely not your typical 16-year-old. And I could've only wished that I'd had as much maturity and common sense back then, too—back when I'd been 16.

Adrienne's boyfriend is reflective of her maturity level as well. He is a city fireman, and he is 22 years old. With anyone else that would sound a little on the pedophilish side. But not with Adrienne. Not in the least. You just had to know her.

I pull on my stretch jeans, tucking the fitted ankles inside big slouchy socks. Then I put on my high-top Reeboks—the ones with the double Velcro strap. I am still trying to decide which shirt to wear when there is a knock at the door. Adrienne. I know, not only because I'd been expecting her, but also from the quick, energetic way she has of doing it.

"You're not wearing a shirt?" she asks, dropping her overstuffed duffle bag in the bedroom.

I look down at my lacy push-up bra, deciding that overall, once on the body, the concept of a bra actually pushing something *up* is nothing more than the manufacturer's blatant statement of false advertisement. "Oh, yeah," I tell her. "I just haven't decided which one yet."

"Wanna wear one of mine?"

"Sure."

She digs through her bag, coming up with a cut-off sweat shirt which also has a stylishly ripped neckline. Cool. I slip it past my head, being careful not to graze my hair on the way over.

When we get outside, I notice that she has the T-tops out, and I quickly pull the bottle of mega-hold hair spray out of my pocketbook, misting it all over my already stiff head. While we're out trolling, we listen to all her new tapes; Glass Tiger, Starpoint, Depeche Mode. We end up going through the Burger King drive thru on our way back, then flopping down on the living room floor to consume all the high calorie stuff. Ginger comes up, pawing at my fingers, and I know before I even open the bag that she wants a french fry. I have never seen a cat before who'll eat the stuff mine does. But honestly, if I don't give her one, I think she'll probably end up attacking me. I pull out the longest one I can find, tearing it into little pieces that'll be easier for her to manage.

Later, Adrienne will go over to her boyfriend's house, and I'll go over to mine. I'm sure we'll end up tying up both their phone lines all night, calling back and forth. We always do.

We still have about an hour or so to kill, and I reach for the composition book I use as a journal, tearing out a piece of paper. I begin drawing, and before I know it, I have this perfect caricature of her boyfriend in front of me. The only thing it takes me a little while to figure out is whether I should dress him in his turn-out gear or in his Mother Fletcher's T-shirt. I decide on the latter, and begin to pencil it in. I sit back to study my handiwork, but still, something isn't quite right. And at first I can't put my finger on exactly what it is, but then it hits me. I turn my pencil over, erase his boots, and in place of them, carefully draw two long, tentacle-like webfeet. I sit back to admire my artistry. There. Looks just like him. Adrienne comes to peer over my shoulder then, to see what I'm doing.

"He does *not* look like a frog!" she insists, just as I am writing the last 'ribbit' in the bubble beside his head.

"Yes, he does!"

"No, he doesn't!"

"Adrienne, you can't tell me that this picture doesn't look just like him!"

"Well, maybe a little—"

"Maybe a *lot*!"

"Why'd you draw his head so big like that for?"

But she doesn't wait for an answer. Instead, she goes over to my composition book, rips out a piece of paper of her own.

"Oh, no!" she protests, shielding her work. "Do not even *think* about coming over here until I'm finished!"

Within minutes, she has produced a perfectly sketched orangutan, wearing sun glasses and a karate suit, his huge hairy knuckles dragging the ground beside him.

"Oh—no *way!*" I tell her.

"*Yes*, way!"

"That doesn't even come close!"

"Oh, but you know it does!"

"What's that in his hand?"

"His car keys . . . . He wants to go *parking.*"

We are laughing too hard to hear the phone when it rings.

"Adrienne—do something for me."

"What?"

"You know . . . ."

"*What?*"

"Just once—before you have to leave . . . ."

"No *way!*"

"Oh, come on!"

"Forget it! I'm *never* doing that again!"

"Please—just one time! Just do it for me one more time! I swear, I'll never ask you again!"

"Oh, alright! But this is it! This is the *last* time . . . . I *mean* it!" And she proceeds to make her signature fish-face.

Still, as I am laughing my guts out over it, I know that I have nothing to worry about, that this will be far from the last time—only one of many *more* times—that I'll be given the privilege of seeing the fish-face that I so love.

Later, Adrienne's mother calls back just as I am walking out the door, myself. I tell her Adrienne is in the shower, that I'll have her call home as soon as she gets out. According to our plan, I dial her boyfriend's number and when she answers, tell her to call home. I decide that we definitely have an awesome system going on here. It's just totally unbelievable! And I check one last time to make sure the front door's locked, before heading out to my own car.

* * *

Years later, after graduating from college and landing my first real 'professional' job, I am packing up the contents of my apartment—11 years' worth to be exact—preparing to move into my brand-new house. It's small, only about 1200 square feet or so, but every single square foot of it's mine, and that's a really good feeling. Especially after all the years wasted paying rent.

As I am cleaning out the final stray items in back of the closet, I actually come across these pictures again; these two stupid drawings—the frog and the ape. Jeez, I'd totally forgotten about them. Still, they make me laugh all over again as the crazy memories come crashing back once more. I can't believe they even still exist, and I reach for the stuffed plastic bag, starting to trash them, but something inside makes me stop. Because I just don't have the heart to throw them out—not yet—and I zip them up in my leather attaché instead, deciding to take them to work with me tomorrow.

In the morning, I wait around until I'm sure no one's looking. Then I smuggle the pictures out of the case, sneak them into the multi-purpose room, fax them over to Adrienne's office.

There. I've done my good deed for the day. And do I have any regrets concerning the use of office equipment for such unprofessional purposes, or even for wasting valuable company time that should be otherwise spent? Nah—just that I couldn't be there when they rolled out onto her desk—so I could witness her mutual reaction, that's all.

***BIG** hair rocks on . . . .*

*. . . . and on . . . . and **ON**!*

*Oops! And would that actually be **Martie** we just caught, teasing her roots, too?*

BLESS THE BEASTS

Ginger has her kittens. Five of the fattest, rolly-pollyest furballs I've ever seen. And now that their eyes have begun to open, they are everywhere; climbing the curtains, walking the kitchen cabinets, performing these unbelievable flying trapeze tricks from one piece of makeshift furniture over to another. And when they get tired from all this over-the-top mischief? They just simply drop, fall wherever they happen to be, purring as the rest take turns piling up on the first one to give out. At night, I make a nest for them at the foot of my bed with blankets and pillows so I can have them close by. And Ginger? She is totally proud. You can tell by the way she struts around, carrying her little ones in her mouth, washing them with her own paw, or simply by the way she just sits back and watches them with her eyes in slits. She even has her own way of talking to them, kind of a '*prrrp*' sound that's half 'meow' and half 'purr.' I wish I knew what she was saying to them. But the kittens understand because they always answer, respond by running to her, rubbing against her.

I am getting ready for work—at my new waitressing job across town where most of my friends are waitresses, too—when I realize that something isn't quite right. In the rumbling pile at the foot of my bed, there are only four kittens. I go in search of the fifth, finally finding him hiding behind the front door, his eyes closed. It's the fattest of the litter, the one Adrienne's boyfriend had named 'W.L,' claiming that a cat of that magnitude needed a true redneck name. I reach down, touch his head. He looks up at me, making the '*prrrp*' sound, but for some reason, he seems very week. I take him to Ginger, who is by now, lying on the bed, nursing her brood. But when I put him down with the others, he turns his head away. Okay . . . . weird.

After I finish dressing in my khaki pants and logoed golf shirt, I warm some milk in a little pot on the stove. I find the kitten in the same place as before, hiding behind the front door, and I try to feed him a little of the warm milk from a dropper. Still, he turns his head away, uninterested.

I don't exactly have a vet yet, not since Ginger's vaccinations aren't due for a couple more months, so I pick up the phone book, start calling around. And the second vet I call can see 'W.L.' that morning. But unfortunately, 'no, they do not bill.' They expect payment upfront, so I tell them I will be in about mid-afternoon, when my lunch shift is over. I can only hope that we're relatively busy today so that I make enough tips to cover the visit.

It's 1:00, and I have about $40.00 cash. I clean my station, hurriedly do my prep work, then head out.

At home, I find the little kitten curled up in the same spot behind the door, and for some reason, this time, it totally makes my stomach knot up. I don't even change out of my wrinkled uniform before I pick him up, take him to the new vet. And he is good, sleeping quietly in my lap on the way there. I randomly reach down, scratching the soft fur under his chin, and he makes the weak '*prrrp*' sound.

"Just hang on, Little Guy," I coax him. "We're going to get you some medicine right now. It won't be long at all before you're running around, playing with all your brothers and sisters again."

In the waiting room, I sit in one of the plastic chairs. The nurse doesn't take me back for the initial exam, and I wonder why it's taking so long. But then the vet, himself—Dr. Andrews—opens the door to the waiting room, beckoning to me.

"I want to show you something," he says, and I follow him into the back room. He leads me all the way over to the steel 'exit' door and then stands back so that I can see inside the cardboard box that is sitting there.

I am not prepared at all for what I find. W.L. is lying, limp and shivering, in a contorted heap.

"What's wrong with him? Why is he so wet?" I ask, reaching into the box.

But Dr. Andrews pulls me back, saying, "He's dying."

"*Dying*?" Well, *help* him! Can't you *do* something?"

"No."

"*Please*! Don't let him die!" I begin to cry.

"I didn't," he tells me. "*You* did."

What? I am too dazed to turn away from the shivering kitten.

"You see that?" he asks, pointing in the box. "That's all *your* fault! *You* caused that!"

"No!" I sob. "I would *never* hurt him!"

"You hurt him by letting him be born," Dr. Andrews tells me. "He should have never come into this world!"

"What are you *talking* about?" I know how totally ugly I look when I cry, but I don't care.

"You told me you adopted the mother from the SPCA."

"I *did*!" I re-confirm.

"Well, I'm on the board of directors there, and I happen to know for a fact that when you adopted this cat—or when anyone adopts an animal, for that matter—you signed a form, stating that you would have the cat spayed."

"I just wanted her to have kittens!" I tell him.

"What about what she wanted? Or what about the kittens, themselves? Did you ever stop to consider what *their* needs might have been?"

"Please, just help him! I'll pay whatever it is! I swear I will!"

"I've had to put him to sleep. He had flea anemia, and the only thing I could've possibly done was to give him a blood transfusion, and I know you can't pay for that!"

"But I can set up a plan! I'll come in every week and make payments until everything's paid off."

"No, it's too cruel and unjust to the animal. I've already given him the shot. His heart is stopping."

I am openly sobbing now. "Is he hurting?"

"He won't be for much longer."

I stand frozen, looking at the little cat as Dr. Andrews repeats, "This is *your* fault! You are a *cruel* pet owner! And I'm going to give you *one* hour to go home and bring the mother back in along with the rest of the kittens."

"What are you going to do with them?"

"Well, I'm going to treat the kittens and make sure they go to good homes. As for the mother, I'm going to spay her for you, free of charge."

"No! I don't want you touching any more of my cats!"

"You can either bring them in, or I'll send Animal Control out to get them."

"You can't do that!"

"Yes, I can. And I will."

I stand a moment longer, and now I am shaking as hard as the kitten.

"You can have her back in a couple of days. But she has to be spayed."

"No! I don't want you touching her! And I don't want you *giving* me anything!"

"Look, I'm not asking you to go to *bed* with me. Only to spay your cat."

I glare. He has absolutely nothing to worry about in that category.

"Just go home and get the cat—and the rest of her kittens, too—and I'll take care of this for you."

I continue to stand there, shaking, but he turns to walk out of the room.

"What about the kitten?" I ask.

"He's hardly even conscious anymore. He doesn't know what's going on."

Had I not been so young and foolish, I wouldn't have believed my only option was to simply turn and follow the vet out, leaving the kitten to die by himself. Had I been just a little older, I would have had the sense to be outraged—I would have realized I had every right to be—and I would have pure raised the lid off immortal Hell.

Instead, I go home, gather Ginger and her four kittens, then drive them back up to Frankenstein's office.

As I leave her there against my better judgment, I glare once more, telling him, "I'm not taking *shit* from you! I don't need you to *give* my anything! I will come in every week and make payments until it's paid for."

"That's *your* choice," he says.

"I'm sorry you see it that way—like it's a 'choice' or something."

"It is."

"And simply drive home the fact that I am a 'selfish' and 'cruel' pet owner? I don't *think* so!"

And as I walk out the door, he seems more amused than anything, but it's not *his* expression that I will remember the longest. It's the image of that little shivering kitten, lying helpless in such an unnatural position. And the unsettled feeling that came from not knowing what Dr. Frankenstein did with his small body afterwards. Because he *definitely* didn't have a choice.

True to his word, Dr. Frankenstein spays Ginger, then gives her back. And true to *my* word, I make every single payment until the balance is finally offset. And I can honestly say that I have gained two new lessons from this 'experience.' First and foremost, I will *never* take another animal to him—and probably not to any other vet as well—for as long as I live. Secondly, I will open my home to all cats, whether stray, needy or sickly. It'll be a safe haven they can come to where I'll sit and religiously nurse them back to health—so we can *all* live happily ever after. All except Dr. Frankenstein that is, who has officially earned the very top spot on my 'List.'

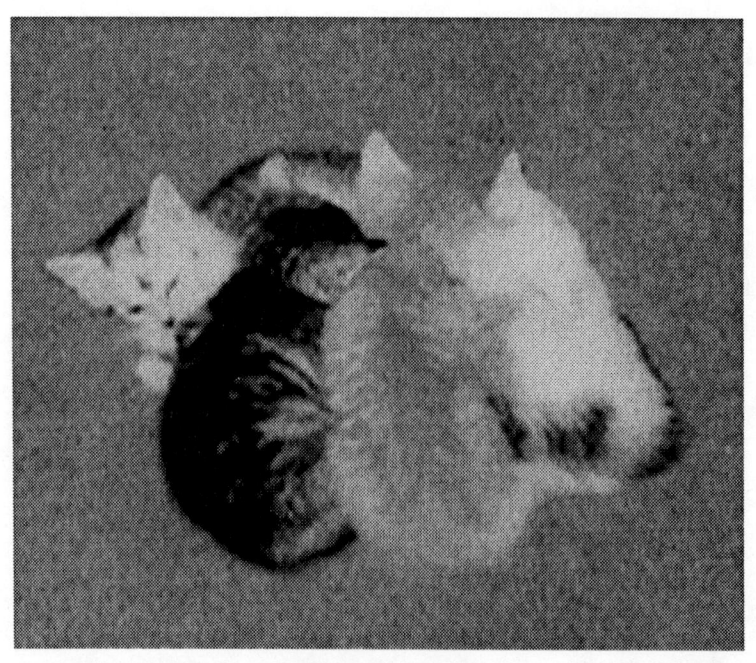

Kittens—at last!

ALL IN A DAY'S WORK

Mimi and Granddaddy are subtly urging me to get a job. A *real* job, that is. One where I work regular hours, get a paycheck, where the words *"You want fries with that"* are not a standard resume requirement or regular interview question. And most of all, one where I don't have to rely on tips (i.e. the generosity of others) to survive.

Find a job? *Me*? Like *where*? That is the absolute equivalent of locating one lone needle in an entire silo. I mean, seriously, what can *I* do? Especially when all I've ever done is run cash registers and wait tables? And that's minimum wage work, no matter how you cut it. And let's face it. It's not like I don't have a clue what it costs to live on your own. Because even though I've been taken care of financially since getting kicked out of the house, I still know what the rent is, what the utility bills register when they come in the mail, what groceries, gas, and car repairs cost. And the list goes on. And on, and *on*. So what the hell are they thinking? All of them! Because this is crazy! Exactly what do they expect me to do? Sell drugs or something? That'd be nice. Then Mama'd be able to proudly say, "I have three daughters; one who's in college at UNCW, making straight 'A's, another who's just in elementary school and always gets the leads in every play she tries out for, and a *third*, who makes a very nice living as her friendly neighborhood 'street pharmacist.'" Yeah. So if I wind up dead in a ditch somewhere, they'll have no one to blame but themselves.

Mimi tells me it's not about getting on my own like tomorrow or something. She just says I need to choose a good field, start a career, and while I'm working to build it, she and Granddaddy will continue to supplement me. Nobody expects me to jump up and take full control of my financial existence immediately. They understand the position I'm in and will do whatever they can to help me get on my feet.

"Start applying at some of these banks around here," Mimi suggests on the phone one night. "They're plenty of teller positions available."

"Banks get robbed," I say.

"That's ridiculous!"

"Well, they do."

"How often do you hear about a bank being robbed around here?"

"Often enough."

"Because Mavis hasn't ever said anything about it being unsafe, and her granddaughter's a teller. So if there was any real danger involved, I'm sure Mavis would *know*."

I end up taking her advice. But only after two months of being told how sorry they are, but I just don't have the credentials they are looking for to fulfill the 'store manager' position. Or the 'Executive Secretary' opening. Or the 'Medical Desk Assistant.' Whatever it is. I mean, I knew it was going to be hard, but I hadn't counted on this; on so much rejection. I'm starting to get the feeling that I'm not needed *anywhere*.

At the final bank where I end up applying, one of the questions on the application reads, "What do you consider to be the most important aspect of a job?" And thinking back over my unsuccessful employment hunt, I quickly write in the blank underneath, '*To be needed. To do something that matters.*' And I guess in the end, that's what they wanted to hear, as stupid as it sounds. Because I wind up getting the job. But rather than a branch, I will be working in the 'Operations Center,' where all the checks and deposits are sent to be processed after the fact. The only catch? I will be working what they call 'swing shift' to start with, the hours being 1:00 in the afternoon until 10:00 at night. Then later, after I'd been working for several months, I'd be eligible to apply out for a daytime position.

Jamey is livid. "Well, I guess this shows how much respect you have for karate!"

"I can't help it!" I tell him. "I have to work!"

Jamey splays out his arms, saying, "Well, so do I! So does everybody else! But you don't see anybody else working those crazy hours!"

"It's not forever," I tell him. "Just until I get established, that's all."

"Get established, my *ass*! *You* are the only one who has the power to establish your life. Not some employer. *You* call the shots. This isn't about 'them,' it's about *you*!"

"So what do you want me to do?" I ask.

"Well, for starters, you need to find a decent job."

"Jamey, do you have any idea how long it took me to find this one?"

"Well, if you were really dedicated to the art, you know where you'd be right now?"

"Where?"

"Out looking."

"But Jamey—"

"That's *it*. *End* of conversation. There's nothing else to say. This is a choice that *you* are making. Not anybody else. Just *you*."

"Jamey, how do you expect me to even pay for karate lessons? I mean, I have to have a job to even do that!"

"Why can't your grandparents keep on paying? It's not like they don't have the money!"

"Because I'm trying to do things, myself. To get out on my own. And I can't do that as long as I keep asking them for money!"

"Well, *you* figure it out, then."

"I don't know what you expect me to do!"

He turns to rey into the classroom, saying, "Where there's a will, there's a way."

I follow him, protesting, "That's not always true! Sometimes things just have to be a certain way for a certain amount of time, that's all."

He turns to me again. "You know what your problem is?"

"No. What?"

"You don't want it bad enough."

"Jamey, how can you—"

He looks at me, shakes his head. "What happened to the little girl I used to know? The one who was so confident? Who knew exactly what she wanted?"

I hold out my hands, saying, "I'm still *here*!"

"No, not anymore, you're not. In fact, I don't even think I know who you are anymore!"

"Jamey, *I* haven't changed!"

He turns back to face me, saying, "Yes, you have. And I've been meaning to talk to you about that for a while, anyway."

"What do you mean?"

"Well, for one thing, ever since you've been screwing around—seeing *Jim*—you've let yourself go."

"What? How do you figure that?"

"Well, first of all, you've gotten fat. Look at the size of that butt hanging off the back of you now!"

"Jamey, I weigh 104 pounds! The doctor says I'm just right! She says I needed to gain weight, anyway! And do you know what? I'm finally big enough to fit into a size 3! Do you know how good that feels?"

"I don't care what the doctor said. And clothes size is nothing but a number, anyway. I'm talking about the way you *look*, and believe me, I'm not the only one who's noticed."

I glance down, back around at my butt. "Who else's said anything?"

"Oh everybody."

"You mean in class?"

"Well, yeah. For starters."

I suddenly have this image of the entire class standing around afterwards, openly discussing the size of my butt.

"Well, screw them! If they're going to sit around and talk about something that stupid, then let them do it! I don't care!"

Inside, my feelings are hurt. Really hurt. But I'll never let Jamey know that.

"That's where you're screwing up again," Jamey tells me. "Because this is about *you*, not about *them*. You have no right to be mad at *them*. They can't help it if you're getting fat. Only *you* can."

"Well, if it's so obvious, why didn't someone say something before now?"

"Nobody wanted to hurt your feelings. Regardless of what you think, they still have your best interests at heart."

* * *

"Does my butt look fat in these jeans?" I ask Mama. I am at their house, doing my laundry—something I've discovered if done over here, can save me several dollars each week.

"*Fat?*" Mama asks, sounding incredulous. "That's crazy! Why would you ask that? You're *teeny*! You always have been."

I shrug. "I was just curious, that's all."

But of course, *she'd* tell me 'no.' She's my mother. And we already know what skewed images mothers have of their off-spring.

"No," Mama tells me. "You're definitely not fat. You've got a cute, little shape!"

"Do I have more of a shape now than I used to?"

"Well, of course, But you should. You're growing up."

"Can you take me to Dr. Pridgen?" I ask. "Just so I can get her opinion?"

"Well, yes—if that's what you want. If you need a doctor to convince you. But I'm telling you, you're teeny-tiny! This is crazy!"

Still, Mama makes an appointment with the doctor, and when she takes me back to weigh me, the scale again registers a solid 104 pounds.

"What's wrong with your weight?" she asks.

"I just feel like I've gained a lot. Especially in my butt."

"But if you read my chart, you're still considered 'underweight,' and just by looking at you, I'd say you have nothing to worry about, anyway."

"But it *is* worrying me. And I want to do something about it before it gets out of hand. Before it's too late."

"How much do you think you *should* weigh?" she asks.

"Well, last year in high school, I was around 97 pounds."

"But that's only a seven-pound difference. And you *are* growing up."

I am so sick and tired of hearing about this 'growing up' shit! But I don't say anything. Instead, I just tell her, "Still, I'd feel a lot better if I learned to control my weight now—you know, at an early age."

I want to add that there's a big difference between growing *up* and growing *out*, incase she hasn't noticed, but I don't. Because now I have another question.

"Can you maybe write me a letter for work, too?"

She looks up from the notes she is scribbling in my chart. "What for?"

"Well, see, I'm in this karate class two nights a week. And I'm in it because it helps me to get stress out. And I've just gotten this new job, too, only it's at night. And I really want them to understand that I need this class, that I need for them to work with me just those two nights a week. Could you maybe ask them to do that?"

"Sure, I don't see how that's a problem."

And she scribbles out a note for me to take to my new banking job, then hands me a print-out of a medical diet consisting of 1,500 calories a day.

"Don't go below 97," she tells me. "You don't need to lose weight, anyway. But if seven pounds is going to make you feel that much better, then go ahead. Just make sure you follow this—that you do it in a healthy way."

At work, my employers turn out to be very accommodating. They allow me to come in on Tuesdays and Thursdays early—from the morning starting time, which varies depending on the amount of work we have, until evening close-out. Then I'm free to go home. Mondays, Wednesdays, and Fridays though, I can keep the same schedule, coming in at 1:00 and working until 10:00. But even with these accommodations, sometimes daytime close-out still runs a little late, especially when it's the end of the month. Sometimes, I don't actually get out until right at 7:00, and sometimes, even a few minutes later than that. Then I am dashing to my car, driving feverishly to karate, trying to change clothes at intersections just so I won't be late. Still, right at 7:30, Jamey has started this thing where he shuts and locks the classroom door so that anyone who is late can't just barge in like that. And it is one of these nights when I have not even had time to change in the car, that I am walking out of the community center, totally dejected because I hadn't made the cut-off, when Sandy, the lady who has worked in the office ever since I've been in class, asks, "Angie, what's wrong?"

I try to pull on a smile, saying, "Oh, nothing. I'm just late, that's all."

She glances down at her watch, saying, "Well, it's just 7:35 now. Go on back and change clothes. You've still got plenty of time."

"I would, but Jamey doesn't like it when we're late. He says it disturbs the rest of the class if we go walking in after everything's started."

"Well, just tell him I sent you on in, anyway."

"Thanks, but—"

"No, go on! I know how much you love that class!"

"Well, the door's locked," I tell her.

"The door's locked?" she echoes. "What for?"

"Oh, he does that to keep things on track, that's all. It sorta makes everybody get here on time, you know?"

"Well, I appreciate his dedication, but he can't *do* that. He's teaching for the *city*, not for *himself*. He doesn't get to lock paying students out."

She picks up her huge ring of keys, heading for the karate room door.

"That's okay," I quickly tell her. "I'm really too tired to work out tonight, anyway."

And before she can protest, I am out the door, walking towards my car. Because I can only imagine Jamey's reaction when he thinks I've gone and tattled like that. And besides, Sandy can't keep him from locking the door. It doesn't matter who he's teaching for. Jamey makes his own rules, and no one in class is going to go against him, no matter what.

I have finally lost weight, and I feel really good. I am back down to 97 pounds. But I haven't used Dr. Pridgen's diet as a guide. I don't eat fruit and vegetables at all—I never have—so there's nothing on it I want to eat. Instead, I just cut back on the things that I *do* like to eat. And at 97 pounds, I feel so powerful for what I've accomplished, I don't even stop dieting there. I go down even further, to 95 pounds, and I like the way my jeans feel loose now, the way they don't fit around my waist anymore, the way I have to wear a belt to keep them up. Jamey tells me I look absolutely wonderful. "You could even afford to drop a few *more* pounds," he says. "Then you'd really look good!"

I decide that's definitely what I'm going to do.

"Besides, I didn't want to have to tell you, but I had a talk with Jim after class a few weeks back. And he said he was planning to break up with you if you didn't lose some weight."

"Really?" I am surprised. Because he'd never said anything to me about it at all. "I can't believe that!"

"Oh, yeah—believe it. He's a nice-looking guy. He's not going to put up with a fat girlfriend. He doesn't *have* to. *No* man with any self-respect ever will."

"Why didn't you say something before?" I ask.

"I wanted to give you a chance to do it on your own first."

He indicates my new frame. "And you did it, too. See, you can do anything you set your mind to."

I am floating—elated—and I can't believe I was going to give all this up—just for a stupid job. What had I been thinking? Still, as the saying goes, 'all's well that ends well.'

After class, Sylvie, one of the new girls, wants to talk to me. She is several years younger, and it inflates my ego, having her think enough of me to ask for my help.

"It's about Jamey," she says, kind of looking back to make sure he's nowhere within earshot.

"Sure. What about him?"

"Well, he's been asking me—I mean, he wants to know—well, it's like, see . . . . it's just that we've got this . . . . he and I, we have this really special *friendship*."

What had she said? "Friendship?" I echo.

Sylvie looks down. "Well, kind of. At least that's what *he* says." Then she looks up again. "But now he's asking me to do these—these *other* things—and I just don't know. I mean, it's kind of weird or something, you know?"

Unfortunately, I do. All too well. Still, I absolutely cannot believe what I'm hearing! I feel so hollow, so empty—so utterly betrayed. Because I'd truly believed I was really special—that there was something very unique about me. And now, how am I supposed to know who I am anymore? How do you even attempt to reconstruct those boundaries? Exactly where do you begin?

It's completely ironic that when I actually land a daytime position at work, I no longer care about attending karate class. Instead, now I have all these nights to sit at home and think about everything that's gone on. I remember the nights Jamey'd worked one-on-one with Tammy, with Karen, with Elizabeth. And I feel so incredibly stupid.

Jamey's come by my apartment a couple of times, too, wanting to know where I've been. I tell him I'm not interested, that it's just not my thing anymore. He refuses to accept that as an explanation, though. Instead, he blames my sudden disinterest on problems with Jim.

"Look—I'll kick him out of class, if that'll make you come back. He doesn't need to be screwing my students, anyway."

Okay . . . . so what a nice way of putting it. It kind of reminds me of the time we'd all been standing around in the parking lot before class, and this pregnant lady had walked by. Jamey'd looked her up and down before finally announcing, "Well, at least we know what *she* does." But overall, I decide it's completely pointless. Because Jamey will never see things in any way, but his own. It's pretty sad, but I honestly don't believe he's capable of it. Still, I tell him not to kick anybody out of class, because no, that will not make a difference. I'm not coming back, either way.

At work, I throw myself into my new position. Still, I don't seem to be going anywhere, regardless of how much effort I put in. In fact, when I'd first been interviewed for the job, they'd referred to everything as belonging to 'the desk.' Like they'd said, "The desk requires that all the high dollar returns be processed within the first hour of duty." Or "The desk has a very high turn-over of employees." And somehow, by personifying the desk, they manage to make me feel completely secondary, like I don't really matter—that's it's all about the desk, not about the employee.

It is becoming more and more difficult to sit at 'the desk' for a routine 8 hours now, doing the very same thing over and over again. The rituals are coming harder and faster every single day, and this really puts a weight on my progress. When calling originating banks to inform them of high dollar returns, I can barely fill in the accompanying form because I have to keep writing over and over the letters and numbers, making sure that all the loops connect, that all strokes have the same amount of pressure applied. Because if one of the letters, or even a part of one of the letters, looks lighter than the rest of the words around it, I have to re-trace it with my pen until it completely matches. And my forms always end up looking sloppy, look like something a first-grader put together. I get up in the mornings and tell myself that today will be the day that I no longer allow the rituals to control my life like this. But for some reason, the harder I try, the worse they become.

Filing becomes extremely difficult because after punching holes in the forms, there is this certain way I have to put them in their respective notebooks, making sure that all three ring binders enter the paper at the exact same time. Otherwise, I have to take it out of the notebook and start all over again. And if I have to start over, then it has to happen an even number of times. The same thing applies to pressing the buttons on the phone. Sometimes I have to dial a number three or four times before I can actually let the call go through. And even worse, I have this sudden extreme need to turn my head—over my shoulder as far as it will go—until it literally hurts, and hold it there for a certain count. On a good day, this is only in groups of twos or fours, and on a bad day, it can range all the way from groups of eight up to groups of sixteen or more. And this new head-jerking thing—I have to do this an even number of times, too, and both the right side and the left side have to match completely. My neck hurts all the time now. (Have I ever mentioned how bad I want to scream?) I can only be glad that my desk is the last one in the row. Because people don't really notice my uncontrollable compulsions as much then. Not like they would if I was sitting in front of them. Still, they *do* see that I'm always dragging butt, always the one bringing up the rear, and the only conclusion they can possibly draw from this is that I'm lazy. They begin to resent me, to make snide comments. Sometimes they don't even seem to care if I hear what they say.

I stop taking lunch breaks because I'm so afraid of getting behind. But my supervisor tells me that it is required by law to take a lunch break. Still, when I am gone, no one will answer my phone when it rings or take any messages for me. Nothing like that at all. And honestly, I can't really blame them because in the same situation, I would probably feel the same way. But still, I wish I could tell them the truth—how I'm actually doing four-times the amount of work necessary—just to make it through each day. Something tells me they wouldn't get it though, even if I did tell them, try to explain it. No one understands why I have these compulsions—not even me. So how can I expect to explain something that I don't even get, myself? All I know is that the compulsions exist, and no matter how much I try, it is becoming harder and harder to function, to actually get my work done. It's almost as if something is taking over my entire body. I feel isolated, depressed. And adding to the depression is the growing knowledge that this is 'it.' That this is life, the way things are, the way things are always going to be. It is a very bitter pill to swallow, and at barely 20 years old, I feel more like I should be around 50 instead.

I meet Mama one night after work to go walking through the neighborhood, something we have recently started doing together for exercise. And suddenly, it hits me.

"I want to go to college." I say it, just like that.

Mama is surprised at first, but still, very supportive. She tells me I can do it, that I can do anything I set my mind to. She knows. She's seen me do it, time and time again.

But I have not bothered to take college-prep classes in high school. I've never been through Geometry or Algebra II. In fact, I have never even taken the SAT. It seems like an impossible feat. But something's got to give. Because this cannot be how life is. There has got to be something better out there.

Once I've spoken it into existence, it becomes real. It becomes my goal. And I want to go to NC State, too, the school where nearly everyone in my family has gone. Pop, Granddaddy, Mama's younger brother, Jimmy. Even Daddy, himself, before later getting married and transferring to Atlantic Christian College where he went on to graduate.

Daddy and I go to the NC State campus one afternoon to look around. Everything seems so big, so serious—so important. I know I am way out of my league. Daddy doesn't think so, though. Like Mama, he believes that this is something I can do, regardless of the obstacles.

We have a meeting scheduled on campus with one of the school's directors. His name is Mr. Bynum, and he doesn't laugh me out the door when I tell him what I want to do. Instead, he offers an alternative way to get into the school. Instead of applying like most students do while still in high school, he recommends a program that NC State offers called 'The Lifelong Education Program.' Anyone can sign up for a class through Lifelong Education, and they can even take up to 12 hours a semester as well. And after those initial classes and applying to the university, if accepted, the hours I have completed through Lifelong Education will count towards my total credit hours required for graduation.

"What I would do," Mr. Bynum suggests, "is to take two semesters here at State, *then* fill out an application for admittance. Because at that point, the only basis they will use for evaluation is how you've done in your classes here. Not on SAT scores or even high school performance."

"So you don't think I'm asking for something that's completely impossible?" I ask.

"No, not at all. In fact, if everyone went to college straight out of high school, or if everyone was judged by their college prep classes and their SAT scores, we'd probably have a much lower success rate and a much higher drop-out rate. Sometimes, students are just not ready when they get out of high school. They need time away from the educational institution, time to grow some. And that's precisely why NC State has this program in place. Just that factor—that one thing—becomes key. Because when students are *ready*, that's when they will succeed."

We thank him for his time before I head back to work. I know I have a long road ahead of me, but I intend to travel every mile of the distance, no matter what it takes.

I sign up for night classes at Wake Tech Community College where I will once again attempt to understand algebra and Geometry. I know there is simply no conquering math at NC State without this basic knowledge. And while I don't intend to major in math—not by a long shot—I still have to take at least two math classes in order to fulfill the criteria for an English degree, according to Mr. Bynum.

It takes me a year and a half to get through the evening math classes offered through Wake Tech Community College. And the thing that has really surprised me is that I am finally starting to understand what I am doing. For the first time in my life, I understand algebra. Still, many nights I get stumped on my homework, and those are the nights that I call Granddaddy. Sometimes the problem will be flipped around differently from the others in the exercise. And other times, there are just 'trick questions,' made for the specific purpose of *trying* to stump you. I read the problem out to Granddaddy over the phone, and he writes it down, works it through himself, then explains to me how he arrived at the answer. Sometimes, if the problem is really tricky, he tells me to let him work on it a while, and then when he gets to the bottom of it, he'll call me back. And even though my teachers at Wake Tech have these nifty little shortcuts that they show us how to use, Granddaddy considers these to be capital sins.

"When you do that—when you *assume* something—you end up forgetting steps. End up forgetting why they're there, what they're there for. And if you want to learn the process, then you need to be consistent."

Sometimes the steps he drags me through seem almost ridiculous. Especially when some of these things are simply givens that everybody knows. Still, he tells me to listen to him—that regardless of how it seems, regardless of how petty each and every step can become—it is still necessary for the system, necessary to condition the brain. He tells me that this is because, "Math is a building process. Each day you build onto what you learned the day before. And if you go skipping steps, that causes you to rely on 'memory' rather than 'system.' And everything's got to be systematic in math. Always. If you want it to work. You just can't shortchange a problem by *assuming* what the steps are. Go *through* them. I *know* what I'm talking about."

And he really does. Because by attacking the problems in a systematic way, I learn that I can solve any that I attempt—even the backwards ones.

In the fall of 1988, I begin the Lifelong Education Program at NC State. I sign up for exactly 12 hours of courses; English 101, P.E. which is required for graduation (though I sign up for the karate class that is offered rather than the traditional P.E. 101, which Merle refers to as P.E. '*run oh run*,' because he says it's all you ever do in there), and Math 101 as well, which I literally sweat and cry myself through. Because even though I've taken all the algebra and Geometry classes that I have in preparation for this, they are still very much watered-down versions compared to what I am faced with here at NC State. And the experience at State will also be the first time in my life that I have ever been introduced to the virtually surreal concept of 'trigonometry,' something that until its introduction at this late point in my life, I hadn't even known existed. But since I have no other choice in the matter, I buckle down, study hard, find ways of opening new avenues in my brain, and learn it.

I befriend several people in my class as well as in one of the higher classes, too, and together, we sit over at McDonald's every morning after our 7:50 and study together. This particular McDonald's is very unique, unlike any other I've ever seen. Transformed from the old Hillsborough Street Theater, it is huge and still has the sloping tile floor and dozens of old movie posters and playbills posted all over the walls. Where the rows of seats had once been lined, there are now rows of booths, and it is here that we sit, eating Egg McMuffins and hash browns, while the TV's mounted in the corners blare the '88 Summer Olympics.

I have not yet learned that a 7:50 AM class 5 days a week is *not* necessary, that parking *arrangements* can be made to avoid parking *tickets*, that no one cares whether you show up to class or not. Because in the end, if you can pass the final exam, that's all that really matters.

I am, in fact, so dedicated to my first classes at NC State that I get up the Monday morning after Thanksgiving and dress for school, like usual, not paying any mind to the fact that I've just had all four of my wisdom teeth out only the Friday before and that I'm still kind of fruity from the pain medicine they've given me. No, the only thing that stops me in my tracks—literally—is the huge tree sprawled across the street. It figures. But that tree turns out to be only one of a gazillion that've been uprooted and slung around—by the series of unexpected tornados that have ripped through Raleigh last night. And the knowledge is shocking. Because that just doesn't happen here. Tornados, I mean. Every now and then we get a watch report, stating that the conditions are favorable, but that's always in the spring, when the changing weather's wreaking havoc. And other than a few bent trees or scattered lawn chairs, that's all you ever really see of it. But this—this is unbelievable, and the governor declares us to be in a state of emergency, declares North Carolina to be a 'disaster area.' We make the national news. They show the same pictures over and over again on all the major news networks; the bare lot off Highway 70 where the K-Mart once stood, the roofless houses and mashed up cars on one side of the street, while the other side has somehow been miraculously spared, left completely untouched. There is footage of a houseless foundation, where in the corner of what was once the dining room, still stands an untouched china cabinet, all its enclosed dishes neatly polished and put away just as the owner'd left them. Someone has even captured a unique picture of a piece of pine straw that has literally been driven through a telephone pole. Further, there is an unbelievable shot of a road sign—a yellow 'Dead End' sign—that's been blown off its post, driven into another telephone pole, then wrapped completely around it, tighter than a doornail. There are even reports of local documents and papers being found in the trees as far away as Kinston and Wilmington. These are the things you only hear about—the things you never actually believe until you *see* the impossible phenomena for yourself.

Back inside my apartment, the phone is ringing. On the other end of the line, I find my grandmother, Mom, who is confused, disoriented. After Mom had her stroke a couple of years ago, she and Pop had moved to Raleigh into a plush apartment complex that catered specifically to the needs of the elderly. That way, with them so close by, Mama could help look after them as well. And in the time that they've lived up here, Pop has really made a spot for himself in the small, exclusive community, joining all kinds of committees and clubs, then on top of that, throwing the highest score on the entire horse shoe team. But Mom has been a different story. Though Pop has complete faith that she will make a total recovery, she still has days when her mind wanders completely off into left-field, today being one of them. Though I can't make out exactly what it is she's saying, I am able to figure out that she's looking for Mama, and it's only then that I realize where they live—in the very heart of where the tornados have struck. I ask her to let me speak to Pop, who confirms that they are okay, other than lots of trees being down and everything being in such a mess. I tell him I will find Mama, have her call them as soon as she can.

"But she's already called us," Pop says, sounding a little confused.

"You mean today? This morning?" I ask.

"Yes," he says. "In fact, she's on her way over here right now."

"Does Mom know that?" I ask him.

"Well, I *thought* she did. Maybe I'd better tell her again."

I hear him muffle the phone away from his face, saying, "Kate—"

I don't think she ever really got it, though, and when Pop comes back on the line, I tell him that there are a lot of trees down over here, too, and to be sure and not worry if it takes Mama a long time to get there.

Next, I call Daddy, who says they are all fine, and confirms that Mama's on her way over to see about Mom and Pop. When I dial Mimi's number, she tells me that everyone in Wendell is fine, too, but points out what a close call this has been for all of us, and how we should say a prayer to God, thanking Him for sparing us the total devastation, and in some cases, for even sparing our lives.

"You can always get a new house, new furniture and everything. But your life is the only one you've got—at least as a mortal, and we should all be very grateful that God has allowed us to remain here, to serve Him further in this lifetime."

I ask about Granddaddy, and Mimi assures me that he is okay, too.

"He's gone down to the store right now to see about the damage done there," she tells me.

He *would*. Only Granddaddy would *so* do that.

"The cat freaked out," Kay tells me when I call her. "That's about it, though."

She and Merle, who are by now married, have a new house in Wake Forest, which Merle and his father'd built, themselves. In fact, they owned their own building company, and almost every single one of the houses in the neighborhood were built by them. You could always tell the ones that were because they had special extra features that none of the other builder's houses had, like odd-shaped little windows tucked away in unexpected places, small adjoining rooms—usually sunrooms—leading off the larger, main rooms, sometimes even a white picket fence outside, surrounding the entire yard. And it was these extra features that made their houses so marketable, earned them awards in the Parade of Homes every year.

I am surprised to learn that school is not closed today, and I wonder how they expect us to get there. But later, I will learn that the university rarely ever closes its doors, since if it declares a day off for any reason whatsoever, it has to pay all the staff and professors, anyway. But if they declare it a "use your own judgment day," then mandatory payment is not required. Still, it's just this understood thing—the professors tell us not to come if the weather's bad because they, themselves, will not be in attendance.

It is hard to get used to the new 'landscaping' in Raleigh. If the absence of familiar trees and landmarks isn't enough, then the glaring foundations where houses once stood and the partially blown down office buildings'll end up doing it for you instead. It is unlike anything else I've ever seen before, almost as if the storm, itself, had been able to hand-select its own victims, though there is no rational explanation for any of its choices, whatsoever. It kind of makes me think about the Fear—makes me wonder why, out of all the people on earth, it chose *me* to torture. Because as far as I'm concerned, there is simply no explanation for that decision, either.

COLLEGE CO-ED

In the fall of 1989, I am accepted into NC State University as a full-time student, based on my performance from the previous year. Overall, everyone's really happy, but I have to say my two head cheerleaders are definitely Granddaddy and Pop, who're both beside themselves because I've managed to land a coveted spot in their much-loved alma-mater. At first, Granddaddy'd been a little concerned about my getting lost, in more than just educational ways, too, once immersed in the vastness of the university campus. But the reality of it is that I like the anonymity of the huge school, the fact that no one knows who I am. Because this way, they're less likely to pass judgment, to label me as 'weird.' Here, I am able to be just another student, walking around with an overstuffed book bag, like everyone else.

In the Lifelong Education Program, I have managed to pull mostly A's for both the fall and spring semesters, as well as in the Biology class I'd taken over the summer. (In Math 101, I grab the 'C' I manage to snag and totally run with it, like it's the final pass in the fourth quarter of the Super Bowl or something.) Since I have declared a major in English, I will only have one other math requirement to fulfill, and for this class, I choose an alternative one—Philosophy of Logic—which will count for my second credit. It is different than anything else I've ever seen before, kind of a cross between diagramming sentences and Geometry, where you prove the validity of statements through identifying key words, then using their implications to write out a proof.

The class, itself is taught by a graduate student who wears frayed jeans and a scraggly beard. And even though the actual session doesn't begin until 11:05, he still brings a cup of coffee in with him every morning. Lots of the students do that, though. Bring coffee to class. Or drinks, or snacks. Whatever. It's like anything goes here. No one's uptight at all, and the carefree atmosphere it creates is very soothing, calming. Often, students even slip in to class late, quietly taking their seats like it's any other day, and still, no one seems to care about this, either.

I slowly begin to relax in this new world, to feel less struggle with the Fear. And while the compulsions are still there, they don't riddle every single move I make—at least not quite as bad as they did when I was sitting at my desk all day at the bank. And even though sometimes I know my compulsions are probably pretty obvious, again, like the snacking and the concept of time around here, no one really seems to care. No one passes judgment. In fact, no one cares what you wear. No one cares where you live. The only thing they *do* care about is life, itself, and how we, as individuals, affect the world in which we live. Because here, on the college campus, 'superficial' is a meaningless concept. It has no use, no significance, whatsoever. We are all our own people—individuals who will eventually find our own ways in this world and then later, come back together, converge, adding our own contribution—our own individual piece—to this puzzle we refer to as life. We all have a place—an individual role—and the purpose of college is to help us decipher that calling.

Regardless, the Philosophy of Logic class is the most useless one I've ever encountered. I fail to see the point of it, in spite of the interesting exercises we are learning to do. I mean, what's up with the statement '*if it's raining, then it's raining*?' Because if it *is* actually raining, that's pretty obvious, I would think. So why is it necessary to go out of your way, just to prove the validity of a dumb statement like that?

Still, there's one thing about this class—one thing that I am becoming all-too aware of—and that is the growing fact that things *don't* happen because they 'just sometimes randomly do.' No, everything that takes place—absolutely everything—has its own cause, it's own effect. It's the only logical explanation, and everything has to have a logical explanation. I begin to question the compulsions, the Fear, the reasons why they exist in me. Because given this new knowledge, there *has* to be a reason. Because to believe that I am just a random individual, hand-chosen to suffer the consequences of this unknown fate is simply *not* logical. It goes against all common sense—all the hypotheses and theories that science so readily offers us.

In my Anthropology class, I learn that the kinship relationships we use to identify our family members with here are not necessarily the same ones that other cultures use. Like, in some remote tribes, cousins are considered to be brothers and sisters. Okay . . . . so that means that they still have the same relationship, they just call it something else. "Not necessarily," my professor points out. He is 60-ish, close-cut gray hair, big, thick-framed glasses. He looks just like one of those the scientists you used to see on public television who wore the lab coats and conducted complicated experiments with outdated test tubes and ancient glass beakers.

"You've got to figure," he tells me. "That if your *cousins* are your brothers and sisters, then their *parents* share the same relationship among *their* siblings as well."

This whole concept is hard to grasp, forces me to open all these new and backwards avenues in my brain. And if I consider what he says from just the right angle, concentrate on the points he is emphasizing, I can sort of understand. It's like looking at a 3-D cube in such a way that if you stare at it long enough, it eventually changes direction on you.

I begin to question things I've never considered before, become more accepting of different opinions, become concerned with ethicacy and worldly issues.

At what would be considered approximately lunch time most days, I make my way over to the bagel shop where I sit outside at the patio tables with the other radicals, listening to Duran Duran, U-2, Jesus Jones. I have given up my acid-washed jeans in lieu of second-hand Levis, tie-dyed T-shirts. I have further traded in my high top Reeboks for more alternative clunky Doc Martens. And going to the mall now? That's been ditched with the newfound respect for consignment shops and Goodwill Industries.

Most days between classes, I have a couple of free hours, and I choose to spend those studying. Usually, if the weather's pretty, I lie on the manicured grass in front of the 1911 Building. Since most of my classes are in Tompkins Hall and Poe Hall, which flank either side of the 1911 Building, it's a pretty convenient place to relax, while all around me, groups of shirtless guys play Frisbee, or sometimes individual games of Hackey Sack. Though I've never put this theory to the test, I'm willing to bet that none of the dictionaries or reference books throughout the entire expanse of this campus include such words as 'rush,' 'hurry,' or even 'late.' In fact, the only certifiably acknowledged time piece I know of around here is the Bell Tower, whose chimes serve more as a pleasant addition to a sunny afternoon than they do for the purpose of alerting the hour. Erected as a monument to fallen American soldiers, the Bell Tower, itself, is beautiful, with it's carved stone and four-sided numeric face. Back in the late 1930's when Granddaddy'd been in school here, they'd just finished building the Bell Tower, and Granddaddy, himself, had been one of the key participants to initially wire the tower, so that the chimes worked, so that the afternoon and Sunday hymns played on-cue.

When I think about it, it's hard to imagine Granddaddy, or even Pop, for that matter, being college students here all those years ago. I'm sure it must've been different back then, anyway. I mean, I can pretty much tell that from the ancient fraternity picture that Granddaddy'd shown me, where instead of jeans and sandals, they are all wearing suits and ties. And instead of lounging randomly on the grass, they are sitting stiffly in a semi-circular arrangement of old-fashioned chairs, hands placed uniformly on their knees.

Aunt Sue, who has always been immensely interested in the family's genealogy, swears that we have relatives who're buried right beneath the site where the Bell Tower now stands. In fact, she could even tell you their names and exactly what their kinship is to us, if you asked. And if anyone should know, it would definitely be Aunt Sue, who, on more than one occasion, took us—along with the whole posse of cousins—on these all-day outings where she'd drive to some remote field out in the absolute middle of nowhere, lead us two or three miles through thick underbrush overcome with years of Kudzu, only to locate a certain tree, beneath which she'd point to a dent in the ground, proudly telling us, "That's where your great-great-great grandfather's uncle-by-marriage's first cousin's brother, *Esophomous*, is buried." Unfortunately, at this point, I am usually too tired to roll my eyes, and besides, what was that Sue'd just casually mentioned to us—about watching out for *snakes* on the three-mile trek back to the car? Okay .... right. And for someone, like myself, who has issues with simple corn worms, this is so *not* a cool revelation. Mama'd probably die if she knew where we were right now, anyway.

"What happens if we see one?" we ask her.

"Just don't bother it," she says. "If you don't hurt him, then he won't hurt you, either."

But what Sue just doesn't seem to get is that the sight of a single snake, alone, is by and far enough to make me hurt *myself*. Forget the snake trying go help out. But when Sue gets on a roll about something, there is absolutely no stopping her at all. She will push, dig and prod until she finds exactly what it is she is looking for. And of the relatives buried under NC State's infamous landmark Bell Tower? I have only one request for Aunt Sue; "Just wait 'till *after* I graduate before you start exhuming dead bodies, will you?"

Ironically, in spite of the vast genealogical knowledge she has managed to amass over all the years, Sue herself—just like everyone else in the family—is still unable to properly explain Aunt Gladys.

Probably the most interesting concept about this new college-campus lifestyle is that the very things that had ostracized you before are now the unique characteristics by which you identify yourself. Individuality is highly valued, though it is not judged by the clothes that you wear or the things that you have. Instead, it emanates from the beliefs you hold, the unique characteristics that ultimately make you who you are.

I begin to take on a strong, new interest—a prodding curiosity—about the characteristics that ultimately make me who I am—how they'd come about. Who, in my ancestry, am I most like, and why? It is a culmination of this curiosity, coupled with the new insight I have gained from the biology lab, the anthropology class—that drives me to begin the tangled job of digging up my roots, unearthing skeletons that have long since been buried.

Granddaddy's fraternity at NC State
(Granddaddy is the one seated in the center, both feet on the ground.)

An 'aerial view' of NC State's campus taken by Pop in 1933

THE BRIDGES OF ROBESON COUNTY

I don't have to go very far to find out things about my family, my heritage. Strangely, most of these things are ones that I've already heard, already known about all along, but just hadn't paid any attention to. Until now. Like Mom and Pop, for example.

Mama'd always talked about how Mom would get depressed and go to bed, sometimes for days at a time. I mean, I'd known about that all along, but I'd just never considered the impact it must've had on her kids—on Mama and her three brothers—when they were growing up. It was just something that had happened. Mama'd told us she always knew when Mom was in one of her funks because when she'd get home from school, the house would be totally dark, shut up tight with all the shades drawn against the reality of day, and there'd be no familiar sounds coming from the kitchen, the TV or the radio. And Mom, herself, would be lying on her bed, backwards. Always backwards, with her head where her feet should've been, and her toes facing the pillows. And when she was like that, lying so still and quiet, Mama would go in and try to talk to her, try to coax her to get up, to at least say something. But Mom would never respond. Instead, she'd just act like no one was there at all.

And Mom did other unusual things as well, like vacuuming the house at 4:00 in the morning, or gathering a load of clothes to wash at midnight. Mama said her friends never knew how her mother really was, that she always put up a jolly front when they were around.

On top of Mom's unusual habits, she and Pop had always had a hostile relationship as well, where most of the time, they argued and fought. As a result, Mama had grown up with a nervous stomach, often sick in the mornings before she went to school.

Mama swore she'd never be like that—like Mom—when she grew up and had kids of her own. And when she and Daddy had first gotten married, Mom used to write her these long, intense letters, talking about how depressed she was, and how she didn't want to go on living anymore. It'd made Daddy pretty mad at the time, and because of all the pain it caused Mama, Daddy had come to resent Mom for it. But Mama argued that he shouldn't feel that way because Mom, herself, had had a very tough time growing up.

Mom's real mother, Kate Vernon Dickens-Shirley, had died in childbirth while having her. Regardless, Mom had still been issued her mother's name—Kate Vernon Shirley—to use as her own. Immediately following her ill-fated birth, she'd been sent away to live with relatives because her father didn't know how to manage a newborn all by himself. As a result, Mom and her two older sisters had grown up more or less like cousins instead of the siblings that they actually were. And Mom's aunt, who raised her, whom she'd called 'Mama Min,' had had some pretty weird ideas of her own as well, adding to the already complicated situation. Like for example, she wouldn't buy shoes for Mom that actually fit her feet. Instead, they were always too little because Mama Min believed that by doing this, it would prevent Mom's feet from growing, cause them to always remain small and dainty, like the Japanese Princesses' feet. And as they'd tried to grow in the too-tight shoes, her feet had ended up bowing in the middle, causing a deformity. Mom had told Mama that what she remembered most about it was walking home from school, how much her feet had hurt then. And Mama'd said when she and her brothers were growing up, Mom had always made sure that they all had plenty of 'growing room,' that new pairs of shoes were almost too big, before she'd even think about buying them for her own kids.

When Mama'd been very little, Mama Min had come to live with them. She'd developed bone cancer in her old age and grown too sick to look after herself. In order to keep her comfortable, Mom was constantly responding to her morphine-induced outbursts, carrying the broom into the back bedroom to knock imaginary spiders off the walls and ceiling.

Now, thinking back on all these things, I can't help but be touched by the irony of it all—by the fact that Mom had gone so far out of her way to make sure she didn't do the same things to her kids that her aunt had done to *her*, yet the sadness and the pain that she must've experienced as a girl had caused her to lash out at her own children in other ways, which were probably just as bad. But sadness and pent-up anger have a way of doing that—of finding other routes by which to escape.

Mom had never had any real contact with her biological father, and she believed that it was because he blamed her for her mother's death. Mama, herself, had only seen Mom's real father once. It had been at a funeral, and he'd been leaning against a column out on the porch when Mom pointed him out, saying, "That's my real father over there." Even then, at the time, Mama said it'd seemed strange to her that they hadn't even gone over to at least speak to him. But they hadn't approached him at all.

Back in high school, Mom had been voted the 'Best-Looking' in her class. Mama shows me old pictures, old playbills from high school productions, in which Mom had had the lead role. Pop, who had gone to school with her, had been involved in just as many activities as she had. Still, it's really hard to think of them as ever being actual high school students. I mean, it's hard enough to imagine Mama and Daddy being that age. But Mom and Pop? It's almost like 'forget it.'

Mom and Pop hadn't started dating until after school, until after they'd both graduated and become adults. And Mom had always told Mama that the only reason she'd ever married Pop in the first place was because he wouldn't quit asking. Still, I find this explanation to be very inconsistent with the memoirs Mama'd saved from their old house in Lumberton, where they'd lived for so many years. It'd been a few years back, when they were downsizing, getting ready to move into the retirement community here in Raleigh, that Mama'd gone down to help them pack, to sort through the years of memories and debris—to decide what needed to be saved and what did not.

In this box, there are letters disclosing secret meetings between Mom and Pop, romantic plans, valentines declaring undying love. I mean, these are the things that you just don't write, let alone feel, unless you truly care for someone. And in all the old pictures of her, Mom is smiling, happy. One photograph in particular, I find riveting; she is running through the fall leaves, her long coat blowing back in the wind, and in front of her, a little dog runs, too. But the thing that really catches my eye is the open way in which she's laughing, with her head thrown back in the fading sun, like she doesn't have a care in the world. So what happened to her? To the girl who appeared to love life so very much? How did she turn into this other woman who was always depressed and who claimed to have not felt any real love for her husband, whom she'd often declared 'would never amount to a hill of beans?' Certainly, her perception had been skewed; because Pop had been very successful, highly intelligent. And he'd looked very dignified, too—like a senator or something—along with possessing immaculate manners to go with his appearance. Mama recalled that it'd actually taken her moving out of the house—when she went off to college—to see it, though. Because Mom had said those things so much about Pop, Mama'd just pretty much accepted them as 'givens.'

Still, Mama did tell me that Mom had had this other boyfriend she knew about, back in high school, with whom she'd been very much in love. They'd planned on getting married as soon as they graduated—at least until he'd had his accident. Mama is not sure exactly what type of accident it actually was, only that he'd become disfigured in some manner that he found unacceptable. And though Mom claimed it didn't matter to her, he still washed his hands completely of their relationship.

It wasn't until much later, after Mom and Pop had moved from their first retirement community in Raleigh to another one which had more accommodating facilities for the aging, that Mama learned of the old boyfriend's death, and she debated for a long time over whether to tell Mom or not. And when she finally decided that Mom needed to know, it appeared that a little more of the remaining life had drained from her already dying spirit. It was as if she'd almost based her whole life—found solace in the fact—that even though they were no longer together, she and this man at least co-existed somewhere in the same world. I can't imagine anything more sad—more hopeless—than living your life in this manner, basing the validity of your existence on the hope of someone else's. And I wish I could've done something for her, been able to go back in time and find a way to tell her, to let her know that it really *is* okay to love more than one person. I can't help but regret for her all the love she'd kept bottled up inside for all those years—love that she could've given to Pop, love that she could've allowed *herself* to feel. No wonder she'd been so troubled, so depressed. How terribly lonely it must have been for her. It reminds me of this movie I'd once seen—'The Bridges of Madsen County'—where for months after watching it, I'd find myself rehashing some scene or another, each time triggering the same tears that somehow always managed to feel brand-new.

It is after this final move—the one into the latter retirement community—that Mom is finally diagnosed with manic depression. They'd began giving her medication at once to even out the chemical imbalance from which she suffered, and while it took several experiments with the wrong medications before they actually hit on the right one, once they got her evened out, she was like a totally different person. Still, since she'd had another series of mini strokes which had been the whole reason for the move to the more accommodating facility in the first place, she was not always in her right mind, so it'd been hard to tell what her life could have been like, had she received medical help much earlier. But unfortunately, there were no real medications offered back in those days—not like the ones we have today that pinpoint and control chemicals in the brain that have the ability to cause such unstableness.

Going into all of this with Mama again now, I finally see how sad the situation really was. Apparently, depression for Mom was like the Fear is for me, and she probably couldn't help her desperate actions then any more than I can help mine now. Not only had she endured so many tragic situations in her lifetime, but she'd also suffered from a chemical imbalance as well, which only intensified the effects of these things. I imagine she must've felt just as trapped inside as I do. But how awful to go on blaming yourself throughout your entire life for events that are totally out of your control. And having others resent you for the *behavior* you displayed in response to these feelings only reinforces the belief that you *are* somehow to blame for what's going on inside your head. This is something I know first-hand.

"I had this dream recently," Mama tells me, as she is putting the old pictures away. "It was about Mom when she was a little girl. And she was walking down this long hallway, carrying a suitcase. Each room she passed had someone in it that she knew—relatives, friends—and they were all talking about her, how she'd been responsible for this, or how she should be blamed for that. When she walked past the first room, she heard somebody say in this stage-whisper, "She killed her *mother*, you know." And then as she passed the second room, someone else had said, "Because of *her*, the family fell apart." And as she walked past each door, hearing these things, her suitcase became a little larger each time, a little heavier—and by the time she got to the end of the hallway, it had gotten so huge, had grown so much out of proportion, that she was struggling just to push it along."

Mama gives a half-hearted laugh as she tucks the last of the yellowed memoirs back into their box. "I guess it doesn't really take Jung or Freud to figure out the significance of this one—that she'd been given way more baggage to carry around through her lifetime than she should have ever been handed."

'Mom,' as a little girl
(the way Mama pictured her in the dream)

'Mom,' as a happy, young woman
(one of the photos I find most riveting)

Mom and her two sisters, Vearl, (left), and Lottie (behind)
(Mom and her sisters had grown up more or less like cousins
instead of the siblings they actually were.)

Mom's real father, 'Daddy Jim,' (right) whom she'd never really known

Mom and Pop's wedding picture

WORKAHOLICS ANONYMOUS

    I am balancing my corked tray with one hand, grabbing condiments from the bar with the other; a lime for the corona, swizzle sticks for the crown and coke, the seven and seven. Oh, and hadn't the dorky-looking guy who'd pegged himself as the 'designated driver' wanted a lemon in his water, too? I grab a handful of cocktail napkins, mashing them into a circle with my fist, and then I am off again.
    The music is overly loud and obnoxious, usually referring to something about 'Funky Cold Medina,' or walking a stupid dinosaur. But regardless of *how* obnoxious the songs actually are, I can still, by now, recite each one of them word-for-word. Not something I'd probably stick on my future resume or anything like that. Just for common knowledge—just for the common fact of it that I am forced

to endure this environmentally-induced torture night after night—that is, if I want to make any money.

I hold the tray as high above my head as I can, winding my way through the sea of festive faces. On really busy nights, like tonight, if someone has the nerve (or the lack of common decency) to order a frou-frou drink, we're supposed to tell them that the blender is broken.

"You gotta figure," Rob, the bartender who's well I am working out of tonight, tells me. "Anyone who orders a friggin' *daiquiri* won't be much of a tipper, anyway." He finishes pouring the shots he has mixed into matching glasses, then adds, "And I am *not* here every single weekend just for my health!" He tosses the used strainer over his head where it lands effortlessly in the sink.

Neither am I. This cocktailing gig is only one of three jobs I am working around my schedule at school. On Mondays and Fridays, I am still at the bank, and on the days that I'm not, I am working in the pharmacy at Kerr Drugs where Kay is also the bookkeeper. Then, on Wednesday, Friday and Saturday nights, I am working here, at 'Celebrations,' carrying drinks. And usually on Thursday nights, I am doing the same thing at the 'Longhorn.' But since 'Celebrations' and the 'Longhorn' are both owned by the same people, I only consider it one job. And during the summer months, when I am only taking one course in school, I pick up yet another job, waiting tables at Hooters, too, on the nights that I'm not already cocktailing in one of the bars. When business is slow, the manager sends three or four of us out to the end of the restaurant's driveway where Wake Forest Road passes by, and he makes us hula-hoop while we motion towards the entrance of the parking lot. Buddy, who by now has moved away, still comes to visit me at the restaurant, pointing out the unnecessary fact that I now look exactly like a traffic cone. He claims the resemblance is uncanny. Height and everything.

"So just think, Angie," he says. "If you ever need another job, you can always go to the city and apply with 'public works' or 'highway maintenance.' Then you can put your hands together over your head, like this," and he demonstrates, "and tell them you want to be a *traffic cone!*"

Okay . . . . sweet. I drop the platter of 3-mile island wings on his table, then lift the pitcher to refill his beer.

"And guess what, Angie!" he continues. "You'll be the only '*little orange cone,*'" and here he does his bat-fingers all up in the air, "that can hula-hoop out there! They might even put you on the news, make you famous. Then *everybody* will want to hire you!"

"For what?" I ask, replacing the pitcher.

"You know—parties, weddings and things. You can be the '*little orange cone*' that tells people where to turn!" And he laughs, doing the bat-fingers-thing again.

Leave it to Buddy! I go back to the kitchen in search of some Ranch dressing to go with his celery sticks.

"You work too much, anyway," Buddy tells me when I return with the sealed cup of dressing. "You need to take a couple of nights off, you know? Then we could go somewhere and stay out late, Angie! *Real* late! Like we could stay out late enough to look for *bats* or something!"

I smile, remembering those days. But unfortunately, nowadays, when I'm not working, I have to be studying. And when do I do that? On Sundays, like after I get up. Or during the hours I have between jobs. Or the hours between classes. Whenever. Sadly, I'd hate to be the one to admit it, but all these jobs have *become* my social life. Buddy tells me I need a boyfriend, that he'll find me a real good one. But honestly, when would I have time? It's just not the right point in my life now. And besides, I have cats. Lots of cats. I think there were eleven the last time I counted. I tell the apartment people they are strays, though, and that I just feed them because I feel sorry for them. Then, when they call the humane society to come out, I round the cats up and stick them inside. Then we can all sit there and watch out the window while the goofball who is assigned to come pick up the 'large community of feral cats' stands around, scratching his head, like he doesn't get it.

Buddy is not the only one who thinks I should have a boyfriend. Because Teddy, who works at the bar with me, has been trying fervently for the last two weeks to set me up with the manager's best friend. No one knows exactly what it is that Teddy does at the bar, but regardless, we are expected to recognize the fact that his job is very important, anyway. I figure the only reason he even has it in the first place is because he is in close with the Myricks who own both clubs. I wish he'd leave me alone about it, but he refuses to take 'no' for an answer. The sad thing? I don't even know the guy's name. But I can pretty much figure that if he's friends with the Myricks, he's more than likely got to be a cigarette-smoking toothpick-chewer who wears his hair slicked back and exclusive French silk shirts with matching alligator shoes. *Real* ones.

"It's not like you have to date him," Teddy says, acting all superior-like. I guess he thinks he is because his family is friends with the Myricks. Okay . . . . so *that's* a coveted position.

I hold my hands out in exasperation, saying, "But that's exactly what you're telling me to do!"

"Look, all he wants is to spend the evening in the company of a *lovely lady*, that's it."

"Then why don't you set him up with Debbie?" I ask. "I'm sure *she'd* go along with it." I grab my tray disgustedly, getting ready to walk off and end this stupid conversation for good. Because he's just officially sealed the deal. If nothing else had completely done it for me, then the '*lovely lady*, thing has done it now. I've never seen it fail—that men who call you 'ladies' like that are always the worst kind of lounge lizards that exist.

"Yeah, I'm sure she would, too. But he wants *you*, Baby. You should feel flattered."

I glare at him. Because for the life of me, I cannot figure out why he won't just go the hell away and let me do my stupid job—so I can then go home to my cats, my TV, my homework—totally unmolested. I swear—it's all I'd ask for in an ideal world.

"He's got *mo*-ney," Teddy bribes.

Okay, so this is the last straw. *Completely!* The camel's back's finally broken, and I intensify my glare, dropping down into my low voice to tell him ominously, "*Sorry—I do NOT hook!*"

As I am walking away, Teddy calls after me, "You don't know what 'sorry' is yet. Trust me. Because you *will* be!"

* * *

It's a Friday night, and I have been called into the manager's office.

"It's my understanding that you and Teddy had words out on the floor the other night."

I cross my arms, look at him pointedly while I wait. It'll be the same old lecture, about how we are here to support the club whose sole purpose is entertainment. If we are arguing and fighting out where the customers can see us, then we are totally negating that philosophy. We are therefore denying the customers the good time for which they have ultimately paid.

"Wanna tell me what's going on?" the manager asks, tapping his pen heel-to-toe against the desktop in this methodic way that is absolutely driving me bananas.

"He wants me to go out with this guy," I say. "And I don't want to."

He laughs a little. "*That's* what the fight was about?"

"Yeah. Only it wasn't a fight. Teddy insinuated that the guy would pay for my company—*pay* for it—and I told him 'no way,' that I didn't hook. Then he yells this stuff at me about how sorry I'm going to be."

"Well, are you?" he asks.

"Am I what?"

"You know—sorry."

"No. Why should I be?"

He shrugs then, saying, "Oh, I don't know. Maybe for turning down a simple dinner date with a perfectly nice guy, just because you think you're too good for him? Wouldn't that be enough to make you sorry?"

I eye him from a new angle. Because where is this going?

"See, if you weren't so *uppity*, I might be able to overlook the fact that all this beer's come up missing from the cooler in back. The one that only *employees* have access to." He folds his hands on his desk.

"What are you saying?" I ask through gritted teeth, although he has already made that quite clear.

"I'm saying that I'm willing to forget all the beer you stole if you'll come down off your high horse long enough to give a nice guy a chance."

"Oh, come on!" I blurt. "You know I didn't take any beer! I don't even *drink*!"

This is too completely unbelievable!

"That'll be between you and the police to decide," he tells me.

"The *police*? What the hell? Are you crazy? You *know* this is bullshit!"

Suddenly, I am reminded of Lin Tran and her stupid brother.

The manager shrugs. "Maybe, maybe not. Teddy *saw* you, you know."

I stand up. "Teddy didn't see a *thing*! He's a lying little 'Eddie-Monster-wanna—be-brainless-*brat*,' and I can't believe you're going along *with* him!"

"It's your choice," he tells me.

"Okay, so let me get this straight. You're saying if I *don't* go out with your friend, you're gonna accuse me of stealing beer. But if I *do* go out with him, you're willing to let it all ride—forget that it's all a friggin' lie to *begin* with!"

He holds his hands out, like I've just uncovered some deep, dark mystery. *Screw* him! That little weasly bald-headed, gap-toothed ex-Burger-King-manager-*reject*! Because he's right on up there, right along beside the 'Eddie-Munster-wannabee,' vying for the very top spot on my ever expanding 'List.' I suddenly have the strong desire to voice my thoughts.

"You know what? *Screw* you! *Screw* you *and* the horse you rode in on!"

I let him 'fire' me. For 'stealing beer,' no less. They are so full of it—all of them! But before I leave, I point my finger directly in his face, adding, "Maybe you think it's fun, calling me a 'thief' like that. But one thing's for sure—one thing I will never—*NEVER*—be—is a little 'yes man,' like *you*. Not for *anybody*!"

I cannot let this go. I have to do something because it is so *totally* not right. But when I go over to Daddy's, to complain to him about what's happened, he shows me no sympathy at all.

"Well, what do you expect?" he shrugs. "If you lie down with dogs, you're going to get up with fleas."

"What do you mean?" I demand.

"Just that it's common knowledge. Why would you even want to work in a place like that to begin with?" Daddy asks.

"Because the money's good!"

"Not *that* good. *No* money is worth all that."

"Yeah? Well, it's *tax-free*, too!"

"No work is tax-free," Daddy tells me. "That's illegal. So don't tell me about it. I don't want to know."

He goes back to dusting his model trains off. "I'd just chalk it up to luck. Say 'good riddance,' and be done with it."

But that is something I cannot do. Simply say 'good riddance' and forget it like that.

"Sue 'em for unemployment," Gary, one of my friends from the club, suggests. "That'll *really* get under their skin."

I decide that this is exactly what I am going to do. At first, they fight it—tooth and nail. But finally, after six weeks of persistence, the Division of Unemployment decides that I am due benefits from the club. In the process, I've shown them paycheck stubs as well as deposit slips where I've put my tips in the bank, proving the validity of all the wages that I have now lost. We have a 'hearing' to which the Myricks don't bother to show up. Only my friend, Sandra, who worked at both the bank and the club with me, stands by my side. The acting judge shows me the rebuttal that 'Celebrations' has sent back regarding my eligibility, in which they have stated that I often laid out of work, that I took drugs and was very unreliable. But since both the schedules and my time cards for the last year have been subpoenaed, the hearing judge knows this information is incorrect, that in fact, I have worked a lot of extra hours in addition to my scheduled ones. I offer to take a drug test as well, but he tells me it isn't necessary.

"Don't worry," he says, waving it off. "I've dealt with *their* kind many times before." Okay, Daddy—you win. You were right. It *is* all about dogs and fleas.

At the hearing, I am awarded unemployment benefits. But there is still a two-week waiting period before I can get my first check. I honestly don't understand how people who're *really* down and out manage to get through this psycho-circus of waiting. It seems so unfair.

After the two weeks are up, I am scheduled to go back in to the unemployment office one last time to fill out the remaining paperwork. I take a number, sit in the last row of chairs where the TV is less obnoxious. Although I *do* have an appointment—at 10:00 to be exact—the fact that this slot of time has been allotted for me is, in reality, a joke. Because regardless, you are still called back according to the number that you pull from the spindle. So even if your appointment is at 10:00, if there are still five people ahead of you number-wise, they're going to get called back first, regardless. I've just come to the conclusion that anytime you have to show up at the unemployment office, you'd better plan on making a whole day of it. Because that's what it'll be. Maybe it's not really a complete 8-hour period, but it takes up enough of one to screw up anything else you might've planned, so it's all the same.

Beside me, a girl flops down in the cracked chair, sighing, like she's got better things to do. She appears to be several year younger than me, but in her arms, she is holding a baby who is not quite a toddler yet, and at her feet, twin girls play with the faded plastic toys that the unemployment center has so generously donated to the waiting room for that sole purpose. And upon further inspection, I discover that the girl is actually pregnant—again. *Too* unbelievable! I can't help but wonder if she has any clue where the kids are coming from.

Sitting back in the corner, kind of off to himself, is a man who is wearing a collection of gold chains around his neck and some kind of lizard skin shoes that actually look pretty expensive. I can't help but wonder if he knows the Myricks, too. I am unable to tell anything from his expression, though, because he is wearing sunglasses. In the opposite row, a little old lady is perched, talking to herself. She is busily folding and unfolding a handkerchief, and I notice that the out-dated red lipstick she wears has smeared off onto her dentures. I look away just as quickly, telling myself that I will *never* get that old. I absolutely will *never* allow myself to go through that humiliation, no matter what.

Finally, sometime around quarter to 12:00, my number is called. I follow the dumpy woman with stringy hair and huge owl-like glasses to her cubicle, which is separated from all the others by only a partician. She looks just about as excited to be here as I am, and I glance pointedly around for the 'mission statement'—the one that always hangs on the wall of businesses and charities, describing their wonderful policy on integrity and customer service. For some reason which doesn't much surprise me, I don't find one.

She pulls my file out of the huge pile sitting on her desk, then looks it over. I wish she'd just hurry up and give me my check. Because this is taking way too long, and I'm *so* ready to get out of here. Still, it is a moment before she speaks, though.

"Well, Angela—it seems we've got another little delay here. Apparently, it will be *another* two weeks before we can start your benefits."

Oh, no *way*!

". . . . are You *CRAZY*?" I suddenly demand, my voice raising louder with each word. I begin to feel as helpless as I had that night at 'Celebrations,' and it makes me angry. *Very* angry.

"In case you didn't know, I was *awarded* those benefits in court two weeks ago!"

At the surrounding cubicles, all activity has ceased, and everyone is peeping around his respective partician to see what the commotion is. But I don't care. Because this is about more than just some stupid money. This is about justice! And I will *have* it, one way or another!

Owl Eyes blinks largely behind the magnified glasses. "I beg your pardon?"

"Don't beg my *anything*!" I retort hotly. "It's been 8 weeks now— *8 weeks*!" And I hold up 8 of my fingers for her to observe, demonstrating just how many weeks it's actually been. "Exactly *how* do you expect me to purchase food? Would you *kindly* disclose that bit of *elusive* information?"

"I'm sorry, Angela, but I am only abiding by the rules."

I hold up my hand. "First of all, do *not* call me 'Angela!' It's '*Angie!*' And secondly, do you have any *idea*—any idea *whatsoever*—how it feels to be *hungry*?"

Ohmigod! I cannot believe I just *said* that! Where'd *that* come from? Like *I'd* really know! God should punish me. I try not to think about the freezer full of Tupperwared string beans, new-boiled potatoes and sour dough rolls that Mimi makes sure I'm always stocked with. I think there's even some of her signature pound cake up there, too—the kind with the sweet, crusty sides that literally melt off in your mouth.

Owl Eyes doesn't say anything. Just blinks again in that reptilian way she has. When she doesn't answer, I choose to do it for her, continuing on theatrically, indulging my audience.

"I'm willing to bet that you *don't* know how it feels! In fact, I'll bet you couldn't even tell me what color the backs of your *cabinets* are!"

Now I *know* God is going to punish me. Because if *I* can't believe what's coming out of my mouth, then I know for sure that *he* can't. I know I should be ashamed, but this isn't about hunger for *food*, it's about hunger for *justice*, and I will *have* justice, no matter how I have to go about it!

"As a matter of fact," I rant on hotly, "have you ever been so hungry that you go into the grocery store and push a cart around—put things in it that you *know* you can't buy—and then eat them as you walk up and down the aisles—simply because it's less like *stealing* if you do it that way than it is if you actually carry the stuff out of the store *with* you?"

The woman in the cubicle beside mine nods her head in agreement. From another cubicle, I hear a supportive "*A*-men!" arise.

Owl Eyes lowers her voice. "What would you like me to do, Angela?"

"For starters, you can quit calling me '*Angela!*'"

"Okay, then—Angie." She clears her throat. "What would you like me to do?"

"I would *like* you to give me my check!"

"Unfortunately, I can't do that."

I stand up. "Well, you better '*unfortunately*' find someone who *can!*"

I'm starting to really like this prima-donna bitch-thing. I never knew I had it in me before. At least, not to this extent—not until the episode at 'Celebrations,' anyway. But I guess after all the years of dealing with the Fear, with the compulsions—with all the unfair treatment those conditions ultimately bred—I was destined to get totally fed up, to simply blow one day.

"That's a decision that was made by a different department."

"Are they higher than *you*?"

"I beg your pardon—"

"Can *they* make decisions?"

"Well, yes. Ultimately, they are the ones who do that."

"Then I want to talk to *them*. Right now!"

"But I'm afraid that's hardly possible—"

"Right *now!* See, I don't want to talk to the 'little yes man' around here anymore! Because for 8 weeks now, I've *been* there, *done* that! I want to talk to the one who can *fix* this situation! Because we're *way* past that point!"

"Oh dear," she sighs.

I sit back down in her chair, cross my arms. This is *my* appointment, and she can just wait. It's not like they didn't make *me* wait. Since they seem to think I have all the time in the world anyway, I am going to show them first-hand how right they actually are.

I get my unemployment. In fact, I am issued a check before I even leave the office. They explain that they'd simply made a mistake, that in fact, I *had* met all the eligibility requirements. Okay .... so what a convenient *coincidence* for them to realize this now! But still, I don't say anything. Because this time I won the battle *and* the war. The only stipulation is that as long as I am drawing unemployment, I have to be actively seeking a job. I have to make at least two contacts in person every week, then keep a documentation of where I went and with whom I talked. Then, at benefit time, I have to bring that record in—turn it over to the clerk—before I can receive my check. Okay. I can play that game. *No problem!*

I show up, unannounced, at IBM's corporate headquarters 'human resources' department—wearing flip-flops. And at the grocery store where I apply for a position as a cashier, on the application, where it asks if I have any disabilities of which they should be made aware, I write in '*yes*,' that I am '*severely dyslexic.*' I even go back and rearrange the '*s*' and the '*y*' in '*dsylexic*' to prove my point—in case there is any question about it at all.

I end up drawing unemployment off 'Celebrations' for over a year. The Myricks are truly pissed—they end up banning me from every club they own. Not that I care—or even learn this because I try to go there or something, but because Gary tells me about it instead. I want to laugh. Because there is nothing better than getting paid to *do* nothing, and besides, it has given me some much-needed extra time to study. Still, I know what Daddy'd say about all this, and I wonder how long it'll actually be—before I have to go out and buy the econo-sized jug of flea powder, that is.

At one of my cocktailing gigs in the mid '80's . . . .

*. . . . and later, in 'Hooters' mode
(We are celebrating my 24th birthday after a grueling shift of slaving over a hot hula-hoop.)*

FAMILY TREE WITH MISSING BRANCHES

If it'd been interesting to be reintroduced to Mama's side of the past, then it is nothing short of educational to learn what I do about the other side of the family. To start with, I'd never known there was an actual reason for my great-grandfather, Mallie's, so-called 'peculiarness.' Though I know he'd never been formally diagnosed (simply for the fact that this type of knowledge was not available during his lifetime), it was later decided by all the experts and professionals (after Daddy'd described his symptoms) that Mallie had probably suffered from something akin to 'Tourette's Syndrome.' But it wasn't the so-called 'funny' kind that you always hear about where people go around, constantly blurting these random curse words. Instead, his was more of what they referred to as an 'affliction,' where he had all these strange ticks and things. Like he'd tap his foot constantly, or tap objects against other objects. Often, he'd randomly shake his arm, his head, make sudden, indistinguishable noises that no one was prepared for. And he liked to touch things—repetitively. Okay, so this is just a little closer to home for me than I'd like to admit. But while there is *some* comfort in at least knowing that I'm not quite as alone as I'd thought, I still can't ignore the fact that now I'm officially 'abnormal.' And then there is the nagging fact that Daddy, himself, has always suffered from panic attacks, just like me. I don't know why I never really considered it before—how I am so much like him. I guess I just never paid much attention to it because he went on and did the things that had to be done, and he rarely complained about the obstacles he must have felt.

It'd been back in the 11th grade, when my parents had taken me to one final psychologist in a last-ditched effort to quell the anger, when I'd first been introduced to the idea of 'OCD.' Though at the time I'd figured it would be pretty much pointless (since after all, it always *had* been in the past), I still attempted to tell him about the Fear, the voices that weren't really voices, how I had to touch things so repetitively all the time, how my conscious existence seemed to be overridden with numbers, counting, and these complicated patterns that, even if I wanted to, I could neither explain or rationalize—not for the life of me.

"You'd think I'd be real good at math, seeing as I'm so obsessed with numbers," I'd told him at the time. "But the truth is, I really suck."

He'd just shaken his head, telling me, "This has nothing to do with math. "You have OCD."

"I have *what*?"

"Obsessive Compulsive Disorder. It's one of the symptoms that can sometimes result from a chemical imbalance in the brain."

"So I'm crazy?" I'd panicked. What if that remote idea that'd first manifested itself all those years ago was really true? I'd absolutely kill myself! Or at least hope to die trying.

"No, it has nothing to do with crazy, either. People use 'crazy' too liberally. It's this blanket concept that doesn't deal with the real issue."

"So then I'm *not* crazy?"

He held up his hand, telling me, "I want you to get that word out of your mind. Totally forget it. Because there really is no such thing as 'crazy.' There're only varying forms and degrees of 'mental illnesses,' that's all."

"So does that mean I'm 'mentally ill?" Because if that's what he's saying, then it's no better than being crazy. It's like simply calling a 'turtle' a 'tortoise.'

"Most people do have some form of mental illness, though some forms are less invasive than others."

"Like what?" I am scared, skeptical.

"Well, for example, biting your fingernails can be a form of mental illness. It's just a milder form of 'self-mutilation,' that's all."

"Self-*mutilation*?"

"Yes. It's a disorder where the person feels compelled to cut him or herself, or to inflict some other injurious act upon his own body. Slicing, cutting—it can embody many different forms."

I stare at him. "You mean there're actually people who get off on *hurting* themselves?"

"It's not that they 'get off' on it. It's just something they feel compelled to do, kind of like your being obsessed with numbers and counting."

Okay, so now he's linking my counting with self-torture. Groovy. Maybe I'll shave off my eyebrows next week. Or if I'm feeling a little bolder, maybe I'll even go so far as to slash my wrists. I'm sorry, but this guy is just totally off the wall. You know, like '*mad scientist meets reality*.' Like Uncle Fester or something.

"I hate to tell you," I begin. "But you're way off. Because I just don't see it—what you're getting at. I mean, you just don't understand. I have no tolerance for pain at all—zero, zilch—so there's really no chance of me going out and carving some guy's initials in my arm or anything like that."

"That's because it's not the disorder that you have. Yours is Obsessive Compulsive Disorder. Likewise, to someone who is a self-mutilator, your symptoms would probably seem just as strange."

"I'm sorry," I tell him. "But incase you didn't know, there is this huge, identifiable difference between counting steps and slicing your body open."

"Symptom-wise, maybe. But it all stems from the same cause, which is a chemical imbalance in the brain."

"So did I do something to cause it?" I ask.

'No, it's not a result of anything that you did. Usually, these disorders are hereditary. Or sometimes they can even be triggered by the onset of a childhood illness."

"But either way, you're telling me that I can't help it? That it's not my fault that I touch everything or count all the time?"

"That's right."

I feel like the bottom has just fallen out from under me, like I'm no longer in control of my own life.

"How do I make it go away?" I ask.

"I'm afraid there's no cure for a chemical imbalance. But there are things you can do to reduce the symptoms."

"So you're saying I'm just stuck like this. Forever."

"If that's the way you want to put it, yes. But again, there are treatment options—behavior therapy, new medications. Sometimes a combination of both."

But as far as I'm concerned, these things are *not* options. At least not for me. Because my days of being a drowsy, beached-whale with dried-out gums are over. *Kaput.* It'll never happen again, so don't even attempt to go there. You'll just be wasting both your time as well as mine. And I refuse—*refuse*—to spend the rest of my life, being tortured by this so-called 'chemical imbalance.' Come hell or high water, I will defeat it. I will find a way around it, a way to control it. And though I don't know when it'll be, I *will* live a normal life someday. That is a promise I am making to myself, though the irony of it all isn't totally lost on me; the fact that I wouldn't know a 'normal' existence if it slapped me right into the middle of next week. Actually, if the truth be known, a crash-landing into the middle of next week would be much easier to fathom than life without all these excessive numbers.

At night, now that I'm not working quite as much, I spend lots of time in the huge library at State, where I search the computer database for books on 'chemical imbalances.' Sometimes, I'll be sitting there, lost somewhere in the stacks, reading about Attention Deficit Disorder, Body Dismorphic Disorder or Bipolar Disorder, so engrossed that I won't even realize how late it's gotten—until the 11:00 warning bell rings, alerting all the stragglers that the library is getting ready to close.

I learn that in addition to OCD, I also possess Panic Disorder, thus explaining the Fear. The excerpt that I read from one of the psychological digests states that often Obsessive Compulsive Disorder is accompanied by Panic Disorder. But whether one actually caused the other is still a mystery; did the compulsions come about as a way to ward off the Fear, or does the Fear exist simply as compliance leverage to ensure that the rituals will be followed through with? I mean, it's like the chicken and the egg theory. I also learn that OCD is a direct 'cousin' to Tourette's Syndrome, and that often Tourette's Syndrome can be misdiagnosed as Obsessive Compulsive Disorder—and vice-versa—due to the repetitive actions and behavior that they both breed. Taking the psychologist's heredity information and pairing it with this new information about interrelated symptoms makes sense; it connects me to Mallie. But if he, in fact, actually did have Tourette's Syndrome, then where had *he* gotten it? And the person who'd passed it on to Mallie, from whom did *they* get it? It's simply a never-ending circle. I mean, it's like being in a bathroom with mirrors on both walls, where they each reflect the other into complete infinity. One thing I had learned from Aunt Sue was that Mallie's parents (Sue's grandparents), had been first cousins. And if that's the case, then there is always the genetic-thing to consider. But upon further research, I find that this type of union is pretty doggonned common for the old South; cousins and distant family members marrying, I mean. Apparently, people just didn't travel very far from home back then, so there wasn't a whole lot of opportunity to meet others who were not connected to your family in some way or another. In fact, people often got married in those days for the sole purpose of producing off-spring who could later help out with the chores. So if this theory—this *inbreeding* theory—holds any truth whatsoever, then why aren't *all* families descended from the old South afflicted with numerous birth defects and acute mental illnesses? There's always the possibility that maybe they are and no one's really connected it before now. Or there's also the possibility that maybe defective genes are less common than we think, therefore, not as responsible for causing the abnormalities we always tend to blame on them. It's one of those questions that probably can never be answered, which unfortunately, leaves me standing right back in square one, all over again. I tell myself it's not about blame, though. It's not just so I can one day narrow it down, point my finger at the right culprit and ultimately say, "*She's* the one who did it! *She* caused all this!" Instead, the curiosity—the *need* to know—is borne out of this identity crisis I have been experiencing for the past 25 years, otherwise known as my life.

But overall, the one thing I find to be completely overwhelming in all my new research is that there is a disorder for absolutely everything! And I mean *everything!* I honestly don't know how anyone can possibly exist on this earth without possessing at least one of them. And if I hadn't lived my whole life with OCD and Panic Disorder, I would think these were nothing more than psychological excuses. I can certainly understand why people get so disgusted with the idea of it all—of making excuses for inappropriate behavior—because the number of disorders that have been 'diagnosed' is staggering, and even though I've lived with it day-in and day-out for my entire life, I still find some of these afflictions hard to swallow, myself. I mean, chemical disorders are actually broken down into several categories, according to the 'Diagnostic and Statistical Manual,' otherwise commonly known as the 'DSM-IV.' They are 'Anxiety,' 'Childhood,' 'Eating,' 'Mood,' 'Personality, 'Psychotic,' and 'Substance-related.' There is even a category dubbed as 'Other' for those afflictions that cannot be made to fit into any of the above referenced. And each one of *these* categories, in turn, breaks down and branches out into sub-categories. Both of mine, 'OCD' and 'Panic Disorder,' fall under the 'Anxiety Disorder' category. Interestingly though, Tourette's

Syndrome, though it's supposed to be so closely related to OCD, falls in the 'Other' category for some reason.

It hits me one day, just out of the blue—and I am reminded of the little girl in kindergarten that I left behind so many years ago. Are there other kids out there, just like me? Kids who struggle every single day with the simple act of getting up and trying to feel normal? I mean, it doesn't matter what form the disorder takes on, because if it's the one you have, then one's just as bad as the next. Maybe, in a sense, I don't *have* to leave the kindergartner behind. Maybe instead, she is showing me a way I can reach and take her outstretched hands after all, to bridge the difference between the two planes on which we exist.

Now it is solidified—written in stone. I will be a teacher, and I will locate them—kids who suffer from a chemical imbalance—and I will walk *with* them instead of leaving them out there, alone and afraid, to find their own way. I mean, I'd always considered the possibility of being a teacher before, but now the idea has a calling—a true calling to which there is a need, and to which I will respond.

YOU REAP WHAT YOU SOW

One thing I've found I have to do in college is to modify—*constantly* modify—to come up with creative ways around the compulsions in order to get things done on time. When reading Shakespeare's late plays, I have to allow time for the repetitive starting and stopping that always riddles my reading, the getting 'stuck' on random words—literally have to make time for these things, to figure it into the schedule. I mean, I know it sounds excessive, but if this is what it takes in order for me to succeed, then it's just a modification I'll have to accept. In class, I have also been forced to make modifications as well. Like, for instance, I no longer use a pencil to take notes during the lecture.

Instead, I always use pen. The reason behind this? Because when I use a pencil, I constantly feel compelled to erase stray marks, to fix little loops that don't quite connect, things like that. And before I know it, I am lost in the pursuit of letter perfection and the lecture has marched on without me. With a pen, I feel less compelled to do this, probably because it isn't possible. Sure, there're things I feel I have to write over, ends I have to make meet, but with a pen, I am less likely to get left so far behind.

Still, with all the intricate modifications I've had to make, the anger I'd always felt while growing up regarding the compulsions, is no longer there. Because when you are in college, you tend to decentralize yourself, especially when you take the time to look around and see all the people who're dealing with disabilities every day, too. Some aren't as bad as yours, some are worse. But the bottom line is to accept what you've been given in life and to make the best of it. It's all you've got.

By my junior year, I am well into my major, and I begin what they call 'field work.' My actual 'internship' will come next year, with student teaching. But all of these visits and activities I do within the school system now are things with which to 'get my feet wet.' Sometimes, I just sit in the back of a classroom and observe. Other times, I create fun activities to do that will give me experience with the students, something my professors tell me I'll find invaluable next year. I find these experiences to be fun, and I love creating activities to ingrain into the lesson the students are currently working on.

In a 9th grade grammar class where the students have just finished reading 'The Wizard of Earthsea,' which is a novel stressing the importance of 'mind over matter,' I decide to do a karate demonstration. I will walk into the classroom, sporting my 97-pound frame, and break 6 inches of concrete with my bare foot. Because if *that* doesn't get the concept of 'mind over matter' across, I don't know what else will.

My karate demo is a hit. The kids laugh, I laugh, we all have a good time. After class, though, while I am cleaning up the broken concrete, sweeping up the residue, one of the students approaches me. She is small, quiet, shy.

"How long have you taken karate?" she finally asks.

I sweep the remains of the last cinderblock into the trash bag, saying, "Many years. But I don't really have time to do it now because I have so much homework, so I just try to stay polished up on what I know until I have time for a new class."

She laughs, saying, "Tell me about it!" Again, she is studying me. "I take karate, too, you know."

"Do you really?" No wonder she has such a strong interest.

"Yes. I'm a green belt now."

"That's great! If you just keep up the good work, you'll have your black before you know it!"

"Yeah, that's what my teacher says. He says I'm going to be his first female black belt."

Okay . . . . don't even go there. Still, I have to ask. "So where do you take class?"

"From this guy over near my house—he's just gotten his own studio and everything."

"Really?" I ask. "What's his name?"

"Jamey. Jamey Everett."

Oh *god*.

"So do you like him?" I ask casually.

She hesitates. "Yeah, he's really nice."

"Well, that's good. It always helps to have a nice teacher."

"Yeah, that's what he says, too. We talk a lot—like after class and all. He says we have this . . . . you know . . . . special *friendship* . . . ."

I *know* I did not just hear that—there's no way. It cannot be happening.

"What kind of friendship?" I hear myself asking.

"Oh, you know . . . . we tell each other things, do things together. Stuff like that."

"Does he touch you?" The question literally falls out of my mouth before I can take the time to phrase it in a different manner.

She looks skeptical. "What do you mean?"

"Does he like to rub your shoulders, put his arm around you? That kind of thing?"

She looks surprised. "How did you know?"

I have to think fast, to do something. "I know some people who've been friends with him before," I tell the girl.

"Do you *know* him?" she asks.

"No, nothing like that," I quickly lie. "Only by what other people have told me about him. About their friendships with him, too. But one thing I *do* know is that some of the things that Jamey asks them to do with him are not really the kind of things that friends have to do with each other—in order to be friends."

"You mean like hugging?"

". . . . and touching."

She doesn't say anything at first, only looks down.

"Who're his other friends?" she finally asks.

I hesitate, but when she continues to look at me in that questioning way, I end up telling her, "Other girls, like you. You know, young and pretty. That's the kind of friends he likes to have."

She is skeptical, distrustful. "I don't believe you!"

I reach for her hand, saying earnestly, "If it isn't true, then how did I know the kinds of things he wants you to do?"

She pulls her hand away.

"Have you told your mother?" I ask.

But she only laughs it off, saying, "My *mother*. Yeah, like she'd really get it."

"Actually, she probably would."

"My mother is *clueless*! All she cares about is trying to control my life. You know, make me miserable. Even *Jamey* thinks so."

This is all-too familiar, and it is taking me back somewhere that I don't want to go.

"Don't tune your mother out," I tell her. "Don't feel that way about her. You've got to tell her . . . . about what he's doing . . . . because his ideas about friendship may not have your best interests in mind."

She picks up her book bag, saying, "I've got to go. It's almost time for the bell."

"Seriously," I tell her. "Talk to your mother. You've *got* to."

She looks totally skeptical as she slips her thin arms through the book bag straps.

"Promise me you'll talk to her. You've got to promise me that."

She is hesitant for a moment, and I think that maybe I have gotten through to her. But then she says, "I can't," just before turning and quickly walking out the classroom door.

* * *

"I just can't believe it!" I am ranting to an old friend from karate. He is now a police officer, and his beat is Hillsborough Street, where if he sees me walking in the direction of school, he will usually stop and offer me a ride.

"Angie, you *knew* he was like that," Randy tells me.

"But I just thought—I mean, I didn't know—didn't expect—you know, that he'd still be *doing* it! That same stupid shit! Saying that same stupid stuff! It's . . . . it's *sick*!"

"Of course it is," Randy agrees. "But you didn't actually believe he'd *stop*, did you? On his own accord like that?"

I don't say anything then.

"People who molest children *are* sick. They *don't* stop. Not until somebody else *makes* them stop."

"I just don't understand why she won't tell her mother!" I say.

"Yes, you do. Get real. Would you have told your mother back then?"

He has a definite point.

"Angie, you need to say something. Go to the police. Because he's not going to stop. Not until somebody comes forward."

But I shake my head, backing away from him. "I am *not* going there! It is *so* not my responsibility!"

"And see, that's the whole problem, right there. Everybody says it's not their responsibility. And in doing so, you are ensuring that he is allowed to go on, to continue doing exactly what he *is* doing!"

"That's not fair, Randy. Don't put it over on me."

"But you have first-hand knowledge of what he's doing."

"That was 10 years ago!"

"All the more reason you need to come forward."

"Sorry—I just can't."

"Why are you defending him?"

Defending him? "I'm *not*!"

"Yes, you are."

"No, it's not about defending him at all. It's about the fact that it's my word against his. And they're gonna want to know why I waited 10 years to say anything about it. It's about defense attorneys—do you have any clue what they can do to you on the stand? I mean, maybe you're telling the truth, and maybe you think you're doing the right thing, but attorneys have this way of turning things around, of making *you* look like the culprit. I mean, think about it! If they dig in my past, they'll find out that my parents kicked me out of the house in high school, about all the wild parties that I had." I hold out my hands to him then. "Are things starting to come together for you now?"

But he shakes his head, saying, "No, once you say something, others will come forward, too."

"Oh, and that's a guarantee," I point out.

"Nothing's a guarantee. But that's what usually happens."

"Well, somebody else'll have to do it. Sorry, I'm just not up for it."

Randy shrugs. "If that's how you want it. If you can live with that. I mean, you said, yourself, that you didn't know how you were going to be able to teach now, how you'd be able to walk in the classroom everyday and see those kids, knowing you let so many others down all those years ago."

"But if I was going to say something, it should have already been said," I tell him.

"You've been given a second chance now, that's all."

We are at school now, in front of Tompkins Hall where I have a 3:50 English class. I hesitate before opening the door.

"Randy, I'm sorry. I know where you're coming from and all, but I just can't do it. I'm . . . . I'm—I don't know. I'm just not that strong."

"Strength comes in numbers, and it's like I said. You won't be fighting this alone."

"I don't want to be fighting it at all."

"What about teaching?"

"Maybe I won't be a teacher after all."

"Maybe not. It's your choice. But that'd really be a shame. To let him win again. You know what I mean?"

* * *

It is several months before the issue ever gets brought up again. I avoid Hillsborough Street like the plague because I don't want to run into Randy again. I don't know what I'd say. Instead of walking my usual route to school, I cut across, walk through campus. Anything to avoid being seen. I start thinking earnestly about what else I'd like to be. Because this year, I am a senior, and I have to make some quick decisions.

I am working at the bank one afternoon when the call comes. The one from the police department. It is a detective by the name of Heather, who has been officially assigned the case on Jamey Everett.

I feel my blood run cold. "What case?"

"Alleged child molestation. I just need to ask you some questions. When can you come in?"

"Well, I don't know, exactly," I falter. "I'm—I'm a senior this year and all—and I'm working a lot. I don't know if I can."

"What about this afternoon?" she suggests.

"Well, see, I'm working today," I tell her.

"That's okay. I can talk to your boss, let him know that this is very important."

I swallow the lump of cotton that has formed in my throat, quickly telling her, "No, that's okay." I decline her offer to send a car out for me, figuring it'd be best to drive, myself. That is, if I have to go at all.

* * *

The décor in the police investigative division is anything but trendy. The cinderblock walls are painted this plain, asylum-yellowish color. The furniture is old, outdated, and nothing matches. In the chair where I am sitting, the pleather seat has split, exposing itchy white stuffing.

Heather snaps on a tape recorder, but I instantly recoil.

"Why does it have to be recorded?" I ask.

"Well, it doesn't, if you don't want it to. Would you feel more comfortable if I didn't record?"

I nod. Because I don't want any connection whatsoever to this investigation. Hell, I don't even want to be here.

At first, the questions are routine, like asking what dates I took karate class, who was in the class with me, that sort of thing. Then, "Why did you file a report?"

What??

"File a report? What are you *talking* about?"

"The report you filed with Officer Hardison back in October."

"But I didn't *file* a report!" I tell her. "Randy—he's a personal friend of mine. He *has* been since before he was ever a cop. All I did was tell him—you know, as a friend—because he'd been in the class with me. In fact, when he suggested it, I told him I didn't *want* to file a report!"

She tosses a print-out across the desk, filled in with Randy's information, then following with my own.

I shove it back, telling her, "The only reason he even knows where I live is because we're friends!" How the hell could he *do* this to me? Especially knowing how I felt about it! That friggin' *rat*!

Heather reads my thoughts then, saying, "Don't be mad at Officer Hardison. As a cop, it's his duty to report things like this. He could lose his job if anyone found out he had knowledge of information like this, and that he'd withheld it."

"But you don't understand," I tell her. "I was talking to him as a *friend*, not as a *cop*. He had no right to do this!"

"It doesn't matter," she explains. "The point is, I received this report, regardless of how it got here. And I can't just ignore it."

"Can't you talk to someone else?"

She sighs. "I already have. And believe me, your name has come up multiple times."

"What for?"

"Different things that people may've told you, things you probably saw."

I hold up my hands, saying, "I don't want anything to do with this!"

"I can't 'uninvolve' you. Not when you're already involved."

"But I don't want to be!" I tell her.

"Look, all I ask is that you answer a few simple questions. That's it."

"Then I can go?" I ask.

"Then you can go."

I sit back in the chair, waiting.

"What was your relationship with Jamey Everett?"

"He was my karate teacher. And I thought he was a friend."

"What made you decide otherwise?"

"When I discovered that I wasn't his only 'friend.'"

"And how did that make you feel?"

"I don't know. Hurt, maybe?"

"Did you have romantic feelings for him?"

"No, nothing like that. It was just that he'd convinced me—you know—that I was special or something. That I was really this very special person. And I guess I believed it. That's all."

"Did you have sex with him?"

What??

I voice my thoughts. "What?"

"Did you have *sex* with him?"

"No. Never. I never had sex with him."

"Did he try?"

"What do you mean? I'm not sure I understand what you mean by 'did he try.'"

"Did he touch you?"

I have never felt so embarrassed before in my life!

"Is that what he did?" she asks.

"I didn't want him to," I explain. "It wasn't like that at all. It was just that I was afraid that if I didn't let him—you know, go along with it—that he'd start rejecting me, and then so would everyone else in the class."

"And why was that important?"

I shrug. "I guess because at the time, I believed these people were the only friends that I had."

"What about your relationship with Jim?" she suddenly asks.

"What about it? It's been over for years now. I haven't seen him."

"How did Jamey react to that?"

"It kind of ticked him off. Like he said if we brought our feelings into the class like that, then we were shortchanging ourselves of all the knowledge we could be gaining."

"What about drugs?"

Drugs??

"Weren't there drugs in your class?"

"In the *class*?"

"You know—usage among you and the other students."

I hold my hands up in protest. Because I can't believe she's actually going here! "I may have tried pot with them a couple of times, but that's it! I never did any of the other stuff!"

"So there was other stuff?"

"I—I don't know. I never did it, so I don't know!"

"When I talked with Jamey, he said you and the others were always getting stoned together, that you were constantly under the influence. He thinks maybe this is why you have such a skewed perception of what was going on."

"I did *not* get stoned all the time!" I tell her hotly. "And if you don't believe me, then you can ask the other students!"

"I already have. They pretty much confirmed it. Especially Jim."

I come up from the chair. "Now I *know* you're full of shit, see? Because I know he'd never say something like that about me!"

"You never know what people will say when their back's against the wall."

"Why the hell would *his* back be—I mean, what *is* this, anyway Have *I* done something wrong here?"

"I don't know. Have you?"

"*No!*"

"Then why're you so defensive?"

"Because you're *accusing* me, *that's* why!"

"No one's accusing anyone. I'm just asking you some simple questions, that's all."

"Well, in answer to your 'simple' question,' *no, I did not do drugs!*"

I run an irritated hand through my bangs, not even caring if I screw up my hairspray. "I thought you called me in to ask me about 'possible child molestation.' So why is everything suddenly about drugs?"

"I just have to cover all avenues. To make sure that situations weren't occurring in manners that might have been construed otherwise."

"Look," I tell her. "*You* called *me*. I hate that he's doing it and all, but personally, I want no part in this! I just want to be left alone!"

"Unfortunately, you're already involved," she says.

"Then why don't you 'unfortunately' *un*-involve me?"

"It's not that easy," she tells me. "Not when you have information that we need to hear."

"How do you know I have information? Or even if I did, why I'd even want to talk about it in the first place?"

But she takes the wind out of my sails when she asks the same question that Randy had; "Why are you defending him?"

Defending *him*? This isn't about him! It's about *me*!

"Look," I tell her. "I am getting ready to graduate from college. Do you know—do you have any *idea*—how hard it was for me to finally get to this point? And I don't need anything screwing that up! *Nothing*! I am *not* responsible for his actions, so don't try and make me be!"

She stops me as I turn to leave. "I may need you in court."

"I won't say anything."

"Then you'll be confirmed a 'hostile witness.'"

But unfortunately for her, she has no idea what hostility is! None, whatsoever.

* * *

It is only a few weeks before the whole incident is all over the news, in the local papers. Most of the parents who have kids in Jamey's class are protesting, saying how ridiculous the charges are. They claim they will stick by Jamey, right till the end. And I can't help feeling total disgust—that anyone's parents would do this—would take Jamey's word over what might be happening to their very own kid. It's beyond sick.

In the newspaper articles, Jamey and his wife stand together, claiming that the 'false' charges were brought by a 'disgruntled female student who didn't get her black belt.' They are so full of shit! All of them! And Jamey's wife—I absolutely cannot believe her! Is she that clueless? I mean, is it possible?

As it turns out I don't have to go to court. Jamey accepts a plea bargain in which he agrees to a term of probation, doing community service work, turning over all his kids' classes to another adult, and registering himself as a 'sex offender' in his respective county. He still claims he is innocent, that the only reason he agreed to accept the plea bargain was to avoid jail time. It all seems too easy—him getting off like that. Honestly though, I'm just glad it's over with.

But it is less than two years later when Jamey appears in the news again, more charges being filed against him, this time, the victim claiming to have been molested since the age of 9. Like everything else associated with this situation, it is beyond sick, and I wish I could say I am surprised. But unfortunately, it is all-too-familiar. Throughout these charges as well, Jamey still maintains his innocence, and I can't help thinking, "Is he so sick that he doesn't even know what he's done?" But I don't believe that—not for one second. Instead, my thoughts are only that he is too vain, that he sees himself as too slick, to get caught. All he cares about is convincing everyone how he's been done so completely wrong by some disgruntled student, and while he's busy smoothing things out, regaining their trust, he's right there, going at it just as strong as before—molesting *their* kid.

The man handling Jamey's case from the Justice Department calls me in. He introduces himself as Mr. Edwards, telling me he got my number from Heather, from the last investigation. But like the last time, too, I tell him again that I don't want to be involved.

"I didn't turn him in the *first* time," I explain. "Not really, anyway. I just told a friend who went in and reported it *himself* when *I* refused to do it." I give a short laugh then. "Hell, when they first called me in to the police department, I actually thought it was Evie's family that had done it—that had turned him in, I mean. But now, regardless of what happened—no matter how it came about—I am still the scapegoat for all of his problems. It's all *my* fault, see?"

He chuckles then, saying, "It's always somebody else's fault, isn't it? We have no 'guilty' criminals in this country. None at all."

"That's the way it seems," I tell him. "Because criminals are the only ones who have any rights around here."

Again, he laughs. "Believe me, you're only preaching to the choir."

"So why did you call me in?" I ask.

"Mr. Everett's going in front of the sentencing committee next week. I would really like it if you could write a letter to them—you know, telling them what happened to you back then. Because we really need all the support we can get here."

"Why me?"

"I'm not just asking you. I'm asking all of his victims—at least, the ones we know about—to do this."

"Does the committee need convincing that bad?" I ask, surprised.

"No, it's not that they need convincing. They just need to be made aware of his pattern of behavior—to be made aware that this has been going on for a long time, and it is unlikely that he will stop without some sort of outside intervention."

I am still skeptical. "Do you *know* him?" I ask. "Because I honestly think he believes he is innocent, himself. I don't know why he can't see it, what he's done, but I think he could convince the devil, himself that he's innocent."

Mr. Edwards glances down into his hands then, saying, "Yes, I've had the opportunity to interview Mr. Everett—along with the psychologist. And he has been diagnosed with Narcissistic Syndrome."

Okay. Another condition. Another *excuse*. "So what does that mean?"

"It means that Mr. Everett has a very skewed perception of himself. He sees himself as superior in every way—looks, intelligence, behavior—we are all 'underlings' to him in his eyes. It's not uncommon, though. We often find this pattern of mentality in pedophiles and child molesters. Even in serial killers, believe it or not."

I can't help but wonder how one actually gets to that stupid point—to that ridiculous state of mind. Instead, I just say, "I wish I could help you, Mr. Edwards. Really, I do. But what's the point? I mean, if he doesn't think he's done anything wrong, then who is it going to punish?"

He holds up a hand then, saying, "I didn't mean he doesn't think he's done anything *wrong*. Only that he thinks he's too good to get *caught*."

"Well still, I wish I could help, but that's been over 10 years ago—and I'd like to leave it there, you know?"

But he stops me as I am gathering my purse, standing up to leave. "Look, I know how you feel. But if I can't get some people to come forward and do something about it, he's just going to get another slap on the wrist. Or worse, he might even get away with it this time."

"I'm sorry," I tell him. "But I think I've been victimized enough here. I don't think I need to be drug through the 'lier dirt' any more than I already have. Because it truly sucks, you know? Especially when I'm not only innocent, but honest as well."

He reaches in his top drawer momentarily, coming up with a picture. I take it from his outstretched hand, noticing that it is of two little girls—two little girls who look a lot like Kay and I had at that age—and though they are both smiling now, the younger one has obvious tears still streaming down her cheeks.

"Their mother gave me that picture," he tells me. "Said they'd been fighting—arguing with each other—all afternoon. Said it'd taken the photographer almost an hour to actually get a smile out of her."

I remember those days all-too well, and I have to smile, too. Still, I hope this mother knows that one day—when one or the other of them leaves home, goes off to college or something—that then they will finally realize the truth—how much they really do love each other.

He nods towards the picture in my hand, saying, "That's her. The younger one."

I look at him questioningly.

"She was 9. You know, when he started doing it to her."

For some reason, I can't seem to tear my eyes from the picture now.

"This's her?" I ask. Because I never expected her to be real, to have an actual face—the 9-year-old, that is. But yet here she is, a contradiction of tears and laughter, blanketed in her own temporary innocence.

"She had some—some learning problems. Something like that. Didn't get along too well with her classmates all the time. Had issues with her mother, too."

I look at him then.

"Her mother—she cried, too, you know. When she gave me that picture. Said she didn't know where she'd gone wrong exactly. Only that she wished she could go back and hug that little girl. But she can't. The little girl's 16 now."

"He did this to *her*?" I ask, and the voice that comes out of my mouth I don't even recognize as my own. "Jamey did this to her, *too*? Didn't he *know* she had problems?" I don't recognize the stupidity of the question until after I have already spoken it into existence.

"Didn't he know you had problems, too?"

I meet his gaze. "I trusted him back then. I told him stuff."

"That's the kind he likes. Because they're the most vulnerable. The easiest to shape and mold the way he wants."

I don't know what to say.

"He's a predator, Angie. He's the very type who would go out hunting and purposely shoot the baby deer because it's easier to hit than the fair adult game. He is not a nice person. And you owe him *nothing!*"

He pauses for a moment before going on. "I have daughters, too, you know. And even though you don't have kids now, you probably will someday."

"I thought you said he was 'sick,' that he didn't really know what he was doing. Or at least, that's the way the courts would see it."

He meets my gaze then, saying, "Sick or not, he cannot be allowed to get away with this. You've got to figure—*all* human beings have twisted thoughts and desires at some time or another in their lives. It's just human nature, and it's gonna happen. But it's what a person ultimately *does* with those thoughts and desires—how he *responds* to those things—that singles out who the predators are."

Still, I don't say anything.

"Regardless, he's made a choice here. Not a *mistake*. A conscious *choice*. And you need to be very cognizant of that before you decide to wash your hands of it."

* * *

I write the letter. But it is probably akin to what I would consider equal to giving childbirth, as hard as it is. I have to keep starting over—again and again—but not because of the compulsions. This time it is because I am going back to someplace that I haven't been in a very long time, and it's a place that I don't particularly want to go. Sometimes, I have to stop writing altogether, to just put the computer away, because the anxiety attacks are coming so hard and fast I often don't know what's even hit me. But by the time I have finally finished the letter, I am angry. Mostly at myself, though. How was it that I'd simply walked away back then? Because by doing so, I'd probably ensured his free run, allowed him the ability to reach lots of other girls—young girls, to whom it otherwise may not have happened. How could I have fought so hard for something as stupid as *unemployment*, especially after I'd let something as important as *this* just go? I feel hollow, selfish. And as I turn my letter in to the DA, I only have one regret; that I didn't have the common *balls* to come forward way back then—by myself. That after Randy'd gone in and filed the report on my behalf, I'd actually seen fit to skitter around in my own shadow, totally afraid of being 'caught.' And now, all I can think is, 'for *what*?' Exactly what was it I had thought he'd deserved? Because the truth is, he's done this to himself. No one else is to blame. There are no '*disgruntled students*,' no '*x-female members with an agenda*.' What ever he gets now is exactly what he deserves, and someday, whether he admits it or not, he will know this.

In the paper, there is an article about the alleged molestation, how it's the second time this has happened in less than a two-year period. At the bottom of the article, there is a quote by none other than Jim, who it'd turned out, been the one to take over the kids' classes. He'd said something like, "I hope to God it's not true." This time I am not angry, just amazed. And though we haven't seen each other in years, I feel compelled to call him, to let him know that yes, unfortunately it *is* true.

I have to look his number up in the phone book, and when I find it, I dial from my cell phone. But instead of getting a person, I get an answer machine, which maybe I should have expected since it is so early in the afternoon. Still, though it's awkward, I leave a message anyway, hoping that the number still *is* his. Because otherwise, what a totally weird phone call to have waiting for you when you got home from work.

QUESTIONS WITHOUT ANSWERS

May, 1993. After fulfilling all the necessary requirements, a task that takes me a total of 5 years to complete instead of the customary 4, I am free to graduate. To walk. My time is my own again. And I have never been so scared before in my whole life.

I don't go to the big graduation—the one in Carter Finley stadium where they give all the important speeches and everyone turns their tassel. Instead, I go to the small, departmental one afterwards where we will receive our actual diplomas. Our particular department holds its ceremony in a church across the street from the college campus. When they call my name, announcing my newly acquired BA in English, Granddaddy—highly conservative *Granddaddy*, whose trousers and obligatory tie embody the same shade of subdued brown—stands up from his row of pews and cheers. Out loud. Pop, who is sitting next to Mama, is showing his school spirit as well, but in a more subtle fashion; he is wearing his NC State red vest underneath his sports coat. Daddy is videotaping the whole event, whether for my sake or for his—proof that this day actually occurred at some point in time—I'm not sure. But either way, it is a tape I will always treasure, not just because it has recorded this monumental climb I have finally managed to achieve, but also because it is the last tape we will ever have of Pop and Granddaddy. (It is less than a year later that both will die, only a month apart from one another—Pop, from complications following an illness and several mini strokes, then Granddaddy, from Lymphoid Cancer.)

After the departmental graduation, there is a reception held for us in the fellowship hall downstairs. Daddy is still following me around with his video camera, and Kay, who is by now severely pregnant with her second baby, is busy snapping pictures of her own. Granddaddy and Pop sit over by the window, intricately studying my leather-bound diploma, their heads close together like they're in serious conversation or something. Maybe they're simply contemplating its validity. Because after all, how can this whole thing seem real to them if it doesn't even seem real to me? Though I know it *is* real, that I've worked very hard to finally reach this point, something still doesn't seem quite right. Something is still missing, though I can't put my finger on exactly what that is. I mean, I'd expected that when this day actually arrived, I'd finally know everything I've always wanted to know, that I'd have all the answers to all the questions I've ever asked. But when I'd returned to my respective seat, sheepskin in hand, I realized that not only had I failed to acquire all the answers I'd been seeking, but now I actually had more questions than I ever had before. Some part of me feels lost, afraid. It's almost as if something inside is saying, "So what was it all for?" To counteract this weird thought, one piece of consolation I can offer myself is that if for no other reason, it at least gave me a break from the real world—5 more years to grow up, to try to figure out who exactly it is that I am.

Since I am no longer sure that I want to go into teaching, I begin to explore other possible options. The one thing I *do* know is that I definitely want to do something for the good of humanity, something to help people—preferably people like me, who don't understand what's going on inside their own heads. I flounder from one do-gooder job to the next, trying to find my exact niche. I figure if I keep on going at this rate though, in just a few more years, I'll have enough printed business cards to wallpaper my own personal shrine. Yeah, that'd be pretty cool, wouldn't it? Then they could dedicate it to the most directionless person to have ever walked across the face of this earth. But as far as my actually putting down *permanent* employment roots, it just doesn't seem to be happening right now. I know I should be worried about this, but for some reason, I'm just not. I mean, as long as I manage to scrape together enough money each month to pay my living expenses, all is good in the world. I try not to acknowledge the guilt I feel for taking advantage of my family's generosity—how they all made sure I had everything I needed during those college years—and of the scholarship I'd been awarded 4 consecutive years from the local newspaper office—Mama's place of employment, where a special program of this nature was offered to employees' dependents. Still, when I'd applied for it, I'd been completely gung-ho about teaching, though. I mean, there was nothing else in the world as far as I was concerned, and I was going to be this exceptional, extraordinary 'gift' to the department of education. One they simply could not live without. But the reality of it is, the only gifts I am actually offering these days are wedding presents—to my ever-dwindling string of friends. And though I know that someday I will truly want all this, too—the American Dream, that is—the house in Suburbia, the white picket fence, the 2.5 kids, just like everyone else, I also know that now is just not the right time in my life. There is so much I want to do, not to mention the unfinished business I still have to take care of as well. Because even though I've literally been searching everywhere I can think of for the past 5 years, I still have been unable to find myself. This concept is actually somewhat amusing, considering that before I went to college, I hadn't even known I was lost in the first place.

In November of '94, I find myself working in a city-sponsored program that doubles as kind of a 'tourist-guide (slash) resource-for-the-homeless.' I think it will be an honorable thing to do, and I plan to go in and drastically change the lives of all the downtrodden, to remove the hopelessness from the eyes of all the lost souls who roam the city streets out there. Maybe helping others to get on the right path will ultimately lead me down my own. I grandly accept the position along with another girl about my age and an elderly gentleman—a sweet, old man who, in time, I'm sure will end up reminding me of my grandfather. And I'll be so good at what I do, they'll call me 'Sunshine.' Because that's exactly what I'll be; a burst of sunshine and a breath of fresh air, all rolled into one.

* * *

"Hey, *Sparkplug*! D'you tell Peewee he could come down here and borrow our newspaper?"

I turn away from the air-conditioning unit, fanning myself instead. It is absolutely 110 degrees outside, and I'm supposed to be walking around out there, looking for lost souls. Instead, I am holed up here in the police sub-station that I now work out of, trying to tell myself that 'spontaneous combustion'—no matter what I may have previously believed—just does not happen. It's scientifically impossible. It has to be, right? And sitting out in the kiosk that is officially assigned to the 'City Guides,' is just as bad; because that's where the 'sweet old man' comes back after his walks, then proceeds to compare parts of my body to various fruits and vegetables, sometimes 'accidentally' bumping me with his nasty fingers. I *so* do not want to be out there with him! When several of the girls actually got up the nerve to say something about it and finally turn him in, the police department more or less said we'd done something to invite his attention, that we'd brought it on ourselves somehow. I wonder if they can really be that stupid. But I figure it's more of a case of them not wanting to deal with it instead, their way of intimidating us into dropping it all.

It is totally ironic that the two things I used the least in college turn out to be two of the most *important* things around here; first, there are my three years of Spanish, which I draw upon heavily in order to halfway communicate with the huge Hispanic population around this area—and the second one would be the econo-size jug of flea powder, which I thought I'd left at the final culmination of all the 'Celebrations' events. I mean, who'd had ever guessed I'd need it here, in the 'professional' world?

"Yo! *Sparkplug!*"

I turn around irritatedly. "No! I did *not* give him the newspaper! All I told him was if he'd come down here, I'd look in the classifieds for him and write down some of the job opportunities, and that was it."

"Well, there ain't no reason why he can't just walk across the street to the Econo Mart and buy his own toilet paper. Because he *ain't* wipin' his ass with my sports page!"

I roll my eyes, but as usual, it goes unnoticed around here.

"He was looking for a job, *not* bathroom accessories."

They all laugh then. "Peewee *work*? Now why's he gonna do that? Especially when he gets 'the check!'"

Still, I cringe at the thought of having to go in to the Econo Mart for anything. The whole time I've been working here, it's never earned above a low 'B' sanitary rating, and the guys swear that the chicken wings they sell are really pigeon wings. And it is the only place I've ever seen where someone can actually walk right in and pick up a single cigarette out of the fish bowl on the counter, and purchase just that *one* for his immediate consumption. And 50 cents a pop at that. I can only imagine the profit the foreign guys who run the store must be making around here.

I'd never imagined that working out of a unit with 10 policemen could be so utterly painful. I mean, when they pull you over and stuff, it's like, "Drive carefully, Ma'am." Or "Have a nice day, Ma'am." But here, behind the closed doors of the innermost 'inner city' substation, it's all about teasing, picking. Scaring the absolute shit out of you, which is something they find hideously amusing. There are loose wallets on the floor rigged to explode when you pick them up, Styrofoam-headed dummies swinging from their necks in the darkness of the bathroom, incoming prank calls on your city-issued cell phone, ancient-Chinese-torture sounds—like continuous beeping—coming from the pager tucked safely out of reach inside one of the guy's lockers. And if the teasing doesn't do it for you, then the atmosphere definitely will. The sub-station, fabricated from an old service station, resides in about a hundred year old building. The back, which had formerly been the car bays, has now been turned into stalls where the mounted police house their horses during the day. I mean, I love animals and all, and we'd had horses back when I'd been growing up, but still, I don't remember them smelling like *this*. And of course, along with the hundred-year-old status, the building, itself, is equipped with its very own rodent club and a generous share of roach infestation. And the guys actually sit there and wait, and when the overgrown roaches crawl out of the cracks in the floor, they catch them, holding them with their thumb and forefinger, while they paint numbers on their backs with whiteout—like stupid race cars or something. Then they make these charts, keep track of how many times each one emerges during their shift, make bets on them. Once when the other girl and I had been making our friendly rounds, we'd stepped into one of the stores only to find ourselves being stared down by the biggest *I-don't-know-what* we've ever seen before in our lives. I mean, if I had to guess, it *looks* like a rat, but it is the size of a dog. No, I will not even *venture* to guess. I will not go there. Later, back at the sub-station when we report this shocking information to the sergeant we work under, he just laughs, telling us, "Oh, you mean one of the *wolf rats*?"

One of them? Pray tell—how many *are* there?

"Oh, dozens. Maybe even hundreds." He indicates the direction of the antique store where we'd made the gruesome discovery. "The one you saw up there this morning—he was just out, *shopping*. See, he really lives down *here*."

Sweet. I suddenly wonder why I'd ever had issues with corn worms.

Then there is the other stuff, too, like when the 300-pound linebacker-sized 'Wilbur' starts chasing you—all through the park—and you run like hell to get back to the safety of the kiosk. And once inside with the door locked and your breath coming in heavy spasms, Wilbur stands at the window, looking all disappointed, saying, "Aw shucks. Don't choo wanna be my friend' anymore? I don't have nobody ta play with now."

One time the other winos who hung out around the bus station came up with the brilliant idea of stealing 'Cheetah's' clothes while she was busy working a john over in the stairwell—a skimpy tube top and micro-mini skirt—and convincing Wilbur to put these on, then go across the street and perform ballet in the park. Not pretty. *So* not pretty!

When the guys in the sub-station run out of things with which to amuse themselves, they resort to other means of torture, like when they hide the only roll of toilet paper in the entire building. Or like the time the quiet, sneaky one—Tim, I think it is—swiped my shoes when I was changing them, and in the bottom of my city-issued skips, where the 'specially designed air pockets' for the 'purpose of walking comfort' are placed, saw fit to take his folding knife and cut slashes, thus replacing the 'comfort air pockets' with semi-deflated flatulent holes instead. I swear, I cannot walk across the floor now without them all dying laughing and calling me 'fart feet.' Okay. So I can see where they get 'fart feet' from. But what about 'Sparkplug?' I mean, what hell is *that*?

"Well, it's just that *real* dynamite usually tends to come in much bigger packages, that's all," the one raring back in his chair tells me.

"Yeah, so if the *shoe* fits," the one who'd taken liberty to vandalize my property chimes in. "I guess you gotta wear it, you know?" Then they are all laughing again.

O-*kay* . . . . I feel *too* special. So what ever happened to just plain old 'dig-a-dig?'

By the end of the day, it is absolutely enough to make one cry. But I can't. Not now. Because at this precise moment, I am dealing with the dead squirrel placed in the back seat of my car instead—

the one I'd called animal control out to come get off the sidewalk much earlier, and which, mysteriously, they were never able to locate.

But easy as it may be, instead of crying, I come up with another solution instead—a much better one. Because this is it. The final straw. Now that the first shot has officially been fired, let the war begin! I retaliate, finding some used rags, holding my breath while I pick up the decomposing clump of fur and bugs. I walk over to Tim's truck—the bright new gold one with the tinted windows and great big shiny wheels, which I seriously doubt have ever actually seen a trace of real mud before. I pull open his gas tank, unscrew the cap.

There, I feel much better now.

* * *

When I leave work the next afternoon, there are three empty bottles in my back seat; a couple of Thunderbirds and one Wild Irish Rose. And if I'd thought the squirrel stunk . . . .

I fill the bottles up with hot water, then replace the caps, though I make sure they are plenty loose. I stuff them down in Tim's duffel bag, underneath his bullet-proof vest, down below his gun belt, where he'll be totally sure to *not* find them—at least not until he sees fit to finally unpack the gargantually overstuffed load he always lugs around with him. And do I think it's overkill? Nah—my only regret is that I can't be a fly on his wall when he discovers it, that's all.

* * *

A year later, we are married. I ask both Adrienne and Regina to be in my wedding, along with my two sisters and Tim's niece. The wedding, itself is beautiful. We are married in a small chapel on the grounds of Historic Mordecai Plantation. For music, Mama and I have hired a string quartet made up of members from the NC Symphony. After the wedding, they, too, will go to Wendell, to my parent's new house on the pond where the reception will be held, and where they will provide the music as well.

For our honeymoon, Tim wants to go somewhere like Bermuda, but since I have never flown before, I don't want to add anymore unneeded stress to an already stressful day, so instead, we drive to Florida, to 'Disney Land,' which I think is as much fun as Bermuda would've been, anyway. And out of all the places we've visited, theme parks included, 'Gator Land' is my favorite, where I fall in love with the real-live pink flamingos. I didn't know there really was a such thing. I thought somebody'd made the 'pink' thing up just for the sake of tacky plastic yard birds.

"The reason they're pink," Tim tells me, "is because they eat so much shrimp."

I look at him, trying to decide whether he's teasing or not. Because after all, he *is* the same person who'd told me that 'mountain' goats have two shorter legs on one side, just so they won't get tired of standing on a slope all day. He'd claimed it was a 'genetic mutation' or something stupid like that.

"But what if they walk around to the other side?" I'd asked. "Then aren't their legs twice as long over there?"

"They don't do that," Tim explains. "They only stay on one side."

"For their entire lives?"

"Sure."

"But what if they don't?"

"Then they'll probably fall off."

While I am trying to contemplate this new bit of information, he gives in, laughing his butt off at me. Having grown up in the country—and more or less on a farm at that—he finds my ignorance regarding livestock and other related issues pretty humorous.

"Seriously," he tells me, pointing out a small group of flamingos gathered at one end of the lake. "Look at the baby—how he's kind of gray. It's only the adult ones that're pink."

I notice that this time, he is right, though.

* * *

When we return home, we fall back into the daily routine of our lives. By now, we've both sold our respective houses and bought a bigger one together. Tim is well into his 'police career,' and I start to think seriously about the path mine will take. Though I haven't completely ruled out teaching altogether, I begin to consider first going back to graduate school and enrolling in a more specific master's degree program, one which would allow me to take on classrooms with actual special needs students. And though until now, my writing has only been a hobby, I also begin to contemplate the possibility of writing a book, of telling my story, in the hopes that it will enlighten others out there who suffer from similar symptoms. Because if I've learned one thing in my lifetime, it's that gaining the knowledge that you are not alone in the world truly is a key factor towards finally accepting yourself for who you are. And learning that there are other people out there who understand how you feel as well? That's even more important. Again, this is something I know first-hand. Finally, though it has taken me nearly 30 years to realize this, I am beginning to see what I'd always cursed as my 'unfair cross-to-bear' in a whole new light. One in which I can actually take all the bottled up anger I'd stored over the years, and then positively turn it around—to redirect it into a valuable learning tool—one that will open all kinds of avenues into the minds of those who suffer from chemical imbalances. And given research and time, who knows exactly what this could mean?

* * *

I am well into my graduate program at NC State, and just starting to put together the outline for my new book when I decide I have to go back. To Carver Kindergarten. Just one more time. There is still unfinished business there I have to take care of before I can truly move on.

But this time, when I turn into the parking lot, I am beyond stunned to realize that the little school *is* no more. It has been completely shut down, its doors locked and chained to the outside world, its long windows boarded up with haphazardly nailed plywood. Along the walls of the building, both the bricks and wood have been littered with graffiti from a black spray-paint can. The little tin roof covering the sidewalk has collapsed in the middle, and now its jagged edge hangs menacingly in the way. The playground equipment has long since been removed, and the grass, now growing wildly, has taken over the entire school yard. Regardless, I continue on—over, around and through all of the varying obstacles—my vision set firmly on the chain-link fence at the far end of the playground, where I can still make out the little girl, standing there all by herself, waiting. As I approach, she recognizes me, finally letting go of the fence to which she's been forced to cling for so long. She smiles and reaches up to me, and I as I take her smaller hands into my own, the different planes on which we'd forever existed finally merge, melt into one. For the first time in my life, I am able to take her with me.

A further 'updated' family picture

At the reception after my college graduation (Granddaddy and Pop sit behind us, probably discussing the validity of my new diploma.)

A year later . . . .

. . . . we are married

Tim, at the entrance of 'Gatorland' . . . .

*. . . . . my favorite of all the theme parks
(where I fall in love with the real live pink flamingos)*

Tim, having been with the police department since the age of 21, continues to steadily climb the 'career ladder.'

I, having floundered through so many jobs since college, could literally wallpaper my own personal shrine with left-over business cards.

EPILOGUE

We are all sitting in the living room of the beach cottage, folding clean clothes. At least we all *were*. But now Martie has had to jump up again for the umpteenth time and chase after her 2-year-old son, who, since the discovery of his own legs, has been into absolutely everything. I don't care what anyone says. Boys are programmed differently than girls, all the way from the start—all the way from *before* birth. And that 'socialization' thing? Sure, maybe it helps out and all if you buy your *male* child toy trucks and your *female* child dolls and frilly dresses, but overall, I think it's pretty innate. We are who we are from the very beginning, and nothing can change that.

The guys have gone off to play golf this morning, a holy ritual they insist on performing every single year when we take this family trip to Sunset Beach. For them, it's like visiting Mecca or something.

And they always go first thing in the morning in order to miss both the crowds and the blistering heat. Still too early to go out on the beach, it gives the three of us time to catch up on laundry and dish washing; whatever needs to be done around the cottage. Most importantly, just time to catch up with each other.

Kay is settling a stack of towels against the back of the couch when I ask her if she remembers the trip we took to Yaupon Beach, back when we were all so young, when we'd all shacked up in one motel room together—for three whole incredible nights. Honestly, I wouldn't wish that kind of torture on anyone—not even the bravest contestant to ever grace the cameras of 'Fear Factor.' Kay has to laugh at the recollection, and she shakes her head, saying, "I was so *mean* to you! Why did I do that to you?"

I shrug, laughing with her. "I was pretty mean to you, too, so I guess it was a mutual thing."

I don't think the irony is lost on either one of us—how such bitter enemies of young sisterhood could turn out, in the end, to be such 'best friends' in adulthood. Who'd have ever guessed?

On the couch, suntanned legs dangle over the edge, long blond hair falling carelessly over the armrest. These belong to Mandy, Kay's oldest, who is thoroughly engrossed in early morning cartoons. In the other corner of the room, playing quietly with her dolls, is Mallory, the younger of the two. Her face is innocent, lightly freckled from the sun. She, too, like Mandy, is blond, though a darker shade, and she is just as suntanned. I *so* remember being that age. Sometimes I wish I still was. I wonder, though, if we had the chance— if we *could* go back—would Kay and I do things differently now? Would we appreciate each other more if we knew then what we know today? I'd like to think that we would. Still, since the invention of her own children, there is *one* thing I have yet to do for Kay, and all of a sudden, right now—at this precise moment—it seems as good a time as any.

"Hey, Mallory," I suggest slowly, thoughtfully.

She stops, mid-play, looking over at me with growing interest, and her full attention is mine for the taking.

"I want to ask you something—something *really* important."

She waits patiently, her eyes large and alert.

"Do you, perchance, happen to know—" and here I pause, just like Mrs. Waddelson taught us to do way back in the 8th grade before continuing on dramatically, "what a '*dig-a-dig*' is?"

Kay looks at me. She does not smile. "You *better* not . . . ."

The guys, on their annual 'Mission to Mecca' golf trip at Sunset Beach
(from left) Merle, Tim and Matt

Mallory and Mandy
(Kay and Merle's kids)

Jack (who has since been joined by Kate)
(Martie and Matt's kids)

Printed in the United States
42389LVS00002B/44